D0276150

Praise for
QUEEN OF THE COURT

"In her memoir, QUEEN OF THE COURT, Serena shares with us her evolution from a girl to a woman to a world champion. From the first time I met her, when she was very young, to watching her capture the U.S. Open, Serena has always amazed me with her ability on the court, her curiosity away from it, and her overall love for life."

—Billie Jean King

"Ascending from nowhere to the top of the world, she has run an exciting zigzag course transforming darkest days into bright victories on her way to the International Tennis Hall of Fame."

—Bud Collins

"On the court, Serena is the most challenging opponent I've come up against, and off the court, she is a loving sister and a true friend. Serena has been a role model for me and an inspiration."

—Venus Williams

QUEEN OF
THE COURT

SERENA
WILLIAMS
WITH DANIEL PAISNER

SIMON &
SCHUSTER

London · New York · Sydney · Toronto

A CBS COMPANY

First published in Great Britain in 2009 by Simon & Schuster UK Ltd
A CBS COMPANY

Copyright © 2009 by Serena Williams

This book is copyright under the Berne Convention.
No reproduction without permission.
All rights reserved.

The right of Serena Williams to be identified as the author of this work
has been asserted by her in accordance with sections 77 and
78 of the Copyright, Designs and Patents Act, 1988.

1 3 5 7 9 10 8 6 4 2

Simon & Schuster UK Ltd
1st Floor
222 Gray's Inn Road
London
WC1X 8HB

www.simonandschuster.co.uk

Simon & Schuster Australia
Sydney

A CIP catalogue copy for this book
is available from the British Library.

ISBN: 978-1-84737-543-8 (Hardback)
ISBN: 978-1-84737-544-5 (Trade paperback)

Designed by Charles Sutherland

Printed in the UK by CPI Mackays, Chatham ME5 8TD

This book is dedicated to my daddy. Your vision
and undying dedication made everything I do possible. I love you.

London Borough of Barnet	
Askews	Sep-2009
796.342	£17.99

ACKNOWLEDGMENTS

When people congratulate me after Venus and I win a doubles championship, I always tell them I didn't do very much—except for pick the right partner and then stand back and let Venus do all the work.

That's how I feel about this book, because from the very beginning I was blessed to work with good, creative people. First and foremost, I have to give glory to Jehovah God for allowing me to have this opportunity. My mom—thank you for your support, your unconditional love, your strength, and your smile. Without you this book would not have been possible! Daddy—your confidence in me has led me to become a champion not only on the court but off. I love you both!

This couldn't have been done without my sister and business advisor, Isha. When I wanted to give up on this project she urged me on, kept me motivated, and saw this project through from beginning to end, never missing a beat. Isha, I can't say thank you enough!

I would also like to thank my agent and friend at the William Morris Agency, Jill Smoller. You have been in my corner for both the ups and downs—thank you for seeing me through this project. You mean so much to me! Also thanks to Evan Levy; he is invaluable to my team.

I also owe thanks to Suzanne Gluck, the head of the William

Morris literary department. I couldn't be Serena without my lawyer, Keven Davis, his colleague, Theresa Simpson, and my business manager, Larry Bailey. They've all taken turns keeping me on track since I was nine years old.

Of course, I can't accomplish anything without the endless support of my other sisters: Yetunde, the world's best big sister; Lyndrea, my heartbeat; and Venus, my best friend! Yetunde, you live forever in my soul and you're in my thoughts every day. My sisters keep me grounded and love me no matter what, even when they found out I broke their piggy banks!

I am indebted to my coauthor, Dan Paisner. Dan ended up chasing me all over the world to put my thoughts on these pages. Yeah, we did it, Dan!

At Grand Central Publishing, I am grateful to Karen Kosztolnyik, our editor, who did a great job helping me and Dan shape and polish our manuscript. Karen, your insights really helped make this a fun yet empowering book. I want to thank all the amazing people at Grand Central who helped behind the scenes, including Karen's assistant, Celia Johnson; publisher Jamie Raab; editor-in-chief Deb Futter; associate publisher Emi Battaglia; production editor, Tareth Mitch; director of publicity, Jennifer Romanello; publicist, Jimmy Franco; publicist, Linda Duggins; art director, Claire Brown . . . and everybody else who had a role in turning me into a real author.

Finally, I want to thank all my readers and supporters for traveling on this journey with me through these pages. Go forth with an abundance of courage and the confidence that you can do anything you set your mind to.

CONTENTS

"When you fail, you fail alone."

—Sign posted on a public tennis court by
   Richard Williams to inspire his young daughters

PROLOGUE

September 3, 2008

Arthur Ashe Stadium. U.S. Open. Head-to-head against Venus. Under the lights in front of a packed house. I hate that it's just the quarterfinals, but it's always a battle when we meet. Last time we played was in the Wimbledon final just a couple months back. Venus got the better of that one, but I came out strong. First two or three games, I was dominant. Fearless. That's how you have to play it on grass. You have to go for those winners early, but then I started thinking too much and the match got away. That happens sometimes, especially against a tough player like my Big Sis.

That's what I have to keep reminding myself going into this one: how good Venus is. How strong I'll have to be to counter. How carefully I'll have to defend. All week long, since I first saw the draw, I had this quarterfinal matchup with V in my head. She's the best player on the tour—with a huge serve. When she's on her game, no one can touch her. Well . . . except for me.

We've gone back and forth in these matches. In the beginning, V beat up on me pretty good. Then I beat her up in the finals of four straight majors. Now we're back and forth again. We've played against each other so many times, we know each other's games so well, there aren't too many surprises. Venus tends to strategize a lot more than I do before a match, so I know she'll mix things up;

she'll go another way with her shots; she'll work a new set of angles; she'll show me something different on her serve, some new disguise. I tend to react more than V, so I plan to be ready for whatever she throws at me.

Warming up, I'm thinking she'll have to completely reinvent her game if she hopes to win. I've been playing so well. All year long. Solid. Consistent. No, I haven't won a major, but I've come close, and I've won a bunch of tournaments along the way. I even won a gold medal in women's doubles with Venus at the Beijing Olympics. And I've been healthy. This is key. This appearance at the Open is the first time I've played all four majors in back-to-back years, so I'm happy with my fitness and my energy and my focus. It spills over into my game, because the more I play, the better I play. Venus knows that about me, too. She knows she has to bring . . . something. And I know that she knows. And she knows that I know. Like I said, there are no surprises.

My plan is to start fast, maybe catch Venus before she's locked in. A lot of times, even top players fumble through the first few games of a match. I'm guilty of it, too. It's like we're sizing up our opponents, afraid to make a mistake, so we play tight until things loosen up. These early games are a little like a boxing match: two fighters circling in the ring, each waiting for the other to make the first move. It's a tentative dance, but my thing is to pounce. Doesn't always work out that you get that chance, because sometimes the game doesn't give you what you need, but that's the idea.

We'll start on my serve. That's huge. A big serve like mine can set me up for the whole match. Already I'm thinking, *Okay, Serena, here's your edge.* But then I step to the line and I don't get the ball quite where I want it on the toss, and I end up hitting my first serve into the net. It lets out a little of the air from my game plan. Not a lot, but some. I try not to place too much weight on the first point of a match, or the first serve, because it's not like they're worth any more than any of the other shots you'll need to make to get the win. You take that first point, you've still got to grab a hundred more. Some players, they're just the opposite. They want to get on the board first and start playing with a lead, but I don't worry about that. I don't even worry about the first game—unless, of course, I'm serving. Then I'm all over it. Then I can't let the other girl break.

Venus takes my second serve deep to the notch at the baseline, forcing me to short-hop the ball on my return. It's a shot I've been working on in practice with my dad—and I guess Venus has been working on it, too. It's a difficult shot to defend because it's right at your feet, with pace, and you're a little off balance coming out of your serve. There's not much I can do but wrist the ball back over the net, where Venus is waiting. Luckily, she tries to do too much with it and goes for a sideline winner to my forehand side, missing wide.

I take a deep breath. Doesn't matter to me if I beat my opponent or if she beats herself. As long as she's beat. Even if it's my sister. I love her dearly (she's my best friend!), but that gets tossed while we're play-ing. For now she's just like any other girl on the other side of the net, trying to keep me from what I want. She feels the same way. We tell each other we can be sisters later.

Venus gets the point right back. I basically give it to her, on an un-forced error off her return, right into the net, so I take another deep breath to settle. I think, *Come on, Serena. You can't be giving it away like that on a nothing shot.*

At 15-all, I'm caught flat in the middle of a long rally. Venus pow-ers a low return that looks to me like it will catch the net, so I don't move toward it the way I should, and I end up paying. Actually, I don't move toward it at all. You only get a split second to move toward a shot, and here I let that split second pass, so Venus's ball falls softly to the court, just out of reach. I want to smack myself on the head with my racquet—that's how disappointed I am in my own effort. I know better than to give up on a point before it's done.

One of the great things about tennis is it doesn't give you any time to dwell on your mistakes. Spend too much time on one and you'll make another. And another. There's always a next point to occupy your full attention, so I set that mental error aside and step to the line. Now it's V's turn to give it back with a mental error of her own—a long return that knots the game at 30–30. Next, she gets the ball where she wants it but tries to be too fine and sends it wide to the same sideline where she'd missed that previous shot, putting me up 40–30.

Here I take an extra beat before serving . . . then, a rifle shot, nearly on the T, curling away from V's forehand. My first ace. Glad to get that out of the way, along with this first game, but once again there's no time to dwell on it because there's no changeover. We change sides, but that's it. I try not to make eye contact with V as we pass. I have this mean, steely look when I play, so I'll just stare down my opponent if our eyes happen to meet. No big thing. But with V, I worry I'll smile or break out laughing, so it's better not to look and maybe cut the tension. Better to let it build and tighten and try to use it to my advantage.

Usually, I don't think about this. In fact, during the first game of the match I make a special point of crossing on the opposite side of the court, as far away from my opponent as possible. I've never seen anyone else do this, but it's become a ritual for me. My thinking is, What's the point of crossing in front of the umpire if there's no changeover? I'd rather steer clear, unless I feel like I need a sip of water or some type of equipment change, so that's the way I play it here.

Venus opens with her first serve, and I manage only a short return, which she crushes for her first winner. I can barely get my racquet on her next serve, and as she goes up 30–0 I think, *Dang, V, you keep serving like this, I'm in trouble.*

At some point during Venus's first service game I reach up and notice that one of my earrings has fallen off. (Hardly a fashion emergency, but worth noting, don't you think?) Working with my Nike designers, I'd put together a dynamite outfit for this tournament—a fun red dress, topped by a wide red bandana and highlighted by these giant hoop-inside-a-hoop-inside-a-hoop earrings. I love the look, but of course that's no edge when I'm up against my sister, who loves her look, too. I glance across the net and see she really does look great, in one of her own designs. Black. Stunning. I think, *Okay, so that's a push, V. All even on style points.*

I reach up and touch my left ear, where those giant hoops had been. Nothing. But I leave the other earring in place, and as I turn momentarily from the net I take time to laugh to myself and think, *Better be careful, Serena. These earrings are heavy! Don't want to list to one side!*

I turn back to the game, and it starts to feel to me like neither one of us wants to stamp this first set. It's early, but we're just trading miscues. I take the next point, when Venus sits back on my return and hits it long. I take the next point, too—on a double fault. I'm happy to have it, but I can see V is frustrated, and when she gets frustrated she usually follows with an extra effort—and that's just what happens here. Another monster serve that I'm fortunate to reach, but that's about it.

Now Venus is up 40–30, but she double-faults on the next point to put us at deuce.

Deuce. It's such a compelling point of pause in a close game. When I'm receiving, I always think it puts me in a good position to break; one mistake and my opponent will be backed to the wall. And yet when I'm serving, it feels to me like I'm in control. We're on different sides of the same stalemate, but it means different things depending on your perspective, and here my perspective is that Venus is struggling. It's early, I know. We're both a little sluggish, I know. But she's already double-faulted twice, and kept me in a game I don't seem to particularly want or deserve, so it's a good time to make a move.

Venus doesn't give me a chance: she reaches back and delivers a big serve, and then on my weak return she finds some funky new angle to my backhand side that I don't anticipate, passing me for another winner. Then, on her advantage, she hits another big serve to take the game.

I think, *So much for Venus struggling.* I also think, *Can't sit back and wait for Venus to give it up, Serena. You've got to take it from her. Now.*

These are my marching orders to myself as I approach the baseline—but I'm still not sharp. Venus catches me leaning the wrong way on a miss-hit, and I don't have time to recover, so she takes the point to go up 0–15, but then another ace brings me right back. (Love those aces!) I go up 30–15 on the next point, when Venus hits another return long, and I start to think neither one of us will ever get it going tonight. We're just a couple games in, but the match has no personality, no rhythm, no excitement. We're trading points, taking turns.

Can't be a whole lot of fun to watch, I realize. I think this way a lot, I'm afraid. About wanting to play thrilling, high-level tennis. About giving the fans something to cheer about. Don't misunderstand; I want to win. That's the single most important thing, but I want to win in an exciting way. I love playing in front of big crowds. I love that all these people spend their time and money watching me play. It's such an honor, especially here in New York, where the fans have always been so supportive. They appreciate good tennis here, and I feel a certain responsibility to give them a memorable effort, to get them on their feet—and this match is starting out like a snore.

It's probably not a good idea to think along these lines while I'm out here trying to win a tournament, but I can't help myself. Plus, I guess I'm not just worried about the fans losing interest. I'm worried about me. I'm like a lot of players in this way; I need to be dialed in to play well. I need to be focused, charged. I can't just go through the motions and expect to prevail. I started out feeling all jazzed and pumped, but ten minutes later we're just lulling ourselves to sleep. If I get bored, I'm done, so I tell myself to power things up—also, not a good idea, because you can't get an awesome rally going on your racquet alone. It's a two-way deal. There's a give-and-take, an ebb-and-flow. Every match takes on its own personality, and a part of me knows I just need to give this one some time to find it, but another part hurries my next couple serves and I end up double-faulting, to even the score at 30–30.

I think, *Aw, Serena, now look what you've done.*

I miss my next serve after that, and on my second serve Venus hits a return that I'd handle easily nine times out of ten—but here on this tenth time (apparently), all I can do is hit it weakly back into the net to go down 30–40.

Here's another thing I love about tennis: it switches gears on you double-quick. I don't love it so much when it takes me on a downshift like the one I'm nearly into here, but you've got to take the bad with the good, right? All of a sudden, I'm in a hole, but I don't get a chance to dig out: Venus catches the net on the next point, and the ball deflects onto my side in a crazy way and I've got no shot, so just like that she's got her first break. On a lucky bounce.

Lucky for V. Not so lucky for me.

During the changeover, I reach for this funny little match book I keep during every tournament. I begin a new book every year, and I've kept every one of them since I've been on the tour. I fill each book with pointers and messages and aphorisms. Whatever I can think might inspire me during my next match. The idea is I read it over and over before I take the court, and whenever I feel the need I sneak a peek during changeovers. For the most part, it's just a bunch of quotes, or reminders to capitalize on a certain weakness in my opponent's game, or to correct a certain weakness in my own game.

Last night, looking ahead to this match, I wrote: "Relax. Don't hit every ball hard. Start strong. U R younger sister, so pressure is on V. Toss high on serve. Don't let ball drop." I also wrote this, just before the tournament: "Your destiny has just begun, Serena. Remember your people. I'm proud of you. Keep it up. U R capable of anything."

There is just enough time to take in both messages and a couple sips of water before the umpire calls "Time!"—and as I set the book back in my tennis bag and press a towel to my face, I softly speak these same words into the fabric: "You are capable of anything, Serena."

I stand and start to move to my side of the court. I think, *Here you go, Serena. Here you go.*

U R the one with 7 Grand Slams, not her. U R #1. Play with a purpose. U will move forward. U will look at balls. U R the best in the whole world. U R amazing. It's on U, only on U. <u>U</u> R here to win, not her. Send her packing to the left, to the left. (Beyoncé!!!) U will add spin. U will fight for every point. U will not be afraid. It is not in your vocabulary. It is not in your nature. It is not in U, period. NO FEAR!!!

—MATCH BOOK ENTRY

ONE

Ride a Little, Bump a Little

My first tennis memory? People always ask about it, but I'm afraid I don't have one. I just remember playing, all the time. It's like tennis was always there, like going to services at Kingdom Hall. Like breathing.

I saw a picture once of Venus pushing me in a stroller on a tennis court, but I don't actually *remember* this moment. I've seen pictures of me holding a racquet taken around the time I started to walk. I don't *remember* those moments, either. I've heard all the stories, of course. The ones that have somehow passed into urban tennis legend, and the ones that still get kicked around in my family. Some of them are even true.

Best anyone can recall: I was three years old. It was a Saturday afternoon, maybe Sunday. My parents took us out to the public courts at a park in Lynwood, California, not far from where we lived. It was a total family affair. There was me, my older sister Venus, and my mom and dad, together with our older sisters Lyndrea, Isha, and Yetunde. The older girls had been playing for a time, while I had been trudging along, but then one day my dad announced that I was ready to take my swings, too. He put a standard, regulation-size racquet in my hand and positioned me a couple feet from the net. Then he climbed to the other side and started soft-tossing until I managed to hit a couple over.

"Just look at the ball, Serena," he kept saying, in that patient tone and sweet Louisiana drawl I'd come to hear in my dreams. "Just swing."

Years later, he took to calling me Meeka—a variation on my middle name, Jameka. Tunde pinned that nickname on me when I was about six and it stuck, and I used to love to hear it from my father. He still calls me Meeka, and whenever he does it puts me in mind of how things were between us when I was little, when I was first learning to really play. Say what you will about my dad (and folks have said an awful lot over the years), he had a gentle demeanor when he wanted to, especially when we were just starting out. He made a game out of it, encouraging me to swing as hard as I could. Didn't matter to him where I hit the ball, or how I hit it, just that I hit it.

After every toss, he'd offer a word of encouragement, a point of praise:

"Good job, Serena."

"Way to go."

"That's it."

My sisters looked on and cheered and chased the balls I missed or hit to the next court. They'd been down this way before, taking their own first hits—Venus, just a year or so before. I'd been around the court long enough to know what I was supposed to do. It was just my turn, is all. At last. Wasn't any kind of ceremony to it. Wasn't really any kind of big deal, except when I look back and see how far I've come—how far we've all come, really. My sister Isha even remembers what I was wearing: a white tennis skirt, with gathers in the middle, decorated with pink, gray, and purple flowers; my hair braided in cornrows and bunched in a ponytail at the top of my head. Even then, I was styling. We didn't have money for proper tennis clothes, but I wanted to look *good*.

I was tiny. People have a hard time believing this, considering how tall I am now. Venus was always tall for her age, but I was way on the small side. That regulation racquet was probably bigger than I was, but we couldn't afford a junior racquet. Over the years, I've wondered if that might have put some kind of stamp on the way I played, taking my very first swings with a racquet that was too big for me. Maybe that was the first instance of my dad setting things up so that success was something I had to reach for. It might be there for the taking, but I would have to rise to meet it.

My parents taught themselves the game so they could teach it to us. It's one of the first things people mention when they talk about my career or Venus's—and yet for some reason it's not always seen as a positive. I don't get that, because there's nothing wrong with learning about something and passing it on to your children. Yes, it was a calculated move. At some point my dad was watching a match on television, and he couldn't believe how much money these women were making, just for hitting a tennis ball. He's told the story so often it's been burned into me. He was watching a match being played by Virginia Ruzici, the 1978 French Open champion. The announcer mentioned that Ruzici had just earned $40,000 during one week of tournament play—more than my dad had earned all year. It didn't fit with how hard he worked for a living, how hard my mom worked, how hard it was for everyone they knew to get and keep ahead. And so the story goes that my dad went out the next morning to pick up a newspaper to confirm Ruzici's earnings, to see for himself if tennis players could actually make so much money in such a short stretch of time. When it turned out to be true, he came home and said to my mother, "We need to make two more kids and make them into tennis superstars."

At least that's the line he used to tell reporters after Venus and I started playing on the tour. It became a real fish-out-of-water story and a symbol of what people can do with a little vision and determination, when they reach beyond what they know for something new.

Now, tell me: what's wrong with *that*? Coming upon some rewarding new path your kids might follow and pointing them in the right direction? Doesn't seem to me there's anything to criticize here, but people are certainly quick to criticize, don't you think? In any case, I'm sure the story of how my family came to tennis has been embellished over the years, but at its core that's just what happened. And there's been some resentment layered onto it as well, because for whatever reason there's this notion that if you didn't grow up around the game, if it wasn't in your blood to begin with, you had no real claim on it. Tennis is like that, I'm afraid. There's a sense of entitlement, of belonging. Like you have to be born to it. Like you have to play it at a high level, before you can teach it. For the longest time, it was that sense of entitlement that probably kept a whole group of potentially talented minority and underprivileged kids from taking up the game. It must have felt to them like a sport of advantage—and I guess it was. Indeed, I've always believed that sense of entitlement is reinforced by the language of the game: advantage *me*!

No, the doors to the game weren't *really* closed on anyone, but they were essentially closed. If your parents didn't play, there was no reason for you to play. If no one in your community played, you'd never think to reach for a racquet in the first place. If you couldn't afford to be a member of some fancy country club, it might never occur to you to pick up a tennis racquet and teach yourself the game on some public court. But my dad saw tennis as a way to open doors for his daughters, probably thinking that the more doors that were open to us the better, so he ordered some instructional books and videos and taught himself the game. His idea was to kind of make it up as he went along. He'd do his homework, borrow what he liked from this or that coach, and find his own way to pass it on to his daughters.

My mother was pregnant with Venus at the time, and she was out on the court with my dad, working on her forehand and learning drills, technique, strategy. They were both good athletes, so the tennis came easy. They were both strong, physical, coordinated. They took to it right away. Before long, they felt like they could hit well enough to demonstrate proper technique and game strategy.

The idea, my dad took to saying, was to teach his girls to be champions, just like the professional players he saw on television—like Virginia Ruzici!—but that really came later. That was part of the lore that attached to my family after we started to have some success. The mental toughness, the single-minded focus, the positive affirmations, the mind of a champion . . . all that came later, too, after we took to the sport and started to show some talent for it.

Absolutely, Daddy believed tennis was our ticket up and out of Compton, the rough-and-tumble neighborhood in Los Angeles where we lived, but he also knew we had to take to it. He knew it wasn't enough to simply teach us the game and train us to be champions. If that was all it took, then everyone would be doing it. We had to have some God-given talent and athletic ability. We had to develop a passion for the game and an iron will to succeed, and all these things would take time presenting themselves. Or not. And so at first tennis was just something to do, a way for us to be together as a family.

Don't get me wrong: tennis became a real focus for us. Very quickly. It became Daddy's focus, certainly. And what a lot of people don't realize is my mom was with him every step of the way. This was her deal, too. It wasn't just that she supported my dad's vision. She saw what he saw; she wanted what he wanted; she worked for it just as much as he did. She had her own ideas on how we should train—and even now, she's one of the best at helping to break down my game and figure out what's working and what's not. When I was little, I actually spent more time hitting with my mom than I did with my dad. Venus was usually on the next court with my dad. And then, when it was time for my older sisters to hit, Venus and I would start picking up balls for them.

We all played, all the time. It was our thing. It got to where people would know we'd be out there on those courts every day after school. There were just two courts at the park in Compton, so the few recreational players there would know to get their games in during the day, because when three o'clock rolled around

Richard Williams would be pulling up in his Volkswagen mini-bus, dirty yellow with a white top, with his five girls spilling out onto those courts like they had their names on them. There were a few more courts at the park in Lynwood—maybe six—but we always used the two at the back, and the people there knew we'd be coming, too. It's not like there were too many people playing tennis on those public courts back then. If it happened that the courts were occupied when we arrived, we waited our turn. We'd do some drills, or some stretching off to the side, maybe work on our swings. My dad never minded the wait. His thing was: no problem, we'll fill the time.

The courts themselves were in sorry shape. There was broken glass every here and there. Cracks in the cement. Weeds poking through. Soda cans, beer bottles, fast-food wrappers . . . I've read articles that say there was drug paraphernalia littering those courts and that we girls had to sweep the syringes and tubes and plastic bags out of the way before we could play, but I don't remember any of that. When I ask my dad about this, he says, "Why you want to dwell on the negative, Meeka?" In other articles it says we could hear gunshots ringing out while we were playing, from all the drive-by shootings. That I remember full well, only the shots themselves didn't sound all that terrifying until I learned what they were. At first, I just thought someone was setting off firecrackers or popping some balloons, but once I learned what the sound meant it would shake me up pretty good. "Never mind the noise, Meeka," Daddy used to say whenever gunfire rang out. "Just play."

Wasn't exactly Center Court at Roland Garros, but it was all we knew.

We bounced around a lot, from public court to public court. There was one place we used to play that had these great chain-link nets. You'd drill a ball into the net, and you'd rattle the cage and feel like you really accomplished something—even though we were supposed to hit it *over* the net, of course. My dad tried to mix it up for us, but for the most part those courts in Lynwood and Compton were our home base. We branched out, though—and if we didn't like a certain park, or a certain neighborhood, we wouldn't go back.

Once, at Lynwood Park, a group of kids started giving us a hard time. I was probably five or six. Venus and I were hitting. My sisters were chasing balls. I don't remember what my parents were doing, but they must have been there, somewhere. These kids kept taunting us. They called us Blackie One and Blackie Two. It was so cruel, so arbitrary, but we kept playing. Finally, Tunde stopped chasing balls and chased these kids instead. She was the oldest, so she felt a responsibility to look after us. She had our backs. I don't know what she said to these kids when she caught up to them, but they didn't bother us anymore after that.

As kids, I don't think we heard those taunts as racist remarks. They were just taunts. Those kids were just being mean. If Venus and I had been more typical California golden girls, these kids might have called us Blondie One and Blondie Two. We were just different; that's how I took it at the time. We stood out. Might have been something more to it than that, but I was too young to recognize it. But maybe Tunde heard these remarks a little differently, and that's why she chased these boys down.

However it happened, and whatever it meant, I looked on and thought, *Someday, Serena, you won't need your sisters to fight your battles for you.*

Over time, Daddy collected all this equipment—ball hoppers, carts, cones, whatever he could find to make our sessions more like the ones in his books and videos. He really tried to create a professional environment for us on a nothing budget. For a while, the routine was we had to take out the middle seat in our van so my dad could fit the shopping cart he'd somehow managed to acquire, which he would fill with tennis balls and wheel out to the court. We must have made an odd picture, crammed into the van like that with a shopping cart. I'd sit up front with Venus, sharing a seat belt. The big girls sat in back. The cart would be jammed in the middle, alongside a couple brooms so we could sweep the court. It always felt to me like we were rumbling along in that van from *Scooby Doo*, our equipment jammed in so tight we'd have to stick our arms and legs out the windows to make room.

My mom would usually meet us at the courts after work. Eventually, it got a little tiresome lugging that cart back and forth each day with all the rest of our gear, so my father started locking the cart to the rusty fence surrounding the court. Saved us a lot of time and trouble. This was another example of my parents' approach: when something worked, they stayed with it; when it no longer made sense, they tried something else. We still took the balls home with us every night, in buckets and boxes and milk crates and whatever else we could find to carry them, but now it was much more efficient; now they took up a lot less room.

Man, those balls were precious to us. They were like money in the bank. I don't recall that we ever retired a ball from our collection. Daddy would take the oldest, baldest, flattest balls and turn them into a drill. He'd keep them in the mix with all the other balls, but when he pitched one of these special balls to us he said it would help us with our speed, our footwork, our concentration. I hated going after those balls—they just wouldn't bounce!—but Daddy kept them in play.

"At Wimbledon," he'd say, "the balls will bounce low, just like these special balls, so you have to be ready."

Occasionally, we'd hit a ball into the woods or out onto the street beyond the fence, and we'd have to go looking for it before giving it up for lost. I hit more balls over the fence than my sisters—not by accident, necessarily, but by design. See, I discovered that when Daddy sent me across the street to collect the ball after one of my errant shots, it meant a break from the hard work he had us doing on the court, so I learned to play the angles at an early age.

Also occasionally, Daddy would add a new can or two to our

collection, and that was always a real treat. Those fresh balls really popped. You could follow them all afternoon, up against the faded yellow of all those tired old tennis balls. It always felt like I had to bear down a little harder whenever a fresh ball reached the top of the pile and was put in play; there was a little more hop to it; it bounced off my racquet with a little more purpose and authority. Plus, it *sounded* great—the music of the game. I never liked to waste one of those new balls with a bad shot. It was like a missed opportunity. New balls are like that. To this day, whenever I smell a can of just-opened balls it puts me in mind of those new cans my dad used to bring out, when those brand-new balls made me feel like a real tennis player. They were so clean, so yellow, the felt so fine like the hairs on the back of your head . . . it was almost a shame to get them dirty.

Of course, they all got dirty, eventually. Soon, they'd lose that fresh bounce and they'd get all dirty and there'd be no telling the new balls from the ones at the bottom of the pile—but that didn't mean we stopped playing. No, sir. It only meant we'd have to get all these other balls to pop with the same purpose and authority, until my father could get us a couple new cans.

That was the way of things for the first while. We developed our own little routine, our own little family dynamic, built around this funny little game. We were little girls smacking a ball around inside a box, that's what Daddy used to say. And, at first, that's all it was. But then we started showing flashes that we could really play, when I was about five or six and Venus about six or seven, so my parents changed things up on us. They went at it harder. They pushed us harder. That might have been their plan all along, but they didn't go harder until we showed them we were ready. And when we were, we went from playing just a couple hours a day four or five times a week, to three or four hours a day every day of the week. Some days, we'd even be out for two-a-day sessions, starting up at six o'clock in the morning before school, and then again after school, usually until dark. In the morning, we'd sometimes get to the court before the sun was all the way up, and Daddy would have us stretch or practice our swings until we could see well enough to hit.

I still do that, by the way—head out to practice at first light. It's my favorite time to hit, because everything's so quiet; you've got the whole day in front of you. I hate getting up early—*really!!!*—but I push myself. You can put in a full day's work before your opponent even gets out of bed, and that can give you an incredible psychological edge to carry into your next match, knowing you're fully prepared, knowing the other girl is sleeping in while you're out there sweating. And in those moments when I'm waiting for the sun to finish rising I'll think back to those early mornings on those public courts in Compton and Lynwood, keeping busy until my dad gave us the nod to start playing.

It got to be a grueling schedule, but none of us really minded it. Or we hardly noticed. We were all together. It was what we did, that's all. We didn't know any different. We didn't have a whole lot of friends outside of school. There was only time for each other, for tennis. My dad tried to make it fun for us. Every session had a theme, a structure. He'd set up all these creative games, with cones placed around the court, and there'd be a series of challenges we'd have to meet. Sometimes he'd put up little messages or sayings on the fence around the court to help motivate us, or maybe just to make us smile.

If you fail to plan, you plan to fail.
Believe.
You are a winner.
Be humble.
Say "Thank you."
(This last saying was one of his favorites.)

He'd write out these empowering messages on big pieces of paper or oak tag, or sometimes he'd have us write them out. Then he'd hang them up all around the court. If there was a theme to one of his sessions—like "Focus"—all the messages would have to do with the theme. He really put a lot of time and effort into this part of our training, because he believed it was important. He wanted these messages to resonate, for the visual image of the word to linger in our minds long after we'd left the court. Years later, when we moved to Florida, he had some signs made professionally, with his most effective messages—and those he put up permanently.

Basically, he was fooling us into thinking we weren't working, with all those games and messages, but after a while we caught on. We didn't care, though. We didn't mind working hard. I mean, we were kids, so of course we grumbled from time to time. Of course we did our little celebration dance whenever it rained, because that meant we wouldn't have to practice. Of course I hit a ball or two over the fence to buy myself a break while I went to retrieve it. But it wasn't so bad. Every now and then, my dad would reward us with some time to play in the nearby playground, or in the sandbox. That was another great treat for us girls. I used to love doing cartwheels. Whenever I had a five-minute break, I'd be in the grass alongside the court, flipping around. I spent a lot of time on the monkey bars, too, as I recall.

Even when we weren't playing tennis, our games were tennis-related. One of our very favorite family games was UNO, which I always thought was fitting for us. We played that game all the time—and I mean *all* the time!—and it really instilled a champion-type mind-set. After all, the point of the whole game is right there in its name—to be number one! No, UNO's got nothing to do with tennis, not directly, but it's a great teaching tool for any individual sport. It instills such a killer mind-set. Every game produces a winner, but UNO is one of the few games I can think of where you need to announce yourself as the winner just before you actually win, when you're down to one card, so everyone else around the table has a shot at you. It goes from every-girl-for-herself to every-girl-gunning-for-the-leader in a flash, and in this way it can really prepare you for the kind of competition you might face in a crowded tournament field. At first, it's just on you to take care of your own game, but then everyone is looking to knock you down. I don't know if my parents had this in mind when they introduced us to the game, but that's the way I always played it.

Sometimes, our competitions were more straightforward. When it was just us girls, playing in the yard at home, we used to play a game called Grand Slam. Usually it was me and Venus and Lyn. I don't know how we came up with it. Basically, it was like box ball, or four square. We'd hit a tennis ball back and forth with our hands. The court was just a square on the sidewalk. If the ball hit the grass, it was out. Sometimes, we threw some dirt on the sidewalk and it became a clay court—the French Open. Then we might throw down some grass—Wimbledon. I won so many majors right there in Compton, all because my dad had us thinking, breathing, *living* tennis so much it seeped into our regular childhood games.

It was everywhere and all around. As I look back on those moments playing hand-tennis with my sisters in front of our house at 1117 East Stockton Street in Compton, California, it puts me in mind of something my mom used to say when we were kids. "Whatever you become," she always said, "you become in your head first." That was a real mantra for her. Daddy took to saying it, too. Whatever it was we wanted to do or become, they'd tell us to see ourselves doing it, becoming it. It's tied in to what my dad was trying to do, getting us to visualize those words in our minds once we stepped away from his posters and signs. When Isha came home one day and announced she wanted to be a lawyer, my mom said, "That's great, Isha. Now go and be a lawyer in your head and the rest will follow." It was the same with tennis—even hand-tennis. We couldn't become champions *for real* until we became champions in our heads, and here we were, little kids, winning Wimbledon, winning the French Open, and willing it so.

*   *   *

It wasn't long before we sisters started making some serious noise on the local tennis scene. My father hadn't known a whole lot about that world going in, but he was a quick study. He always said he had a master plan for us—and that he was "a master planner"— and part of that plan was to collect whatever tennis insights he could find. He moved about by touch and feel; he added to our game plan by borrowing from the game plans of others; mostly, he watched local pros and picked up ideas and strategies for his sessions with us. By the time I was seven going on eight, and Venus was eight going on nine, Daddy was scouting area tournaments and academies, and following the comings and goings of all the young players in and around Los Angeles. It was a competitive environment—and a close-knit community. Everyone knew everyone else, so it's no wonder people started to pay attention to what he was doing with his girls on these courts all around Los Angeles. Our home courts might have been neglected and underused, but as we bounced around we turned a couple heads, that's for sure.

For one thing, there weren't a whole lot of African-American tennis players on the circuit at any age. That goes back to the entitlement or privilege that attached to the sport. For another, you didn't see too many entire families on those public courts. There were seven of us; we couldn't help but turn heads, and over time Daddy got to talking to all these people and tapping in to whatever was going on in L.A. for kids playing tennis. This was an important part of our development, and the first time we got any kind of exposure as players.

He signed us up for all these different events. One day when I was seven he came home and told us we'd be hitting with Billie Jean King, and of course we all knew who she was. Another big part of Daddy's grand plan was to get us to learn the game by watching the pros. He had us watching so much tennis on television, talking all the time about all these great players, that we were terribly excited. We thought Billie Jean would be hitting with just us, but that's not at all how it happened. There was a clinic, organized by World Team Tennis, and Billie Jean was one of the featured participants.

Even so, it was a big, big day for us. I remember going through our closet with Venus, trying to pick out just the right outfit, because even then I was into how I looked on the court. (In Compton, all five of us shared a closet, so it was always a frenzied time when we were scrambling to find something to wear.) We didn't really have proper tennis clothes, but we wanted to make a good impression. Lyn and Isha played that day, too. We all fussed over what to wear, and then, when we finally got to the clinic and started playing, Billie Jean actually walked over to us during one of the drills. I'm sure she was just being a good ambassador for the sport, making special time on each court with each group of kids—just like I try to do now when I'm asked to participate in one of these clinics, because of Billie Jean's example—but it felt to us like she'd come over just to watch us play. Like she'd heard about us and wanted to check us out. That was the kind of confidence our parents instilled in us when it came to tennis; that was how they had us thinking: there were the Williams sisters, and there was everyone else. Over and over, they kept telling us we were champions, that everyone in tennis would know who we were, and on and on. After a while, we started to believe them, but here at this World Team Tennis event it was too soon for all of that. This was just Billie Jean, making the rounds, working with as many kids as she could. She didn't know us from any other group of sisters out there on that court.

Unfortunately, the meeting meant more to me when I was look-ing forward to it than it did when I was in the middle of it, because I didn't play too well when Billie Jean was hitting to me. Plus, Ve-nus did such a good job when it was her turn, so that made it even worse. I panicked, I guess. (I was so nervous!) I think I hit every shot long or into the net, but that's how it goes sometimes. You look ahead to some meaningful moment and set it up in your mind like it's going to be this huge, consequential deal, and then it just fizzles. The trick, really, is to find some takeaway moment in the fizzle and carry *that* with you instead, and here I managed to shrug off that I'd played so poorly and ended up crying because Venus played so well, and remember instead that I got to hit with the great Billie Jean King. That alone was pretty huge and consequential.

I think back on that Billie Jean King moment every time I look forward to an event or a milestone or a special opportunity. Why? Because it grounds me. It reminds me that we can take pleasure and pride in the thrill of anticipation, but at the same time we must be careful not to invest too heavily into any one situation, in case it doesn't work out the way we've planned. That's life, right? We get disappointed from time to time. But that doesn't mean we shouldn't look forward to anything, or even that we should keep our expectations reasonable. Not at all. What it means for me is to aim high and to know that if I fall short of the mark it was still worth doing. Whatever it happens to be, if it's worth looking forward to it, if it's worth taking aim, it's worth doing.

We went to tournaments from time to time. I remember watching Gabriella Sabatini, and thinking she was so tall and so beautiful, but at the same time thinking, *Man, I can beat that girl.* That's where my head was at as a kid. My parents had me thinking I was invincible. Gabriella wasn't built like the other girls on the tour; she was big and powerful, almost majestic. I kept staring at her and wondering if I would ever be that tall, that graceful, that powerful.

Another time, about a year or so after that World Team Tennis event with Billie Jean King, we hit with Zina Garrison and Lori McNeil. Here I would have been about eight years old, and these two great players were pretty much it in terms of role models for African-American girls on the tennis court. They were doubles partners, so they had a real rapport. This time, it actually *was* a special opportunity my dad had arranged. It wasn't any kind of clinic. It was just us, and Zina Garrison and Lori McNeil. I don't know how Daddy pulled this off, but he did. There I was, still a tiny little thing, thinking I could take it to these two great players.

I actually thought I could beat them—that's how confident Venus and I were in our games. But then we started hitting and I thought, *There's just no way.* Oh my God, Zina and Lori were so strong! So quick! We couldn't hang with them at all, of course, but that was cool. That was just the silent fuel I'd need to put in the tank to keep me going to the next level.

There was another great program my father found for us in L.A. around the same time: "Youth vs. Experience." The way it was set up was they paired an older player, usually someone with experience on the tour, with an up-and-coming kid. Some of the older players were good club players or local teaching pros, and some were former tour professionals. I'd never heard of the lady I played against, so it wasn't any kind of big deal, but Venus drew a woman named Dodo Cheney, who'd actually won the Australian Championship back in 1938. Dodo Cheney was probably in her seventies when she played Venus, and Venus took it to her. She really did. My old lady beat me pretty soundly, but Venus beat her.

I mention this because Venus was really the first to make a name for herself, and it was largely through outings like this one— and her usual strong showings in local tournaments. I still remember the very first article written about Venus. We all remember it, because it set in motion one of our favorite family adventures—or misadventures, I should say. The article was in a local newspaper, the *Compton Gazette*. Here again, I was about seven or eight. The article was about Venus, mostly, but it was also about all of us. How we trained together on the public courts around town. How our parents taught themselves the game. How the tennis world was expecting great things. And on and on.

Daddy was so proud when the story came out that he wanted to grab as many copies of the paper as he could for souvenirs. His idea was to drive around to all the houses in our community on the morning the papers were delivered and swipe them from people's yards. Not the most neighborly solution, to be sure. Not the most practical, either. I mean, here he was, excited that we were finally getting this positive publicity for our tennis, and at the same time negating all that publicity by taking away all those newspapers so folks couldn't read about us. He could have just called the *Compton Gazette* office and asked for some copies, or gone to the local drugstore and bought as many as he needed for about twenty cents apiece, but these options never occurred to him.

So off we went, on our family paper-grab. It wasn't the most logical operation. Daddy would drive the van up and down the street, and whenever he spotted one of those rolled-up newspapers on some driveway or front walk, he'd pull over, get out of the car, and scamper over and swipe the paper. Then he'd race back to the car and drive off. It was such an absurd scene, and we girls were sitting in the back of the van, giggling about it, until finally Isha suggested that they could hit a lot more houses if she was the one doing the driving. The rest of us weren't too happy with this idea, because it meant we'd collect all the papers we needed that much sooner, and after that we might have to go and practice. As it was, we were missing practice for this, and whenever we missed practice, for the weather or for any other reason, it was something to celebrate.

My father thought about this awhile and agreed this might be a better approach. At the very least, he might get us back on the practice court that much sooner. Only trouble was, Isha was just thirteen and couldn't drive. She said, "How hard can it be, Daddy?"

Daddy said, "Are you sure?"

Isha said, "Yes, Daddy. I can do it. I can do it."

That's how it was with us girls. Nothing was out of reach.

So that was the plan. Wasn't a very good plan, but it was a plan. Isha got behind the wheel. I climbed into the backseat with Venus and Lyn. Daddy walked alongside the van, and off we went. Only we didn't get very far. Isha had some idea what she was doing, but not a lot. She didn't have a great concept of space or depth or any of those things you figure out when you're an experienced driver.

She didn't understand how close she was to the cars parked on the side of the street, and she proceeded to run right into one of them. And then another. Took off a couple side mirrors along the way. It was crazy!

Daddy had managed to collect a couple papers before Isha started to lose control of the van, but now he was running alongside and yelling for Isha to step on the brakes. He was yelling, but mostly to be heard. Underneath the loud voice, he was surprisingly calm. He said, "Hit the brake, Isha." And then, when she did, he came up to her window and said, "Are you okay?" His tone was soft; he wasn't mad. Anyway, he didn't *sound* mad, and that was always one of the nicest, most reassuring things about my dad. We were just kids, so I'm sure we set him off from time to time, but he would just take a deep breath and let his frustration pass and then deal with whatever it was in a calm, patient manner.

Meanwhile, in the backseat, the three of us were trying to climb out the window. We were so scared! Isha was crying, crying, crying. Daddy was more embarrassed than anything else. Frustrated, too, because his plan had somehow backfired. Now he had to wait out there in the street and talk to all these people whose cars Isha had hit. Can you imagine! We didn't mention that we took their newspapers, just that we hit their cars, and then we had to drive over to the ATM to take out money to reimburse them for the damage, money we didn't really have to spare. I think it cost us over one hundred dollars, when if we had bought the papers at the newsstand it would have just been five or six dollars.

We laughed about it, though. Right away, we laughed about it. We sat in the back and turned it into a song. Lyn made it up to poke fun at Isha, but we all joined in soon enough. We sang: "Ride a little, bump a little, tear the mirror off a little . . ." It came with its own little singsong melody. It got to be a long-running joke in our family, one of those Greatest Hits–type stories you take out and tell over and over again. Isha gets all red-faced whenever we bring it up, whenever we start singing, because it certainly wasn't her finest moment, but even now, all these years later, that little song can get us going. One of us will fall in to singing, and the others will chime in, and at the other end we'll just laugh and laugh and remember what it was like out there in Compton, back when we were all still making it up as we went along, learning the game by touch and feel, on some level knowing our world was about to open up for us in a big-time way.

Serena, this game is mental. Good thoughts are powerful. Negative thoughts are weak. Decide what U want to be, have, do and think the thoughts of it. Your vision will become your life. Hold on to the thought of what U want. Make it absolutely clear in your mind. U become what U think about most. U attract what you think about most. Think. Do. Be.

—MATCH BOOK ENTRY

TWO

The Greatest Love of All

Away from tennis, we were just a regular family. Sort of. I was the youngest of five sisters. There was me at the bottom, and then Venus, fifteen months ahead of me. I was actually born in Saginaw, Michigan, not far from where my mom was born and raised, but we moved to Compton when I was a baby. Ahead of Venus, there was Lyndrea, whom we all called Lyn, and Isha. The oldest was Yetunde—or Tunde, for short.

My parents established the tone in our house, but you could say we girls held sway. My parents were disciplinarians, but on top of that we were taught to be self-disciplined. My older sisters used to say me and V had it easy, because by the time my parents got to us they were too tired and worn out to be superstrict disciplinarians, but I don't know about that. They were still pretty hard on us, but we were even harder on ourselves. We were expected to do our schoolwork and our chores, and to help each other in whatever ways were age-appropriate. Tunde and Isha could help the younger girls with their homework, say, while Lyn and Venus could help me clean my section of our closet. (Notice that I was the one on the receiving end of my sisters' assists. I knew how to work a good thing, even then.) We went dutifully to our daily practice sessions, but it wasn't entirely without complaint. Actually, we whined more than we complained, but mostly we whined among ourselves. There was an unspoken rule that any real misgivings we might have had about logging all those hours on the court should be . . . well, unspoken. We were meant to practice like it mattered, like there was no place else we'd rather be—because, of course, these practices *did* matter. They were all part of my parents' plan.

My mom worked as a nurse. My dad had his own security firm. What that meant, for most of my childhood, was that he was around. Later on, after he'd turbocharged our tennis schedule, I used to catch myself hoping he'd have to go to work and cancel practice, but that never happened; his schedule was flexible. Our practice times? Not so much. My mom's work schedule was set by the hospital, but as we got older she started to take on more private patients, so there was a little more room. Meanwhile, my dad set it up so he worked at night; sometimes, he worked while we were in school, but it was mostly at night, after we went to bed. When we were home, he was home. Usually, he was trying to talk to one of us about tennis. Trying to get us to watch matches with him on television. Looking ahead to our next practice.

Daddy carved out some special time for each of us, underneath our hectic comings and goings. He'd talk to us about focus and discipline. His big thing was for each of us to have a plan and to write it down. The plan could be about tennis, school, life, whatever. He'd say, "Meeka, did you have a plan for today? Did you write it down?" By writing it down, he said we would be more likely to own it and to see it through. It can be a powerful motivational tool, I guess, but try telling that to a little kid who didn't quite see the point, a kid who would rather be doing cartwheels or dancing.

We sisters all fit into our particular roles. Tunde was the forgiver; she had a heart of gold. Isha was the caretaker; she looked after each of us, and helped to establish a sense of order in our private world. Lyn was our play pal; she was everyone's favorite knockabout buddy, always up for a new adventure. Venus was my protector. I'm not quite sure how the others saw her, but to me she was like a benevolent bodyguard, on the constant lookout for any situation that might cause me trouble or distress. And me, I was the princess; I was everyone's pet. Looking back, I think I was more like a pest, but my sisters let me get away with everything!

What's curious is that we all kept those roles into adulthood. Even now, I'll reach out to Lyn if I'm looking to cut up or do the town, or to Isha, if I need help sorting through the twists and turns of my crazy schedule. And so on.

Another curious side note to how we grew up was that all five girls shared a bedroom, with four beds. Do the math: it meant one of us was the odd girl out, and since I was the youngest that was me. There were two sets of bunk beds: Isha and Tunde, the two oldest, had the two beds on top; Lyn and Venus had the two down below. Every night, I'd have to bunk with a different sister—and here, too, there was a lesson for a lifetime. A situation like that might have messed with my sense of belonging or identity, but that's not how I looked at it. How I looked at it was it brought me closer to each of my sisters. How I looked at it was I had this great gift that none of the other girls had. It might have been a negative, but I took it as a positive. Each night, I'd crawl into bed with a different sister, and as a result we each had a special bond. Instead of feeling like I didn't quite belong anywhere, I felt like I belonged everywhere. It was empowering, really. It made for a series of real, close, substantive relationships, and I had it going on four times over.

I fit myself in, in whatever ways I could, wherever I could—an odd way to look out at the world, but ultimately a healthy one, I think. The constant bed-hopping reminded me yet again that nothing is ever handed to you, not even a bed to call your own. Also, it taught me to grab at what I needed, and to make it my own—and at the same time to make the best of what I had in the first place. There was a lot of love in our house; we were bursting with it. But it took chasing after it each night in this unusual way for me to trust in it; it took reaching for it, and reaching for it, to know it wouldn't slip away.

It all goes to character. The way you're raised. *Where* you're raised.

How you look out at the world. How the world looks back at you.
All of that gets mixmastered together in such a way that you come
out the other side a fully formed person—only it took me a good
long while before I got my game on in this respect. Fully formed?
That wasn't me, not until I was much, much older. I took shape
at my own pace. For a while, I had a real princess-type mind-set.
Maybe it came from being the youngest. Maybe it came from smiling my way into a different sister's good graces each night. Maybe it
came from learning to get what I wanted. Maybe I was just spoiled,
plain and simple. My sisters took care of me, that's for sure, and I
was pretty good at playing one off another to get what I wanted.

Perfect example: we used to put on these ridiculous talent shows,
but after a while Lyn and V never wanted to participate because I
always had to win. That was my thing, winning. Man, I hated to
lose! (I *still* hate to lose!) Isha or Tunde would usually be the judge,
and the rest of us would sing or dance or do a little skit. I always
sang the same song—Whitney Houston's "Greatest Love of All"—
and if I didn't win, I cried. (Wouldn't have killed me to come up
with another routine, but I *loved* that song.) I'd kick and fuss until
the judge made me the winner. It didn't matter if Venus or Lyn deserved to win. It only mattered that I got my way.

I don't know why my sisters put up with me, but they did. Lord
knows, I didn't make it easy for them. Actually, I was kind of
horrible. (*I* wouldn't have put up with me!) Some of the stunts I
pulled were off the charts. But cute cuts you a lot of slack, I quickly
learned, and it buys you a batch of forgiveness. Once, we'd all been
given piggy banks by a Spanish teacher my father had hired to work
with us. The deal was if one of us did particularly well at our lessons, we'd get a porcelain piggy bank—empty, but done up with
traditional Mexican-style painting on the sides. They were really
nice. I think I was the last sister to get one, and when I did I was
so proud of myself—but then I broke mine, and I was devastated. It
was worse than not earning one in the first place. I'd set it to rest on
this wicker bookcase we had in our bedroom, and it toppled over.

Next thing you know, Lyn's piggy bank also broke. After that, Venus's broke as well. No one could figure out why these piggy banks kept breaking. It was a big family mystery, until about ten or twelve years later when I finally confessed: I'd smashed my sisters' piggy banks because mine was broken; I couldn't stand it that they had something I didn't have. It was the only way I knew to cover this lost ground.

My goodness, I was awful. But I was the baby of the family, so I got away with a lot. That's how it goes in some families; the baby gets a free pass, so it took a while for me to figure out this right-and-wrong business. I even struggled with it on the tennis court, where it came up almost as soon as I started competing. Thinking back on it, I can't believe I started playing in matches at such a young age, because at first my parents were only concerned with form and function. They wanted me to hit the ball properly, to work on my ground strokes, to really get a good feel for my game. With me and Venus, it was mostly about hitting. Over and over and over. With Lyn and Isha, it was also about hitting, but on top of that it was about tactics and positioning. (Tunde had drifted away from the game at some point, as we got older.) I never really talked strategy with my parents when I was little. The concept of hitting it where your opponent isn't, of playing to win . . . somehow those things were instinctive with me. By the time I was six or seven, Daddy had me playing in these local leagues, and I knew to move the other girl around. I knew to put the ball away for a winner. I knew from watching all those matches on television, from going to all those tournaments. But I didn't know it well enough to put it into words. I just *knew*. Like it was a part of me.

There was one league I remember in particular, the Domino's Pizza League. I joined when I was about seven, and my mom used to take me to most of my matches because my dad was usually off at some tournament or other with Venus or Isha. I used to win most of my matches, but my teammates lost most of theirs, so we never really won anything. They had it set up so there were four to six girls on a team. We'd compete individually against the girls from the other team, and then at the end we'd tally up our scores, and whichever team had won the most games would win the match. I'd breeze through a lot of my matches and end up playing hopscotch by myself, or dancing and cartwheeling along on the sidewalk behind the courts. I wasn't a very good teammate, I guess. I didn't have it in me to root for the other girls on my team.

There was this one girl, Anne, who always played me tough. She was good, but I was better. She wanted it, but I wanted it more. Can't say for sure *why* I wanted it more, or how I knew to measure my will to win against hers—but this was how Daddy had me thinking on that court. He had me sizing up my opponent, and figuring where I'd find my advantage, without really talking to me about it. It came from all those hours watching tennis on television, watching all those VCR tapes of classic matches. It all just seeped in.

This one time, Anne beat me pretty thoroughly—only I counted it as a victory for me. I was down 5–2 in games, when Anne made the fool move of asking me the score. Big mistake. Why? Well, you have to realize, in little-kid matches there are no referees. The parents aren't even supposed to watch. It's left to us kids to keep our own score and make our own calls, and it was always a special point of pride to me that I called a fair game. A lot of girls would cheat like crazy. A lot of that was because they were just young, and they didn't know the rules or couldn't follow the flight of the ball as it went past and found the line, but a lot of that was because they were cheaters. You'd hit a ball that was in by a couple feet, they'd call it out. They'd serve it way wide and insist it was good. Not me.

Except for this one time, against Anne, when my moral compass pointed in an entirely different direction. For whatever reason it really, really bugged me that this girl couldn't even keep score. I thought, *How can you even ask such a stupid question? Why are you even wasting my time? What's that about?* We were only seven years old, of course, but—still!—it was just counting. We'd been counting since kindergarten. What was so hard about keeping score?

So what did I do? I glared across the net at poor Anne and said the score was 5–2, in my favor. I gave her my most menacing look and claimed three of those games for myself. I don't know why I did it, but I did it. And I don't know why or how Anne bought it, but she bought it. I'm certainly not proud of myself. I don't think I was a bad kid, even though I was clearly in the wrong on this one, and yet I look back and can't even recognize my behavior. I've tried to understand it. Yes, I was pampered at home by my big sisters. Yes, I was used to getting what I wanted. Yes, I liked to win, no matter what. Maybe that's all it was. Maybe I just didn't want to lose. Maybe the fact that this girl couldn't even count was unacceptable to my entitled self. Whatever it was, I announced the score with such conviction that my opponent had no choice but to accept it.

I must have felt badly about it, but I played on. I couldn't lose to this girl, I convinced myself. Especially now. I couldn't steal all those games and not come away with a victory—a victory on paper, at least. I looked at her across the net, with her glasses and her simple, trusting face, and I thought, *How could someone be so naïve? So timid? How could she give back all those games?* Underneath feeling bad for her, I was also angry that we were both out there playing to win, and she couldn't take things seriously enough to keep score.

Then, after a while, a lightbulb must have switched on in Anne's head. She said, "Wait a minute. I think *I* was up 5–2."

"What are you talking about?" I shot back. "*I'm* up 5–2."

We went back and forth on this for a couple beats, but ultimately I prevailed. I was meaner about it, I guess, and yet somehow this girl battled back to 5–5. That would have been a real stroke of justice for Anne if she managed to beat me anyway, but for me, at this point, it would have been a humiliation. I know I'd already humiliated myself, but this would have just been humiliation on top of humiliation. And so, in my narrow seven-year-old worldview, I was digging deep and making double-sure this little girl didn't somehow beat me—even though she already had. It became a real pride thing. A stupid pride thing. She'd been up three games on me, and now she was up three more, and still I talked myself into thinking it would be some kind of victory if I pushed the phony score in my favor.

Shame on me, right? Absolutely. But I was starting to realize that I *loved* to win. At all costs. I loved my family. I loved my sisters. But winning just about beat all, in my developing spirit of competition.

In the end, I held on to "beat" Anne 7–5, and I somehow allowed myself to feel good about it afterward. Like I said, I counted it as a victory. I'd backed myself into an impossible corner, and while I was there I convinced myself that I deserved to win, that I was a better player than Anne, that the win meant more to me than it would have to her. All this nonsense to justify my princess–*prima donna* behavior. And after I held on to legitimately win those final two games, I went right back to thinking I had more integrity than my opponents, because I never cheated them on the lines. Even in this match against Anne, I didn't cheat on the lines. If my shot was out, I called it out. If her shot was in, I called it in. I just gave myself a bunch of games when she wasn't looking.

I was becoming a real player, but I still had a lot to learn.

My goodness, I had a rotten streak. I was horrible—a real witch! To my sisters. To my little kid opponents. I had this double-dose of mischief and rebellion that couldn't help but bubble forth. It even came out with my parents—against my better judgment. But I was smart: I always had deniability. That's what they call it on those *Law and Order* shows I like to watch: *plausible deniability.* I could always point the finger, look the other way, or pretend to have no idea there was any kind of trouble. That's one of the great benefits of being the youngest. People are inclined to see your side because you're cute.

Of course, it's significant to note that I never thought of myself as cute. That might have been my role in the family, but that wasn't my self-image. I looked in the mirror and saw an ugly duckling. Now, all these years later, I look at pictures of myself from back then and think, *How could my mom have let me out of the house looking like that?* I blame my sisters, too. Even then, they had a real sense of style, a sense of fashion, a flash and flair. Surely, they must have noticed how goofy I looked.

But all I got back was that I was cute, so of course I put that to work for me. Once, I "accidentally" hit my dad with a tennis ball, and I used my cute persona to full advantage to deflect the blame. The way it worked, whenever someone was on the other side of the net and a shot got away from us, we were supposed to shout, "A ball! A ball!" Like the way a golfer shouts "Fore!" So one afternoon when I was feeling particularly disgruntled or beaten down by a particularly grueling session, I whacked a hard liner in the direction of my dad, who was picking up balls and had his back to the net. I don't think I meant to hit him, exactly, but it was clear to me that was where the ball was going, and I certainly had time to call out a warning. But I didn't. I just watched as the ball smacked him full-on. Startled him pretty good. Stung him, too.

We giggled on the other side of the net, because there's nothing funnier when you're a kid than seeing a grown-up get thwacked with a tennis ball.

My father said, "Who hit that ball?" He wasn't mad. Or, again, he didn't *sound* mad. He sounded curious.

We giggled some more.

Once again, he said, "Who hit that ball?" He approached the net. We were trying his patience. That was a line we used to hear a lot as kids.

I didn't think I could stand right next to my dad and keep a straight face and maintain my deniability, so before he got any closer I pointed to Venus and said, "Venus hit it, Daddy."

Venus looked like she wanted to smack me with her racquet, but she didn't cover for me. She pointed at me and said, "It wasn't me, Daddy. It was Serena." Then I pointed right back at V and said,

"No, Daddy. It was Venus." We went back and forth like this, blaming each other, until Daddy finally got so disgusted with both of us he walked off and left us to figure it out for ourselves.

There was another time when Venus couldn't have covered for me if she wanted to. We had just finished a hitting session with this guy named Jumo, who used to come around and help out my father every now and then. Daddy collected a lot of unusual characters when we were living in California, people who had played tennis or had been around the game. He was like a magnet for the tennis fringe, and for a long time he had his friend Jumo meet us at the court to hit with us. Jumo was tall and skinny, with a full head of dreadlocks—not the sort of guy you'd expect to see with a tennis racquet in his hands. He drove this big, faded-green delivery truck. But he could play. That was all Daddy cared about. He liked it when other people hit with us, because then he could stand back on our side and talk to us about our footwork or our positioning or whatever else we happened to be working on at the time. Plus, he thought it helped us to have to hit to a lot of different people so we could experience all these different approaches, all these different styles.

Jumo was a good soul, too. He brought us oranges one day, for some reason. A whole bag. I was a little older by this point, maybe eight or nine. We put the oranges in the shopping cart while we were hitting, and then I think we must have forgotten about them. At least, my dad must have forgotten about them, because when it came time to work on our serves Daddy said he was going around the corner to get us some Super Socko. That was always another one of our special treats—a sports drink they used to sell in some of the local grocery stores that basically tasted like lemonade. If he'd remembered the oranges, he probably would have peeled a couple and given them to us instead. But off he went in search of our Super Sockos.

We always ended our practices working on our serves. That's the way they do it at most camps and clinics and academies, I've discovered, but more often than not coaches don't leave much time for it, which is why I think it takes so long for youth players to develop an effective serve. It's just been a neglected part of their game for so long. But my dad took a different approach. He had us work pretty diligently on our serves, and that's probably why it's such an effective part of our game. We worked on it at the very end of our sessions, but there was no clock on what we were doing. He'd have us out there serving until it got dark—or, sometimes, even after it got dark. We'd work it and work it until we had it down. Then we'd work it some more. The whole time, Venus and I would just talk and talk. The time flew, because we'd be chattering up a storm. It was the only moment during our practice session where it was just the two of us, side by side, so it was like we were catching up.

Daddy's routine was to have us toss a football back and forth before we started serving. It sounds like a gimmick, but it's really not; he saw it in one of his teaching videos and it struck him as a good idea, because the crisp, snapping overhead motion you need to make in order to get a football to spin in a tight spiral almost precisely mirrors the crisp, snapping overhead motion you need to achieve a powerful serve. So that's what we'd do. Venus and I would stand across the net from each other, close, and start tossing the football. Every few minutes, we'd take a couple steps back, until finally we were throwing baseline to baseline. Then we'd start serving.

We *still* toss the football around before we serve—only now my nails are a problem. (Daddy hadn't counted on *that!*) Back then, we didn't care about having elegant fingernails, but now I have to catch the football with the heels of my palms so I don't break a nail. Venus, too. It's the one thing we do on a tennis court that looks awkward, but that's the small price we pay for fashion.

So there we were, working on our serves. Jumo was gone. Daddy had disappeared into the store. It was inevitable that we kids would dawdle a bit, with no one watching. Self-discipline took us only so far, I guess. I wandered over to our cart and saw that big bag of oranges on top, and without even thinking about it I started smash-

ing them. Here again, I've got no justification or explanation for
my behavior. It was just that devil streak spilling forth. I picked up
a couple oranges and served them over the fence. Then I started
smashing them right there in the cart. I was like a wild child. I unleashed on these defenseless oranges. I didn't think about it. I just
went a little crazy.

I couldn't sweet-talk my way out of this one, because Daddy
came back from the store and caught me in the act. I was swinging
so furiously at those oranges, I didn't notice him return. He took
one look at all that mess and pulp, and he could tell right away that
I was the one responsible. Venus and the others didn't give me up. It
was on me. I got myself chased from the court—and caught a good
whupping, too. And I deserved it, I suppose.

We tell this story now and laugh about it, but at the time it was
upsetting to me that I could have acted so brazenly, so heartlessly.
To have beaten back a kindness offered by this good man, for no
reason at all. Now, as an adult, I recognize that my actions here
offered a glimpse into the mind of a competitive athlete. At least,
it offered a glimpse into *my* mind. Into *me*, and the young athlete
I was slowly becoming. I've tried to understand it, and what I've
come up with is you need a wild streak if you hope to be a serious
competitor. You need a kind of irrational killer instinct. You need to
put it out there that you're reckless and unpredictable—not just
so your opponents take note, but so that you notice, too. You've got
to convince yourself that you're capable of anything, that you will
not be denied, that you'll do whatever it takes to accomplish whatever it is you're out to accomplish. You need to surprise yourself, too.
And you've got to embrace the wild, rash abandon that finds you
and lifts you and transforms you in the heat of a cutthroat moment.
It's almost like you've got to get to that weird place where you can't
recognize your own behavior, and here I certainly couldn't spot myself in what I was doing. Understand, I didn't *like* what I was doing
too terribly much. I didn't know who I was, smashing those oranges.
It was a little scary. But on the court, I loved it. On the court, it

made sense. And looking back, it's really the first glimpse I had of the passion I'd soon develop on the court. The passion I'd *need* to develop if I meant to grow my game.

The greatest love of all? At first, it was my family. My sisters. But then tennis mixed itself in, and I have to think that emotional attachment to the game was what started to bubble forth that afternoon on the practice court. At the time, of course, I couldn't put any of this stuff into words. It was just me smashing up a bushel of oranges. After it was over it was easier to laugh about it than to think it through, so I let my sisters believe I was just making some mischief and letting off steam. But there was more to it than that.

Be strong. Be black. Now's your time to shine. Be confident. They want to see you angry. Be angry, but don't let them see it. Play angry, but let them see confidence. Play angry, but let them see patience. Play angry, but let them see certainty. Play angry, but let them see determination.

—MATCH BOOK ENTRY

THREE

Me and V

One year. Three months. Nine days. That's the age difference between me and my older sister Venus. These days, it doesn't seem like much, but when we were kids it felt like I'd never fill the gap.

She cast a big shadow, I'll say that. She was taller, prettier, quicker, more athletic. And, she was certainly *nicer*. There was no living up to her. I certainly tried. I wanted to do everything just like Venus. Like Lyn, too, but Venus was first in line. Whenever we went to a restaurant, my mom would make me order first, because if I didn't I'd just order whatever Venus ordered. I'd never speak my own mind. When we were little it was always "Venus this" and "Venus that." "Venus, Venus, Venus." The more we developed as players, the more I became the tagalong kid sister. That was the perception.

I still remember this one national newspaper article about Venus that suggested I'd never be anything more than a footnote to Venus's career. It talked about how in tennis the younger sibling never amounts to much, and how that would be my fate, too. That article came later, after we'd started playing in some tournaments, but it put me in mind of how I felt when we first started playing seriously.

Imagine somebody writing something like that about a child. Declaring that a younger sibling would never amount to much. It's harsh, don't you think? That's why I always have all this sympathy for the younger siblings, for people like Eli Manning and Patrick McEnroe. Everyone counts you out before you even get started. For our whole life, growing up, we're like the underdogs.

I promised myself I'd never forget that article, that one day I'd prove the reporter wrong. It was such a cruel thing to say, but I turned it into some more of that silent fuel. I filed it away for later. Everyone took it as such a big positive for Venus, and for all of us, and for the most part it was just that. With all the excitement in our house when it came out, I thought we'd be off on another one of Daddy's paper-grabs. There's no denying that it put us on the tennis map. *All* of us. But Tunde read between the lines and saw what I saw. She felt what I felt. As the oldest, she was the furthest removed from my runt-of-the-litter perspective, but she understood. She took me aside and said, "Don't pay any attention to that article, Serena. You'll have your day. You'll have your time. And it's gonna be even bigger."

I never forgot that. Filed that away, too.

Growing up on those tennis courts in Compton and Lynwood and all over Los Angeles, it sometimes felt like nobody believed in me. I suppose I understood it on some level. Clearly, Venus was the phenom, the prodigy, the rising star. But on another level it hurt. Even my dad, who's always been my biggest supporter, was spending more time with Venus, more time on her game, more time talking to reporters and coaches about her. The more he talked to people about us, the more he took us out to these events, the more connections he made in the game, the more it became about Venus.

She was the main attraction. I *get* that now. I *get* that Venus deserved all that extra tennis attention. I *get* that you can raise only one champion—until you look up one day and realize you've raised two.

My parents believed in me, in their own way. Absolutely, my mom believed in me. Wholeheartedly. That's a great word for how she felt about her girls. She believed in all of us, with all her heart, and she had each of us believing in ourselves and in each other as well. We could do anything we wanted, be anything we wanted, accomplish anything we wanted. She had this great way of isolating each of us and making us feel special. Didn't have to be about tennis. It could be about school, or dance, or gymnastics, or the way we'd decided to wear our hair. She singled us out and allowed us to shine.

It wasn't just my parents who believed in me. Venus knew I could play, too. Even when we were kids, she knew I could play. She didn't understand why she was getting all the attention. She used to tell me I was a clever player, but I think that was her way of putting a positive spin on my game. I was good, but I was more of a counterpuncher. I wasn't strong, like Venus. I wasn't an intimidating presence, like Venus. I didn't have a superaggressive game. I eventually found one when I got a little taller and stronger, but when we were little I was all about lobs and really, really long baseline rallies, and doing whatever I could to break my opponent.

Venus never held it over me, that her game was bigger and better; she didn't rub my face in it. She had such a good, kind heart. (She still does!) She was always so positive and generous and accommodating. She just told me to work hard and to play my game. "The rest will come," she used to say. "Your time will come."

As I got older, I started sleeping more and more in Venus's bed. Even when Tunde moved out of the house and there was a bunk bed to call my own, I still crawled in with Venus most nights, and we'd talk about these kinds of things. You'd think we'd get enough talk of tennis during the day from Daddy, but Venus used to take the time as we drifted off to pick me up and set me right. She could see when I'd had a tough day, when I needed a lift.

One of the reasons Venus cast such a big shadow, of course, was because she was so tall. Always, always. I used to watch her play and think she was like a fierce swan out there on the court, with this incredible wingspan, able to reach every shot. I just couldn't get the ball past her. (Nobody could!) In contrast, I was really, really small—the runt of the litter. That's how I felt, growing up with all these big, beautiful sisters. And it wasn't just Venus who dominated me on the court. Isha, too, had some serious game. That's another thing people don't know about our family, that for a long time Isha was a rising star, too. She could never quite touch Venus's game, but she was good. In her own right, she was good. She was training to be a champion, just like me and Venus, up until she was about thirteen, when she started to have some trouble with her back and had to step away from the game. That was a real heartbreak for Isha, and for the rest of us, because she had a real shot. After that, she took some time off and returned a couple years later to become a strong high school player, but it was at a different level. And so, when we were kids, I was competing with Isha, too. That made two shadows for me to hide behind.

By this point, Tunde and Lyn had drifted from the game. Tunde always said she didn't have an athletic bone in her body, so she was happy to give it up. Lyn was a good athlete, but she started running track in middle school and said she didn't have time for tennis. Plus, she loved writing and music—she had an artistic soul. From time to time, Daddy would work on Lyn to get her to take it up again because he said she showed a lot of promise, but she didn't want to play. She'd had enough, she said. So that just left the three of us.

I didn't start growing until I was fifteen or sixteen years old, and my "clever" game was a direct result of my size. It came from necessity; I had to compensate. I learned to be resourceful on the court, to work on my shot placement, to out-think my opponent, because there was no way I was overpowering anybody out there. Physically, there was just no way.

That observation I made earlier about never cheating my opponent on the lines? It didn't apply against Venus, because the only way I could beat her was to cheat. She knew I was cheating, and I knew she knew I was cheating, but I cheated anyway. If the call was close, it was mine.

I look back now and hate myself for cheating my big-hearted, generous, accommodating sister. Really, I'm so embarrassed by my behavior, but at the same time I recognize that it goes hand in hand with how I cheated that girl in the Domino's Pizza League, when I felt I needed to. When my back was against the wall. When it was the only way I knew to compete. I wanted to win so badly that I'd stoop to this, but I guess I didn't see it as stooping. It was just reaching—in the wrong direction.

Daddy had us play against each other in practice. Not all the time, but a lot. He tried to get other hitting partners for us, and we'd hit with local teenagers or college players from time to time, but the default option was always me against Venus. We were always around. Anyway, we weren't really competing against each other in these practice matches. Things weren't like that between us. They were like that in my head, but only in my head. I was definitely competing with myself. I was competing against the low expectations everyone had set out for me, against the high expectations they had for Venus. Plus, I still hated to lose, and I knew if I played Venus straight I'd probably lose. So I called balls out that weren't. I insisted some of my shots were clearly in, when they clearly weren't. My justification was no justification, really. Venus was better than me, that's all. Way better. This was just my way of trying to win. It was wrong. I admit it. But it felt to me like I was doing what I had to do to keep pace.

Venus never seemed to mind. She certainly never said anything. She just accepted my calls and played on—and in this way, I guess, we pushed each other. She pushed me to get good enough to beat her legitimately. I pushed her to get good enough to beat me so badly I couldn't cheat my way from losing.

Daddy had this idea that he didn't want us to play in proper tournaments. He didn't want us to have to face all that pressure. Also, he didn't want so many sets of eyes on us, I think. He wanted to give us time to develop as players, before people had a chance to check us out and weigh in on what he was trying to do. He didn't care for second-guessing. He liked that we could just do our thing on these different public courts, on our own timetable, without having to deal with these know-it-alls in the tennis community who always seemed to have something to say.

Venus was ready to play in tournaments before I was. First of all, she was older, so she qualified. Second, and more important, she was so physically impressive that I could no longer give her much of a game, even with my not-so-generous calls, and the players Daddy brought around weren't much competition, either. Very quickly, Venus got to where she really wanted to see how she'd do in a proper tournament, just like the players on television, but my parents wouldn't allow it. I joined in on the argument, of course. I might have been a notch or two below Venus, but I was pretty good, too. I wanted to play, too. Finally, we wore Daddy down. He said if Venus could beat him straight up, he'd let her play—and I knew that once that happened, I wouldn't be too far behind.

We all looked forward to that match between Venus and Daddy like it was a Wimbledon final. We talked about it the whole time leading up to it. At least, Venus and I talked about it. At night, before we'd fall asleep, Venus would say, "Do you think I can beat him? Do you think I really have a chance?"

I had no idea if she could beat him, because Daddy was such a good player. He was much stronger than Venus, obviously. He was bigger. And he was smart. He really understood the game. Plus, we were so young! Venus was only nine or ten. How could she hope to compete against a full-grown man? But I didn't say any of these things to Venus. Most likely, it's only in retrospect that I recognize them. At the time, I probably just thought, *Yeah, sure, Venus can beat him. Why not?* So that's probably what I said.

The day of the match finally arrived. It was set up at night, at one of the public parks. We all went out to watch. (You can bet Daddy opened a couple new cans of balls for the occasion.) I remember it as a real exciting moment, a highlight family event, and Venus beat him. She did! I don't remember the score, but I don't think Daddy eased up to let her win. It was a hard-fought match. Daddy was sweating. He was trying, most definitely. We were all there; we all saw it. But Venus beat him, she really and truly did, and we went to bed that night so happy because it meant that Venus could start playing in tournaments. It meant we'd both be playing, before long. We talked and talked and talked about it under the covers before we finally fell asleep.

Sure enough, that's what happened. Venus started playing, and we started bouncing around as a family to all these tournaments. For me, it was a mixed blessing. I was happy for Venus, and I really wanted her to do well, but now the focus shifted even more in her direction. Now Daddy started to spend even more time on her game. This was around the time they started signing me up for all those local recreational leagues so I'd have more of a chance to compete against kids my own age while Venus was out doing her tournament thing, but I wanted what Venus had. I wanted the chance to beat Daddy in my own match, so I could play tournaments, too.

Every day, I'd say, "Daddy, let's play. Give me a chance. I want to play in tournaments, like V."

But he'd always say, "Not yet, Meeka. You're not ready."

I was so mad, so frustrated. I didn't think there was anything I could do but wait for my chance, but then Venus was signed up for this one tournament and I had an idea. Venus was nine, so it was a 10-and-under tournament. I was eight. The germ of my idea was this: I used to play Office a lot with my sisters. It wasn't really a game; it was more of a mind-set; we'd pretend to answer phones and fill out papers and sit at our kitchen table like it was a desk in a real office. It's like playing House, only with phones and paperwork—a way to pretend we were grown-ups. So there I was one day, pushing around all these papers, when I noticed an application for this particular tournament. For some reason, we had two applications lying around, so I filled one out and sent it in. I didn't have a checkbook, obviously, so I couldn't pay the entry fee, but I sent in the entry form. Then, when the tournament came around on the calendar, I went along for the ride with Venus and the rest of my family, just like I always did. I didn't say anything to anybody, not even my sisters.

A lot of times, I'd take my racquet with me to these tournaments, because there was a chance to hit on one of the open courts, and there were usually other little sisters and little brothers running around, looking for something to do. Or, sometimes my mom or dad would hit with me, while Venus was resting between matches. So nobody thought anything of it that I was dressed to play, and when Venus went with my dad to go play her match I walked over to the registration table to see where I was in the draw. Pretty devious, huh? But I didn't think I was doing anything wrong. I just wanted what Venus had. That was all I ever wanted, to be just like Venus—my role model, then and still—so I went out and took my turn like I had it coming.

When I tell this story now, people are amazed that I had the nerve to do something this big behind my parents' backs. They say that for an eight-year-old kid to go against authority like this is fairly remarkable—but I didn't see it that way at the time. I thought there was a good chance I'd get into some kind of trouble over it, but that didn't stop me. I was too excited to play to think of any negative consequences. The only potential negative, really, was that I wouldn't play well, but I wasn't too worried about that. I knew I could beat these girls. As long as I didn't have to play Venus, I thought I had a shot.

My plan almost backfired, because Venus won her match in no time at all, and before long my dad was looking for me. He didn't like that I wasn't around watching my sister. He didn't like that he couldn't find me. People kind of knew who we were at this point, so he started asking people if they'd seen me. He asked one of the tournament officials, and the guy said, "Oh, you mean the younger one? She's playing her match on that court over there."

He nodded his head to indicate the court.

Daddy thought there must be some mistake. He said, "No, sir. She's not playing. She's too young. She's not signed up."

The guy said, "No, Mr. Williams. I'm afraid there's no mistake. She's in the other half of the draw. She's playing right now."

My father couldn't believe it, but the guy walked him over to where I was playing. I didn't know he was there at the time. He stayed back, away from the court. That was just as well, since I don't think I would have noticed him if he'd pulled up close. I was too focused on my match to worry what kind of trouble I'd get into once my parents found out I'd entered the tournament without their permission. Right then, I was only worried about my opponent. I had just turned eight a week or so earlier, but I was determined and single-minded even then. I was trying to run this girl all over the place and tire her out—and I was doing a pretty good job of it.

I ended up winning that match, and when it was over I heard my dad's sweet drawl coming at me from behind the fence. He said, "Meeka! Look at you! You won! You played great!"

He was so positive, so upbeat. Here I'd thought I'd be in for another whupping, but he couldn't have been more encouraging. I was prepared for punishment—at the very least, I thought I'd get a good talking-to—but it never came, and so for the time being I was just happy that Daddy was happy. And he was happy that I was happy.

He said, "I can't believe you won. I can't believe my two girls both won. I'm so proud of you."

And he *was* proud, I could see that. He was beaming. My mother, too. And Venus, when she found out what I had done, she had a smile on her face like you wouldn't believe. Not because I'd won, I don't think, but because I had the brass to enter the tournament in the first place. Deep down, I think she knew I'd win if I had the chance to play, so she wasn't surprised by the outcome. She was just surprised to see me playing.

Right away, Daddy started talking about what I'd have to do to win my next match, the few things he saw in my game I might need to fix before the next round. Venus was in the other half of the draw, so I didn't have to worry about facing her just yet. I had two other girls to get past on the way to the finals. I had never given the finals a thought going in, but after that first match I thought I could do well. My next opponent was a girl I used to play a lot in practice, so Daddy knew all kinds of ways for me to beat her. He said as long as I had entered I might as well go on to the finals.

I said, "You really think I can beat her?"

He said, "Meeka, you can do anything."

It worked out so he could be at that next match, to cheer me on, and then at the semifinal match, against another girl we knew, so he gave me some tips on how to beat her, too.

Now things were getting exciting. It was a 10-and-under tournament and I was the youngest girl in the field, by a lot, so people were coming around to watch, to talk to my parents, to talk to me after my matches. All of a sudden, I had what Venus had. It was the most thrilling, encouraging day. And so much fun! But then I realized these wins now put me in the finals against Venus, and all of a sudden I was intimidated. I knew I couldn't beat her, because it was the final round of a sanctioned tournament. There'd be people watching, so I couldn't cheat. Venus was just too good, and I was just too little.

It was the first time we'd face each other in tournament play—the first time of many. And, of course, it was such a big, big deal in our family. My parents were so excited for both of us. They said afterward they didn't know which one of us to root for. They just wanted us to play good tennis, and to have fun, and to learn from the experience. That became their standard response whenever we'd face each other. Our sisters were also terribly excited for both of us. And I was so excited for Venus. I really was. I tell that to people, and they think it's just a line, but it's the God's honest truth. I always want the best for Venus when she's out there on the court. I want her to make her shots, and hold her serve, and all that. Even if it means I'll have to face her in the end. I just don't want her to do all those things against *me*.

My thinking has always been, Look, she's the best player on the tour. Next to me. If you ask Venus, she'd probably say the same thing: "Serena is the best player on the tour. Next to me."

That's how we felt as kids, too, and it wasn't bluster or arrogance that had us feeling this way. No. It's that we really were good. As soft as my game might have been, it was only that way in comparison to Venus's game. Everyone else my age I could beat. Everyone else Venus's age I could beat. At least, in and around Los Angeles. I'd seen all those girls play. I'd played most of them in practice, or in some recreational league or other. I didn't have the power to beat them with anything but lobs and rallies and placement, but I had the shots. I had that mental edge, that toughness. Daddy had me thinking about my footwork, and moving my opponents around, and working my serve, and that was all fine against these other girls, but we all knew that finals match against Venus would be another story.

Meanwhile, just before the final, my father came over to talk to me about the tournament fee. I think it was forty dollars—and naturally I hadn't paid it. He'd spoken to the director between matches, and puzzled together how I'd sent in my own application, and he thought he'd have some fun with me about the fee. He said, "How you planning to pay for this tournament, Meeka?"

It turned out he wasn't really mad that I had entered. He was happy that I cared enough about playing to arrange this sneaky end around into the draw. And he was happy that I was doing well. But I had no money to pay my own way. I hadn't thought things through that far, so now I had something else to worry about, along with going up against V in the final. It never occurred to me that he was just joking with me. I could see he was smiling, but you could never tell with Daddy. He was always smiling.

He probably thought this would be a good distraction for me, to get my mind off my worries about facing Venus, and I guess it was. And yet, distraction or no, I couldn't keep up with Venus. She beat me easily; 6–2, 6–2, I think. I tried my best, but she was playing at a whole other level. And I was happy for her, too, that she'd played so well. I was sad for me, though. Really. If I was any older, or more mature, I might have given myself permission to sulk or fuss about losing, but I didn't think there was any room in the moment for me to be upset. It was Venus's tournament, after all. I didn't really belong there. I should have been happy for V that she'd won. She deserved to win. She was meant to win. But I was surely disappointed—and I couldn't let on! Here I'd had this great tournament. I'd made it all the way to the finals. I was the youngest girl there. I got a lot of attention. But when you're eight, you don't have it in you to appreciate the big picture, so I remember feeling this huge letdown.

At the awards ceremony right after, they gave Venus a nice gold trophy. They gave me a nice silver trophy as the runner-up. It was my first real trophy, so you'd think I'd be excited about it, but I just kept looking at Venus's gold trophy and wishing I could have somehow beaten her. Oh my God, I wanted that gold trophy so badly.

Venus could see I was upset. After all, she was my big sister. She was used to taking care of me. She knew just what to do to pick me up. She came up to me after the awards ceremony and said, "You know what, Serena? I've been thinking. I've always liked silver better than gold. You want to trade?"

It was the sweetest, most selfless gesture. She set it out like I'd be doing her a favor by trading trophies. Took me completely by surprise, but we traded trophies right there. She was my big sister so I did what she said, and to this day that's the most meaningful trophy I've ever received. I didn't earn it, but I cherish it. It's the only one I keep close—at my bedside, actually. Every night when I'm home, I go to bed and look at Venus's gold first-place trophy from my first-ever tournament and count my blessings. That I have the world's best big sister. That at eight years old I was able to beat all these girls a year or two older. That Daddy never did make me pay him back for that entry fee. That I wouldn't have to play in those silly recreational leagues anymore, now that I had shown everyone I was ready to play in real tournaments. That my whole family was so incredibly supportive of me during that first tournament, just as they have been at every tournament since. And that no matter how many times Venus and I face each other on a tennis court, we'll always be sisters.

We'll battle each other like nobody's business, but the competition will never separate us.

The buzz around Venus's game only got louder as we developed, because she never lost a match as a junior player. Me, I didn't lose many, but I did lose a few. And yet despite that small gap between us in terms of our records, the space between us in terms of our reputations was just huge. Venus was still the rising star, and I was still the kid sister. I started to think maybe that newspaper reporter was right, because our situation wasn't about to change. Venus was still way taller than me, but a lot of times people couldn't tell us apart. They'd call me Venus; they'd call her Serena. But once they saw us play, that made it easier. They could tell the fierce swan from the ugly duckling, no problem.

After that first tournament, Daddy did what he could to make sure we didn't compete against each other in a meaningful match. He put Venus in the 12-and-unders and me in the 10-and-unders. And that was how it was until we both turned professional. Venus went pro first, and I followed soon after, kind of like it first happened for us on the circuit in California. After that, we couldn't really control when we'd face each other. We could only hope it wasn't too early in the tournament, so we'd each have a chance to get on a roll and reach into the later rounds. Ideally, we'd stay out of each other's way until the end.

The very first time we competed as professionals was in the second round of the 1998 Australian Open. I'm skipping ahead here, but I want to finish out these thoughts about going up against Venus, and growing up as a player in her magnificent shadow. It was my first major (also known as a Grand Slam tournament), so I was pretty nervous. I'd ended the previous year ranked 99th in the world, so I was starting to make my mark. A couple years later, I'd see that 99 ranking on the way down, and it felt a whole lot different to me, but on the way up it felt great. On the way up, it was a real marker, the first time my rank reached into double digits—and then, into single digits. People around tennis were talking about how this was going to be a big year for me—but you have to remember, Venus was already making her mark. She was already ranked in the Top 20. I'd watched her struggle in her very first professional matches, then get it together and have some success. That's why I think I went into that second-round match in Melbourne with a defeatist attitude, because Venus was playing so well, and because she was expected to play so well.

It's not that I was convinced I would lose, but I was resigned to it. It's better to say I was *prepared* to lose—and, of course, that's no way to prepare to win. (Sounds like one of my dad's motivational quotes!) In any case, that's the kind of rookie mistake I used to make when I was just starting out. I'd put myself in the wrong frame of mind before a match, not realizing how important the mental part of the game was in relation to everything else I put out on the court. But my head was cluttered with so many negative thoughts, so many drags on my performance, there was just no way I could have played well.

Yes, I was bigger and stronger than I was the first time I'd played Venus in that first-ever youth tournament. Goodness, I was nearly as big and strong as Venus. But I was only sixteen years old. It was my first full year on the tour. Nobody expected me to win. Everybody expected Venus to win. And even if I did manage to get past V and into the third round, nobody thought I'd have a shot at going much deeper in the tournament, against all that great competition. Most important, *I* didn't think I'd have a shot. Venus, though, she had a shot—and she knew it. She'd been playing well enough to win the championship, so a part of me thought, *Hey, this is my sister. She deserves to win. Better for her to win and go deep in the tournament than for me to win and get knocked out in the next round.* That's how this first matchup had me thinking. Like a loss to V would come with its own silver lining, because she'd get to keep playing. Like if I managed to win it would somehow knock both of us from the field.

I hated that we had to meet so early in the tournament, but that was how it fell. And over the years, that was how it would fall again and again. As we moved up in the rankings, as we earned higher and higher seeds, the draw would be set in such a way that we couldn't meet until the later rounds, but that wouldn't happen for a while. In 1998, before I'd ever played a Grand Slam tournament, it was inevitable that we would meet in the first or second round, so the thing to do was power through and hope for the best—never fully knowing if *the best* meant a victory for me or Venus.

We were both a little tentative in that match. Venus ended up beating me in straight sets, but the first set went to a tiebreaker. She took control in the second set, though, to beat me 7–6, 6–1. Neither one of us played particularly well, like we were careful not to show each other up. I kept looking at the players' box, where my sisters were sitting with my mom, and it was so weird, no one knowing when to cheer or what to wish for. Tunde didn't make the trip—she had kids of her own by this point, and Melbourne was a *long* way from her home in Los Angeles—but Isha and Lyn were there. I felt the same tug-and-pull down on the court. I wanted to win, but I wanted Venus to win, too, if that makes any sense. As disappointed as I was to lose (remember, I *hate* losing!), that's how happy I was that Venus had won.

Later on, people would say we'd set up our matches and figure out beforehand which one of us would win, but that's absurd. It's enraging, really. I bristle every time I hear something like that, but what can you do? People are going to believe what they want to believe and say what they want to say.

I have no response to these kinds of comments, so I hold my tongue. Venus, too. We were raised to believe that a lie cannot stand forever—and it certainly cannot stand on its own. I think of that great line from Dr. Martin Luther King, Jr., from that famous speech he made after his march from Selma to Birmingham. "However difficult the moment," he said, "however frustrating the hour, it will not be long, because truth pressed to earth will rise again. How long? Not long, because no lie can live forever. How long? Not long, because you will reap what you sow. How long? Not long, because the arm of the moral universe is long, but it bends toward justice."

True, Dr. King was talking about something a whole lot more significant than a tennis match, but it goes to human nature, don't you think? *Truth pressed to the earth will rise again.* There's such power in that sentiment, such grace. It's not quite what Dr. King had in mind, but it applies. At least, I choose to apply it here, because the first time I heard that charge against me and V I came away thinking, *If someone hurls an untruth in your direction, it doesn't always pay to swat it back. Sometimes the thing to do is to just let it hang there, unanswered, and wait for it to disperse.*

Because no lie can live forever.

Over the years, these run-ins with Venus have become legendary in tennis circles. People say it's been an epic battle. I don't know about that, but I do know that it's put a stamp on my career. On Venus's career, too, I think. We've played each other pretty close—at one point going into the 2008 U.S. Open, we were dead even in tour matchups, at eight wins apiece—but we've each had our momentum runs. In the beginning, Venus had the big-time edge. Then, for a stretch, I won a bunch of times in a row. More recently, we've traded punches. In 2008, Venus beat me in the finals at Wimbledon; I beat her in the quarterfinals at the U.S. Open. We've been up and down, and all over the place.

Nevertheless, this first-ever Grand Slam tournament between me and V at the 1998 Australian Open was a real turning point in my career. It announced my arrival. I hated that I lost, but at the same time I didn't mind, because the match held out a carrot for me in terms of the player I might become. Throughout my development, there was always Venus to set the standard. At times, when I was little, it seemed like an impossible standard, but there it was. She was the embodiment of my best self. She was the player I hoped to be—the *person* I hoped to be, too. I'd watch her play, and go to school, and order ahead of me when we went to a restaurant, and generally carry herself throughout her days, and I'd think, *Someday, that'll be me.*

During the 2008 U.S. Open, a reporter asked me an interesting question. She had been looking over my history with Venus in all these Grand Slam tournaments, and she asked me how many more majors I might have won if Venus had not loomed in my path on so many occasions. It was a reasonable question. Venus had knocked me from a major on five different occasions, twice in the finals, so just going by the numbers I could see where the reporter was going with this line of thought. But I went another way in my response. Without hesitating I said, "I don't think I would have won nearly as many."

This wasn't exactly what the reporter expected to hear, so I talked about how growing up in Venus's shadow has been such a positive motivator for me. How the impossible standard she set on the court (and off!) was such a powerful model. How she pushed me to be the very best I could be. I talked about how I learn by watching. All my life, that's how it's been. I'm a good mimic; show me a couple dance moves, and I'll have them down. Let me watch you learn your lines and hit your marks on a television or movie set, and I'll do the same. If you *tell* me something, it'll probably go in one ear and straight out the other. But if you *show* me, I'll get it. That's how it was, watching Venus when we were little. At her very first tour event, I was taking all these mental notes. She lost, but I could see where she lost. And when she lost, I lost. When she won, I won. How I played was all tied in with how she played. And so by the time I went out there to fight my own battles, I was ready. It's like

I had all this experience—Venus's experience. Without V to lead the way, it would have taken me longer to get to where I wanted to be. And then, once I started having some success on my own, I still looked to Venus. If she won a major, it fired me up to win the next one. If she went out early to practice on the morning after a big win, I went out early to practice.

Really, I don't know where I'd get that drive, were it not for Venus. I suppose I would have found it somewhere, but it might have taken awhile. Yes, you look at the scoreboard and see that Venus beat me a bunch of times in Grand Slam tournaments. She beat me twice in the finals—at Wimbledon in 2008 and at the U.S. Open in 2001—so right there that might have been two more titles for me. But I don't see it that way. The way I see it is, Who knows if I would have even made it that far without Venus?

It's the difference between a roadblock and an open lane—and it's all the difference in the world.

She beat Venus, so take it to her. Play deep to her backhand. She gets nervous. U have nothing to lose, so play like it. U will set the tone. Make her run. Get her. Remember, it takes courage and discipline to do/be Serena Williams—the best. U R Serena Williams. U R the best. Keep that courage and discipline. Stay relaxed. Be happy.

—MATCH BOOK ENTRY

FOUR

The Fiery Darts of Indian Wells

There's one match between me and Venus that stands out—only it's memorable because we never played. I got credit for the win in a walkover, but I would have gladly taken the loss if it meant we could have avoided all the grief and ugliness that came our way as a result.

It was at the 2001 Indian Wells Masters. I had already won at Indian Wells in 1999, beating Steffi Graf in three sets in the finals when I was only seventeen. That was a big deal. After that, it became my absolute favorite tournament, for a lot of reasons. It was in a small town, just outside Palm Springs, California. I loved the setting. I loved where it fell on the tour calendar, right before Miami. I loved that the fans were knowledgeable and respectful and appreciative. And I especially loved that it was one of the few tournaments that allowed us all to be together, as a family. Palm Springs was close enough to Los Angeles that Tunde could peel away for a few days, and we'd all stay together in the hotel and hang out, and it was so much fun.

I came to Indian Wells at such a positive time in my career that I naturally attached all of these positive feelings to it. But then the 2001 tournament came around and changed things up on me. That's how it goes sometimes. Whenever you're feeling most comfortable, most in control, something happens to knock the wind out of you.

In this way, tennis is a lot like life. You might think you're in control, but you're never really in control. You might have a good game plan, but then you run into someone or some*thing* on the other side of the net trying to move you off of it. You might do everything in your power to prepare for a special moment, and you're still caught unprepared.

I'd looked forward to the tournament for months. Then I got off to a strong start. Venus did, too. We were both happy about that. We always liked it when we both did well—in the beginning of our careers, especially. Venus basically owned me in our tour matchups at that point, with a 4-1 record, but I'd been playing well and I was ready to take it to her. Venus had already won a couple majors by this point, and here I was, her younger sister, starting to make some noise with eight tour championships and a major of my own. I'm sure the Indian Wells people were happy about the possible matchup.

As it played out, we each advanced to the semifinal round. I beat Lindsay Davenport in the quarterfinals 6–1, 6–2. This was a big victory for me, because Lindsay was playing great tennis at the time. It was a real statement match. That's what a convincing win can do for you early in your career against a strong player. It can set you up as a player to watch. Already, with the way we came up and joined the tour, Venus and I were players to watch, but now I was finally playing like the fuss was for real.

Unfortunately, Venus struggled in her quarterfinal contest against Elena Dementieva. She won, but she struggled. The straight-sets score didn't really show it, but it was a tough match, mostly because it was ridiculously hot. That's the one knock on Indian Wells—it's out in the desert and it can get really, really hot, although usually in March it's not that bad. On this day, though, Venus came down with heat exhaustion. The match went on for a long, long time. She was so dehydrated, she started to cramp. She wasn't really moving too well at the end. She couldn't breathe when she came off the court. It was crazy. She hurt her knee during the match, too. She won, but the match took its toll. Privately, she worried if she'd be good to go for the semifinals. I felt terrible for her. It's like I wrote earlier: when she won, I won; when she lost, I lost; and when she hurt, I hurt, too. We talked about it, even though we were playing each other. We didn't care about things like giving the other one an edge. There was no gamesmanship. We were sisters. We each wanted the other to be at her best.

Despite Venus's injuries, we prepared for the match like we normally did, and when we got to the stadium on the morning of the semifinal Venus checked in with the tour trainer and told him she didn't think she could play. She couldn't have done anything before that—and besides, she was hoping to be able to compete. A lot of times, you go to bed in a lot of pain and you wake up in a lot less pain and you're able to play. She wanted to give her body a chance to respond, but when she woke up on the morning of the match she knew she was in no shape to play a semifinal in a Tier I tour event. Her knee was giving her too much trouble. She was completely up front about it. She didn't want to withdraw, but she believed she had no choice.

Daddy tended to leave it to us to listen to our own bodies. Game-day decisions like whether or not we were fit to play were pretty much ours to make, so it was Venus's call.

That is, it was Venus's call until it wasn't.

See, the way it works on the Women's Tennis Association tour is that the tournament trainer consults with the tournament director on all significant injuries. At least, that's how it's supposed to work. If there's a possibility that a player won't be able to compete in her next match, they work it out so they can reschedule another match in its place. They'll slot in a doubles match, or a junior match, or maybe relocate a match from one of the outer courts. It happens a lot, so they have all these backup plans in place, and usually no one thinks anything of it if someone has to pull out. It's a shame, but it happens. It's part of the game.

The key, though, is you have to make this kind of decision in a timely manner. The closer you get to your scheduled start time, the less understanding the crowd and the tournament organizers are likely to be. But on this day, with the two of us scheduled to go at it in such a big match, no one wanted to see Venus pull out. The tournament director didn't want it. The fans didn't want it. The sponsors didn't want it. Venus and I certainly didn't want it. There was buzz, hype, drama . . . and all of that. People said it was good for the game, a match like this, but at the same time Venus felt strongly that she couldn't play. She knew her body. She knew she wasn't able to go at anything close to full strength. More than that, she didn't want to risk a more serious injury, with three majors coming up in just a few months.

No doubt about it, there was a lot riding on this one decision, and Venus was in a difficult spot. If she was an older, more established player, she might have been a little more forceful about the situation. She might have bypassed the trainer and gone straight to the director. But she was a relative newcomer, and the rules said she had to get the trainer's approval before making a withdrawal, so that was what she tried to do. For hours and hours, that was what she tried to do. And for hours and hours she got a kind of stiff-arm from the trainer, who kept telling her to hold off on making any kind of final decision.

It was the strangest, most frustrating thing. I felt so badly for V, not just because she was hurt, but also because she couldn't get anyone to take her seriously. This went on for a while after we got to the stadium. Venus wanted to pull out because of her knee, but the tournament officials were stalling. They kept putting her off. It was like they weren't letting her do what was best for her. They wanted only what was best for them, which was for the match to go off as scheduled. I had no idea what was going on. Nobody did. At one point I said to Venus, "V, what's the deal? You gonna be able to play?" It didn't matter that I was her semifinal opponent; she would always be straight with me.

She said, "I really don't think so. I'm hurt."

I knew my sister. If she said she couldn't play, she couldn't play.

Plain and simple. Plus, I could see she was hobbled. She wasn't right. If she could have gone at sixty percent or seventy percent, she would have sucked it up and played—and she would have given me a tough match, I'm sure of it—but that quarterfinal match against Dementieva had really taken a bite out of her. She couldn't go at all.

That should have been the end of it, but it wasn't. The tournament officials kept dragging their feet, until finally I had to go and get dressed and warmed up. The clock was against us. I had to treat it like any other match, against any other opponent, and underneath these preparations we were just waiting and waiting. I went out and did my usual prematch warm-up. I stretched. I started to hit and tried to find my rhythm. My father came down to the court to watch. Not to talk about Venus, but to watch me hit. I was just working on my game. I hit some forehands crosscourt. I hit some backhands crosscourt. I hit some serves, some volleys, and then I was done. After that, I usually talked to my dad about strategy, but when I'm playing Venus he just says, "Have fun." That's the strategy. As far as I know, he says the flip side of the same thing to V. And that was all he said that morning. Just "Have fun."

Venus came up to me in the locker room after my warm-up and said, "I really don't know why they're not making some kind of announcement. I told them I couldn't play two hours ago."

I look back now and think maybe I should have said something, done something. But I was even younger and less established than Venus. It didn't even occur to me at first to step in, and then when it finally did I didn't see that there was anything I could do. I mean, I was just a kid. I didn't think I had the juice to make any kind of stand for Venus, and even if I did my situation was complicated because I was also her opponent. I couldn't really argue with the officials that my opponent should be allowed to withdraw.

For the moment, everyone was moving around like the match was still on. The fans had all filed in, expecting to see the Williams sisters in this great semifinal showdown. All the VIP types, the sponsors and benefactors were on hand. There was no public indication that Venus might be sidelined until about five minutes before the match was scheduled to begin, when a tournament spokesperson finally got on the loudspeaker and announced to the packed stadium that Venus was withdrawing due to injury.

Well, the place went nuts—and not in a good way. The fans were angry, which I can certainly understand now, considering how things were handled. I would have been mad, too, if I'd paid my money and gone to all the hassle and hustle of getting to the stadium. Understand, all these people had planned their day around this match. They'd looked forward to it. The television people sold a lot of advertising for it. The sponsors were all lined up. But what I couldn't understand was why the anger was directed at us. It wasn't Venus's fault she was injured. It wasn't my dad's fault. And it certainly wasn't my fault. It was just one of those things. Venus tried to pull out in a timely fashion. She did everything by the WTA book. But the late scratch let people think there was some grandstanding going on, or that the Williams sisters had somehow held the tournament hostage to our own way of doing things.

Here again, I thought back to that quote from Dr. King, because of course there was no way to answer these claims. *Truth pressed to the earth will rise again.* That didn't really help us just yet. The whispered charges against us didn't really deserve an answer, but there they were. The tournament officials didn't really do anything to discourage people from this view. They certainly didn't want to take the heat for how things went down—and believe me, there was a ton of heat. I learned later there was even a rumor that my dad was behind all this, that he was manipulating the situation to decide which of his daughters would play in the finals. All of these ridiculous lies were being said about us, all because some bullheaded tournament official was determined to give the fans and the sponsors and the broadcasters what they wanted instead of giving the players the respect they deserved.

It got nasty when they made the announcement, but after that

I thought the incident would pass and I could concentrate on the final. Man, was I wrong! We had to do a press conference right after the match was canceled, and there were questions suggesting that we sisters had somehow manipulated this situation to our advantage. I sat there and thought, What advantage? What did either one of us gain by any of this? In fact, the walkover actually cost me points in the rankings, because if Venus had actually tried to play for a couple games before withdrawing those points would have come my way. But still, we had to answer for it publicly. On the tour, they're always sticking a microphone in your face. Before a match. Right after a match. And, apparently, right after a late scratch, so we had to go out into the press room they had set up at the stadium and do a little dance and put a positive spin on the situation.

I said, "I don't know why everyone is blaming Venus. She told them as soon as she arrived that she couldn't play. Ask the trainer. She'll tell you."

Of course, nobody asked the trainer. Nobody looked at what actually happened. People were only too happy to cast us as scape-goats, when really we were just victims of a stupid system and an abuse of authority. People were pissed and disappointed and they took it out on us. No question, it should have been handled differently, and now here we were at the other end, getting ripped for something that was out of our control. Venus caught the brunt of it, but some of it fell to me. My dad caught a bunch of it, too. I could almost understand why people were upset with Venus, especially if they didn't know what happened, because she was the one who withdrew from the tournament. But I couldn't get why folks were mad at me.

I still had a lot to learn, I guess.

Despite all the noise and controversy, I thought things would return to normal soon enough, so I tried to focus on the finals. I was going up against Kim Clijsters, a strong young Belgian player who was just coming onto the scene and doing well. The year before, she was named as the WTA Newcomer of the Year, so there was a lot of excitement about this matchup. She was only seventeen, and I was nineteen, so it was a real sign that the women's game was getting younger and fitter and more energetic.

Plus, Kim had been having a great tournament. That always adds a whole other level of anticipation to a match. She'd just beaten the number one player in the world, Martina Hingis, in an exciting semifinal match, and she'd knocked off an up-and-coming Justine Henin, her countrywoman, in one of the early rounds. I guess it seems kind of obvious to say someone who reaches the finals in any tournament is having a great run—but that's not always the case. When you're an underdog and you manage to beat a couple top players along the way, it puts you on a roll going into the finals. You start to think it's your destiny to win the whole thing, and it's tough to compete against that kind of mind-set.

I talked to Venus about Kim's game. Venus was always my first and best read on an opponent. She had a good head for tracking a player's strengths and weaknesses. She paid attention to that kind of thing. Me, I tended to just go out there and play my game. My thinking was: as long as I'm on, no one can beat me. Let the other girl worry about *my* strengths and weaknesses. I didn't care if you had a killer serve, or an aggressive ground game, or a vicious drop shot. As a matter of fact, if your forehand was your strength, I'd go to that side all the time, to show you I could beat you on your best shots. I would make you change your game to counter mine. *I* would overpower *you*. That was always my basic plan of attack—still is, by the way—but it didn't hurt to get my big sister's input on a new opponent. So we talked about the matchup and how I wanted to approach it, and all this time it never occurred to either of us that there would be any fallout from Venus's injury.

Here, I drew strength from my previous matches against Kim. I'd beaten her in the 1999 U.S. Open and here at Indian Wells in 2000. I was seeded #7 in the tournament to her #14. She was cer-

tainly solid, but I had a bigger serve and a lot more power. This was
her first Tier I final, whereas I'd made it this far a bunch of times, so
experience was on my side as well.

(A Tier I event, by the way, is a premier-level tournament that
is considered just a notch below the majors in terms of importance;
there are Tier II, III, and IV events, too, and the draws tend to get
a little weaker, and the prize money and ranking points a little stin-
gier, as you drop down.)

By every prematch measure, I thought I had an edge—and yet
there was one all-important measure that would go against me: the
crowd.

I stepped onto the court a couple minutes before Kim, and
right away people started booing. They were loud, mean, aggressive . . . pissed! It was one of those tournaments where they give you
a bouquet of flowers when you go out to warm up before the finals,
and for some reason that struck me as so absurd at just that moment. Me, walking onto the court with a bouquet of flowers while
everyone booed. It's like one of those "What's wrong with this picture?" scenes. It didn't fit. What got me most of all was that it wasn't
just a scattered bunch of boos. It wasn't coming from just one section. It was like the whole crowd got together and decided to boo
all at once. The ugliness was just raining down on me, hard. I didn't
know what to do. Nothing like this had ever happened to me.

What was most surprising about this uproar was the fact that
tennis fans are typically a well-mannered bunch. They're respectful. They sit still. And in Palm Springs, especially, they tended to
be pretty well-heeled, too. But I looked up and all I could see was a
sea of rich people—mostly older, mostly white—standing and booing lustily, like some kind of genteel lynch mob. I don't mean to use
such inflammatory language to describe the scene, but that's really
how it seemed from where I was down on the court. Like these
people were gonna come looking for me after the match.

At first I thought maybe there was something else going on,
some piece of news that had flashed on the scoreboard that had

gotten them all upset . . . *something* to explain the jeering. But then I realized it was meant for me. By this point, Kim was out there on the court as well, with her own bouquet, and she got a big cheer before everyone set their sights once again on me.

There was no mistaking that all of this was meant for me. I heard the word *nigger* a couple times, and I knew. I couldn't believe it. That's just not something you hear in polite society, but I was a long way from polite society on that stadium court. I didn't make the connection to Venus's injury just yet, but it was clear I was the target. And then, just to reinforce how angry these people were at me, when Kim started in with her warm-ups, the crowd stood and cheered for her all over again. Everything she did, they cheered. Everything I did, they booed. It was freaky. And cruel. I'd played in matches before when the crowd was against me and pulling for my opponent for whatever reason, but this was so far off the map of my experience I didn't know what to do.

I tried to block it out and prepare for my match, but it's tough to ignore fourteen thousand screaming people—especially when they're screaming at *you!* It's tough to tune out such ugliness and venom. And it got worse. The fans quieted for Kim's introduction and then gave her a standing ovation. Then they introduced me and the booing kicked up another couple notches.

I wanted to cry, but I didn't want to give these people the satisfaction, or let them know they could get to me.

Just before the start of play, my dad and Venus started walking down the aisle to the players' box by the side of the court, and everybody turned and started to point and boo at them. At Indian Wells, it's such a long, long walk down the stairs to the players' box that I thought they'd never get there, underneath all this booing. It was mostly just a chorus of boos, but I could still hear shouts of "Nigger!" here and there. I even heard one angry voice telling us to go back to Compton. It was unbelievable.

That's when it finally came to me that this was connected to what happened in that semifinal scratch. I should have made the connection sooner, because it was so transparent, but I was rattled. Remember, I was just a kid. What did I know? But now it was clear even to me that these people were angry at Venus and my dad, and that I was somehow caught up in it. I suppose I knew this all along, on some level, but it took watching my father and sister run the gauntlet to their seats, while all around people were shouting at them and pointing at them for me to figure out what was really going on.

Daddy didn't help matters, I'm afraid. When he got to his seat, he turned around and pumped his fist in the air, in a gesture of defiance. I'm sure he meant to send a clear message that he and his family would not be beaten down by something like this. Perhaps he wanted to call to mind that famous black power protest from the 1968 Mexico City Olympics, when two American athletes pumped their fists from the medal stand during the anthem. But whatever his intent, the gesture had the unintended effect of inciting the crowd even more.

My first thought as I took all of this in was for V. I was okay when I thought all this nastiness was meant for me, but once I saw it was directed at my family I got my back up. It set me off. I'm extremely protective of my family, and I hated that Venus had to deal with something like this, after what she'd already had to deal with leading up to our semifinal. She looked great, and I could see she was trying to put on a brave face behind her sunglasses, but I could see that deep down she was hurt by the negative reaction. Truth be told, I don't think any of us knew quite how to handle it, but I had a match to play so I had to do more than just handle it. I had to overcome it. I had to move on.

Now, I don't want to misrepresent the situation, because this incident got a lot of attention in the tennis press. You can dig up videotape on it if you look hard enough. I know I've got a tape of the match somewhere at home, but I can't watch it because it brings back too many painful memories. And so, to be completely objective about it, I shouldn't state that every single fan in that stadium was yelling at me and my family. That's probably not accurate. I'd say there were about a hundred or so people shouting out encouragement, and maybe another hundred or so not saying anything. That seems about right. For every ninety-eight people yelling at me, there was maybe one person on my side and another person just keeping quiet.

It's also not accurate for me to suggest that everyone in the stands was rich, white, and old. Certainly, *most* everyone in the stands was rich, white, and old, but there were probably another hundred or so black faces in the stands, and maybe another hundred or so who lived from paycheck to paycheck, like most people. There was actually one guy in the crowd whose voice managed to make it through, and he was really, really helpful to me. I couldn't tell you if he was black or white, but it didn't matter. He was on my side. He kept telling me to hang in there, not to listen to all these people, to just play my game.

Oh, yeah. My game. For a beat or two I'd forgotten about the match. It was hard to concentrate. I imagine Kim Clijsters also had a tough time concentrating. There was just too much going on. She held her serve in the first game without breaking a sweat. A backhand return into the net. A forehand wide. An ace. Another forehand into the net. Four straight points. Not exactly the way I wanted to start out the match—but then, there was a lot about the match that wasn't going according to plan. With each point, Kim got a bigger and bigger cheer, and it only got worse when it was my turn to serve. I remember I missed my first serve and the crowd was just overjoyed. In tennis, you never hear fans cheer a player's mistakes, but here they were, cheering. It was just awful. And then, the biggest, most derisive cheer of all erupted when I ended up double-faulting. Oh my God, it was such a low moment!

They kept it up for the entire match. No matter what I did, these people booed. Or cheered—a mean chorus that almost sounded worse than booing. Or—worst of all!—sat in stone silence after I won a point. Kim broke me in my very first service game, and the first set went downhill from there. She actually won the first seven points of the match, and a tiny part of me wondered if I'd ever win a point. I couldn't get into any kind of rhythm. I couldn't focus or get anything going.

Kim won the third game, too, and when I questioned a call on a ball I thought was out, it was like these people were ready to string me up.

Somehow, I found the strength to hold serve in my next service game, and then to break Kim back in the following game to bring us essentially even. For a while, it seemed the crowd had quieted, but then I double-faulted again to start the next game, down 2–3, and the crowd was on me all over again.

I look at pictures of me from that tournament—all fresh-faced and excited, looking sharp in my pink Puma jumper, my hair in braids and gathered into high pigtails in back, held in place by my black Puma visor. I looked so cute! And yet these people were just ripping me. I was just a kid, and they were ripping me. I feel so badly for the little girl I was back then. I mean, I was still just a teenager! How can you justify treating a child so badly?

It had to mess with my concentration. Kim's, too. She put out a tremendous effort that day and a stirring show of sportsmanship under difficult conditions. She got off to that great start, on the back of all this nonsense, but I battled back and held serve, then I broke her again to go up 4–3. For a moment, I thought I'd put all that ugliness behind me, but I stumbled in my next service game and let the jeers and taunts start messing with my head. I ended up giving that break right back, allowing Kim to tie things up at 4–4.

Neither one of us was playing particularly well. My first-serve percentage was terrible, and I was making tons of unforced errors. I kept hitting balls wide and long—but they were so far wide and long that they weren't even close! Most of the points I won were on Kim's unforced errors, so she was struggling, too. Everything was just *off*.

Kim held serve, then rallied back to break me again to take the first set. On the very last point of the set, I approached the net, thinking I could maybe force Kim from her comfort zone. I'd only been to the net a couple times to that point, and here I thought I could push the issue and take control of the match. At first, it appeared I'd do just that, as I went to put away Kim's return. I was *right there*, and what did I do? I hit the ball directly into the net, to give the crowd something new to cheer about.

I thought, *Man, I just can't catch a break!*

I looked ahead and couldn't imagine how the rest of the match might go. I was just going through the motions. We stayed on serve for the first few games of the second set, but they were ugly holds. I'd go up 40–0 and then give back a bunch of points before holding on to win. That's no way to win, if you're hoping to put any kind of stamp on the rest of the match. I was defeated, deflated. Emotionally drained. You could see it in the way I carried myself, in the tentative way I returned to the baseline after each point. I didn't think I had it in me to keep going. The booing was just wearing me out.

During the next changeover, trailing 1–2 in the second set, I sat down and cried into my towel. I don't mind admitting it here. I don't think it makes me soft or weak, just human. The crowd was all over me. I was down a set. I couldn't think how I would get through the rest of the match. It seemed to stretch out in front of me in an unreachable, unending way. At just that moment, I didn't care if I won or lost. I didn't want to go back out there. I couldn't. And then I thought, *Okay, Serena. You need to be tough.* I thought if Althea Gibson could fight her way through far worse, I had an obligation to fight through this. And not just fight—I had an obligation to prevail. In my head, it was no longer a battle between me and Kim Clijsters. Now it was between me and this hateful crowd. Now I would not be denied, and so I summoned whatever reserves of inner strength I could find and stood to take my place on the court, telling myself I would not lose this match. Whatever happened, whatever would keep happening, I would not be beaten down by it.

I have to believe there was some racist component to all of this.

If it had been twenty years earlier and Chris Evert had to make a late scratch in a semifinal match against her sister Jeanne, nobody would have booed Jeanne the next day. Nobody would have suggested that the sisters were conspiring in some way, or manipulating the game. Nobody would have booed some blond, blue-eyed girl. And nobody would have shouted down her father with cries of, "Go back to Compton, nigger!" I'm sorry, but that would not have happened—not in Palm Springs, anyway—so you tell me this attack on me and my family wasn't racially motivated on some level. You tell me that this mostly white crowd wasn't beating up on this nineteen-year-old black girl and her family in part because of the color of our skin. Go ahead and make that argument. I'll listen to it. But I won't buy it. Why? Because I was there. Because I was the target. Because you don't know what it's like to have all of this entitled vitriol rain down on you. These privileged, entitled people were up in my face and all over me and my dad and my sister because they were denied their entertainment the day before. That's the bottom line.

I understand that I'm in the entertainment business. I compete at the highest levels of my sport. I know the only reason there's all that prize money and endorsement money is because people buy tickets to watch. I get that. But I also get that I do what I do for me. I'm not out there busting my butt for the blue-haired Palm Springs jet-setter. No, I'm out there for me. People need to understand that. I'm no different than any other athlete. We play to win, and to prove something to ourselves and our opponents. If you enjoy watching us compete, that's great. If you want to root for us and take a little sideline pride in our accomplishments, that's great, too. Go ahead and pull for us because we feed off of your excitement. Go ahead and expect the best from us because we rise to meet those expectations. But don't take it out on me if you don't get what you want out of the deal. Don't ask me to play in a pain you could never endure. (I *always* play in pain, by the way. Every athlete does.) Don't hold me to any standard you wouldn't place on yourself—or your own daughter. That's not part of the bargain.

If I'm on my game, I'm on my game; if I'm not, I'm not. But count on me to give one hundred percent, and I'll count on you to leave me to do my thing.

During that emotional changeover, all I could think about was my dad, and everything he'd been through. He was born in 1942, in Shreveport, Louisiana, and he'd suffered all kinds of oppression and racism in his life. He had a tough time, but he was determined to keep his family from the same tough time. He'd pushed me and my sisters, hard, to become the best players we could possibly be. Somehow, against all odds and against everyone's low expectations, he pushed us to the very top levels of the game. People in tennis seemed to either admire this about him or to resent him for it. There was no in-between. Either way, there's no denying that it was because of him that we were even here at Indian Wells. It was because of him that thousands and thousands of young black athletes could now look to Venus and me as role models. And it was because of him that a great many of those young black athletes were picking up their first tennis racquets. I thought, *My dad doesn't deserve this kind of grief. Venus doesn't deserve it. I don't deserve it.*

I didn't know what else to do, so I prayed. Right there on the court, during the changeover. I said a simple little prayer that just about changed my life. I said, "Jehovah, give me the strength to get up from this chair. Give me the strength to finish this match. Give me the strength to persevere."

I actually spoke these words out loud. Well, not *out loud* in any kind of public speaking voice, but in a whisper I could certainly hear above the din. I didn't ask Him to help me win. I didn't ask Him to help me with my serve. I didn't ask for anything but the resolve and strength of character to power through a difficult situation. That's all. Really, all I wanted was to walk off that court with my head held high and to somehow be a better person because of it.

There's a wonderful scripture in the Bible, Ephesians 6:10–17, that talks about the shield of faith, and I called it to mind here: "Put on the complete suit of armor from God, that you may be able to stand firm against the mechanisms of the devil. . . . Stand firm, therefore, with your loins girded about with truth and having on the breastplate of righteousness, and with your feet shod with the equipment of the good news of peace. Above all things, take up the large shield of faith with which you will be able to quench the fiery darts and burning missiles of the wicked. Also, accept the helmet of salvation and the sword of spirit that is God's word."

So I stood and cloaked myself in that shield and went back to work. I tried to tune out the fiery darts and burning missiles of the Palm Springs set and play my game, to let all that venom fall softly to the stadium floor, and to work my way around it, and as I stepped back on the court I heard that lone voice of support yet again: "Come on, Serena!" It was such a powerful, positive cry! A true Godsend.

The "shield of faith" thing helped, too. It really did. *Stand . . . having on the breastplate of righteousness . . .* Those words gave me the power to believe that these people couldn't touch me. It let me feel invisible *and* invincible. Most of all, it let me get back to the game.

Initially, I thought I'd made the situation worse. I took the court after that changeover feeling recharged and refocused, that the match was now in my hands and in my heart, but then I double-faulted right away. It felt to me like I'd given the power of that moment right back to the crowd—and to Kim Clijsters. Somehow, I managed to string together a few points in a row and hold serve. And then, at 2–2, I took the next four points in a row against Kim's serve, to go up a break. It was a thrilling turnaround and it seemed to quiet the crowd. They were still on me, but now it was just garden-variety-type heckling. It wasn't so personal.

Unfortunately, the crowd wasn't quiet for long, because Kim broke me right back, bringing the angry mob right along with her. They were all over me, all over again, and I allowed myself to get swallowed

up once more. Kim held serve to go up a game. Then she pushed me
to break point in the next game, which would have put her up 5–3
in the second set and serving for the match. It was a key point in the
match, obviously, and I hated that the crowd was so much a part of
it. The only good thing about all that noise and nastiness was that
it seemed to be rattling Kim almost as much as it was rattling me.
By some odd mix of luck, will, and justice, I pushed the game back
to deuce on an unforced error. It was like we each took turns being
pushed off our game by the crowd, and now it was my turn to help
with the pushing. My serve had been hit-or-miss the entire match,
but here I unleashed a 114 mph bullet for an ace—my biggest of the
tournament!—to help me hold and knot the set at 4–4.

Once again, I let myself believe the momentum that had been
sucked from that stadium before the very first point was once again
on my racquet—and I carried that belief into Kim's next service
game. Down 30–40, she misplayed a drop shot that I managed to
reach, which put me back up that all-important break. The crowd
wasn't too happy about this latest turn. They'd been relatively quiet
when it appeared that Kim was in control, but now that I had
battled back into position to serve for the set, they were on me
again. It was like I'd set them off—and now they were madder than
ever, because it appeared I might deny them the knockout jeer they
seemed to desperately crave. At one point during my next service
game, it appeared a line call had gone my way, and the fans started
jeering—*right in the middle of the point!*

I'd never seen such terrible behavior, and I'd certainly never been
on the receiving end! I wanted to climb into the stands and fight
these people, but at this late stage in the match, with the second
set finally within reach, I told myself I wouldn't let this ugliness
push me from my goal. Here again, I was helped in this resolve by
that same lone voice of support coming from the stands: "Come on,
Serena. You can do it."

I heard that and thought, *Okay, Serena. Keep it together. Just hold
serve and you're back to even. Just hold serve and all this energy will*

shift over to your side of the net. I figured I had this one guy on my side and that was all I needed, so I pulled myself together and did just that.

Unfortunately, the seesaw continued to teeter in the third set. I went up 0–40 in Kim's service game to start the set, but she hung on to take the first game. For me, it was one unforced error on top of another, and each one seemed to allow Kim to play with a little more confidence. Until the seesaw tilted back in my direction. Then I'd capitalize on one of her mistakes and go on a momentum run of my own. That's what happened here. I took the next five games, to take a commanding 5–1 lead in the third set, up two breaks.

I thought, *That should keep these people quiet!*

I ended up winning the match 4–6, 6–4, 6–2. I don't know how I did it, but what mattered to me most of all at just that moment was that it was over. It wasn't about winning. It was about powering through. At the same time, I remember feeling badly for Kim Clijsters. She's a great girl. Absolutely, the crowd affected her, too. Neither one of us deserved to be caught in such a hateful moment, and as a result I don't think either one of us got to play our best tennis that day. We'd each been having such a strong tournament, it was a shame for the championship to be decided on such a pair of unremarkable performances.

By the end of the match, a good portion of the crowd had come over to my side. There were still boos, but it was almost like being at any other sporting event. Once I went up those two breaks in the third set, it seemed inevitable that I would win, and the crowd softened. I imagined the fans felt badly about how they treated me and my family at the outset, and that explained why the mood of the stadium turned a little bit. Not a whole lot, but a little.

In the postmatch interview they do on the court, I thanked my dad and Venus and the few people who cheered for me throughout. "And to those of you who didn't," I said, "I love you anyway." My throat was all knotted up. I tried to smile. I didn't want to choke on my words in front of all those people, so I kept my speech short. I held my head high and said what I needed to say, and then I waved to the crowd and disappeared into the runway beneath the stadium.

You want to talk about strength? It was harder—*way* harder!—to get through that postmatch interview than it was to play the match itself, but I would not be reduced by these people. I would rise above them. And it would take every measure of strength in my nineteen-year-old frame to lift myself from this moment.

I was crying when I left the court, but I didn't want anyone to see so I kept wiping away my tears. I was tired and sweaty, so that helped. The tears just blended in with the anguish of the match. I choked up, too, during the press conference afterward, but the whole time I kept thinking of Althea Gibson and how she had to deal with some of the same vitriol. I remembered reading that Althea had to sleep in her car when she was out on the road traveling to all these tournaments, because she couldn't stay in the hotels. I don't know if I could have done that, but she did it so I wouldn't have to. She was a true tennis pioneer for African-American women. Zina Garrison, too, a couple generations later. She had her own trials to get past while she was walking the path Althea had set. And now here I was, all these years later, at my favorite place to play, in a sup-posedly enlightened time, hearing the same garbage all over again.

I look back now and think something could have been done about this situation before it got out of hand. Some tournament official could have gotten on the loudspeaker and explained to the fans that Venus had been legitimately hurt, that I had nothing to do with her withdrawal, that every effort had been made to cancel that semifinal match in a more timely manner. Some effort could have been made to quiet the crowd. But no one did anything. The WTA people just sat there with their mouths open as all these people beat up on a little girl. The Indian Wells people just sat there with their mouths open, too. Everyone was in shock, I think—but that's no excuse.

I could cry about it now if I wanted to, but I choose not to. I could lose sleep over the sight of that little girl—me!—wearing her adorable pink Puma jumper, and her braids, and playing her heart out in front of such an angry mob. But I choose to gain strength from this sorry moment, not to give it away. I choose to recognize it for what it was, to learn from it, and then move past it. And yet I call attention to it because I believe it's instructive, because I think we need to call out bad behavior, especially when it cuts across racial lines and is directed at our children. After all, that's what I was at the time, a child. Say whatever you want about my dad and how he handled our careers when we came onto the scene. Say whatever you want about me and Venus and how our approach to the game may or may not have been different from the approach taken by the other girls on the tour. At the end of the day we were just a couple kids, trying to do our best.

We need to hold each other accountable for our actions, don't you think? Nobody really talked about this at the time, and Venus and I never really talked about it, not even in the car ride back to Los Angeles with our sisters. We all drove back together, and it was the strangest, most unsettling ride, because usually after a big tournament win we'd all be giddy and excited. But here it was like we had been stunned into silence. We all knew what we'd just seen and experienced, and it just kind of hung there in the car with us, like a pall.

In some ways, it's with us still. You can see it in the stand Venus and I took afterward. We refused to return to Indian Wells. Even now, all these years later, we continue to boycott the event. It's become a mandatory tournament on the tour, meaning that the WTA can fine a player if she doesn't attend. But I don't care if they fine me a million dollars, I will not play there again. They can also suspend you from the next tournament, but my feeling is that if I go back to Indian Wells I'll send the wrong message to little black girls who for whatever reason have chosen to look up to me, who might have a dream of lifting themselves up and out of their present situations and becoming something else. If they fine me, they fine me. If they suspend me, they suspend me.

As I write this, it looks like I can keep to my principles on this and I won't be fined or suspended—but I really don't care either way. I have a responsibility to those little girls who look up to me, just as I have a responsibility to myself. They might not even know what happened at Indian Wells in 2001, but I'll know. And I'll know that if I don't make my small stand on this, it will be harder for them to make their small stands when they come up.

It's amazing to me how every year some tour official comes to me and asks, "Are you playing Indian Wells this year?" It's as if we never had the conversation before. And every year I say, "Hell, no. I'm not playing Indian Wells. Are you out of your mind?"

The most amazing thing is that they keep asking, like it never happened. But you don't get past racial tension by forgetting about it. You don't just ignore this kind of prejudice and hope it goes away. That's not how it works. If you sweep it under the rug, one day you'll lift the rug to redecorate and there it will be.

No, I won't go back. I will not give these people the validation. I will not stand down. It's a point of pride. I don't care what these folks say about me, about how I'm vindictive or stubborn or reading too much into the situation. I actually heard that one, early on, from some official. He said I was making something out of nothing. But I don't think so. Remember, I was there. I was the target. I know what I know. What I don't know and what I can't say for certain is whether or not the small stand my sister and I are taking on Indian Wells will amount to anything in the ongoing fight for equality. Probably it won't, but you never know. You don't make these stands to accomplish a specific goal, I've come to realize. You make them because they're right. You make them because, taken together, they add up to something. In all walks of life. At all times. At all costs. You make them because you wouldn't be here if someone didn't make them for you, long before you were even born. You make them to ensure that the doors that are at long last open to you will keep from closing. You make them because you can, and because you must. Most of all, you make them because somewhere some little girl might be watching. This little girl might be black or white or brown. She might be rich or poor. She might be a future tennis player or a doctor or a fashion designer. Whatever she wants to be, she can be. It's like my mom used to always say, all she has to do is set her mind to it and get busy. And all I have to do is set a positive example.

Piece of cake, right?

U stand on the shoulders of your parents and grandparents. Your ancestors made U. Your ancestors made U the best. Think of all they went through for U. Don't let any girl take away your win, your destiny, your dream. This is opportunity. Yours. This is your time. At last. This is your dream. Make it happen.

—MATCH BOOK ENTRY

FIVE

Faith, Family, Florida

Faith. It's at the root of everything I do, everything I believe. It's what gets me out of bed each morning before first light, to head out to the tennis court. And it's what keeps me believing that anything is possible—not just on the court, but all around.

Without faith, what do we have? What's the point? Where's that silent fuel to drive us through our days and get us where we're going? This kind of thinking was instilled in me when I was little, through the values passed on by my parents and sisters, and through meetings and Bible study. Those Bible verses I cited earlier? I come by them honestly. The scripture that lifts me from a low moment like Indian Wells is in my bones. See, we were raised as Jehovah's Witnesses, and that foundation has given me a deep conviction in a higher power, a higher purpose. It grounds me, and keeps me whole and looking ahead. Most of all, it places my life in a kind of context and lets me know I'm not just going through the motions but moving instead to some higher purpose. There's got to be a reason we're all here on this earth—reaching, striving, pushing—don't you think?

Now, I do my share of preaching and teaching the good news, but I don't go door-to-door as much as I'd like, because people recognize me and it gets in the way of what I'm trying to say. Sometimes, I'll knock on a door and people will be so surprised to see Serena

Williams on the other side that we never quite get around to the reason for my visit. Other times, they've got no idea who I am and I'll have their full attention.

I do my share of reaching out, too, but that's not for these pages. What's important to note here is that I feel strongly that we all need to believe in something. Open your heart to the idea that there's something bigger out there, something bigger than we can know.

In our house, our hearts were opened early on. My mom had been raised in a churchgoing family back in Michigan, and she was looking for a place to keep that going once we moved to California. She was anxious to re-create those all-important points of connection in her new community, but that took some time, I'm afraid. If you've ever met my mom, you'll know that not just any church would do. She's a spiritual person, but she's not the most social person on the planet, so those two sides had to fit together. She had to feel comfortable wherever she worshipped. I was too little to know any of this firsthand, but she used to tell my sisters that when she found the right church she'd know it, and that would be all there was to it. Her big thing? She was looking for something real, she used to tell us. Something honest. The truth.

And so she went to a lot of different churches—every week, it seemed, she was trying on another one—but she never really felt a powerful connection until some Jehovah's Witnesses knocked on our front door one morning. It was like some kind of sign, like God had literally answered her prayers, so she went to a meeting at Kingdom Hall. I'm betting she was skeptical at first, because she didn't know what to expect, but she took to it, she really did. She went by herself at first, to make sure it was a good fit. After that, we went regularly to meetings, as a family. Enthusiastically, too. In California, that meant every Sunday, Tuesday, and Thursday. In Florida, after we'd picked up and moved there so we could kick things up a couple notches in our training, it meant every Sunday, Tuesday, and Wednesday. Yes, it takes up some time, but you don't really notice the time when you're at Kingdom Hall. It becomes a part of you, and washes over you, and you're swept up and set down on the other side of the experience in such a way that the time just flies. Anyway, that's how it's been with me. Ever since I was little, sitting next to my sisters, soaking it all in, wanting to be no place else in this whole world.

My dad didn't always go with us to meetings, but he was with us in spirit. He carved out time for us away from practice to coincide with our meeting schedule, because Kingdom Hall came first. We weren't allowed to miss a meeting—for *anything*. He and my mom both believed it was important for us to have religion in our lives. It was a first-and-foremost deal. That, and a good education. Even our relationships with each other had everything to do with this shared search for meaning. It was at the core of our family—and, blessedly, it remains so.

The great thing about being a Jehovah's Witness is it's all about the Bible. A lot of people don't understand our movement, but it's all right there. New Testament. Old Testament. As it says in 2 Timothy 3:16, all scripture is inspired of God, so we read it all. All the way through, and then all over again. We try to learn from it and apply what we learn, both to our everyday lives and to set us straight for teaching and righteousness. In fact, the Jehovah's Witnesses grew out of the Bible Student movement at the turn of the last century, so Bible study remains central to what we do. We seek to understand the stories that have been set down to teach us, to light our way, and to reconsider these stories yet again.

That's basically it. We're Christians. We believe in Jesus Christ. We believe in God, Jehovah. After all, we are Jehovah's Witnesses—bearing witness to Jehovah's word. Up and down, our beliefs are essentially in line with conservative Christian values. But of course there are some key differences. We don't celebrate holidays like Christmas and Easter, for example, and we don't accept blood transfusions—a belief that led in an indirect way to the development of bloodless surgery, a noninvasive alternative to traditional surgery that has recently gained favor in secular communities. We're also big into relief work, which is like a sacred mission to Jehovah's Witnesses. Show us a flood or a hurricane or some other natural disaster, and we're all over it, doing what we can to set things right—only here I don't get how missionary or volunteer work can be assigned to one faith or another. Here it feels like that's an obligation that should be on all of us, no matter where or how we pray.

But like I said, we're Christians—and I was an eager participant as a kid. I still am. I go to the Kingdom Hall all the time, wherever I happen to be. I read the Bible all the time, wherever I happen to be. I read every night, before I go to sleep. I soak up what I can, whenever I can. And, each time out, I'm lifted and transported and set down in a peaceful, spiritual place. I'm constantly looking to build on my spirituality, to make myself a better person, to find all these different points of connection with our God, Jehovah.

After all, it's who I am.

The book of Matthew talks about how Jesus instructs us to go forth and make disciples of all nations, to preach His good news throughout the land. So that's what we do: we preach that good news. The more I go to meetings, the more I learn. The more I learn, the more I look to share. And the more I share, the more I appreciate the value of religion in my life. It's like holding up a mirror to everything you do and all the choices you make, and seeing what comes back in the reflection. Obviously, I'm not perfect. No one is perfect. Obviously, I make some mistakes and some bad choices. Everyone takes a wrong turn from time to time. But I'm working on it, and I believe that as long as I'm working on it I'm doing okay. I'm striving, reaching, pushing. Searching. I'm doing my best to please my God, Jehovah, wherever I happen to find Him in my life.

I find it such a strength and comfort where the scripture says that God reads the heart. A lot of times, because of my crazy schedule, I start to feel like I'm letting Him down, because I'm so focused on my tennis. Because I can't find a Kingdom Hall and get to a proper meeting. Because I let my guard down sometimes and act on a bad impulse. But He reads my heart, and knows at least that I'm headed in the right direction. He knows at least that I mean well—and that I mean to do better. And, just as He can read my heart, others can as well. Lately, I've been focused on what we call informal witnessing, which basically means preaching by the way we carry ourselves. On the tennis court, for someone like me, it can be in the way I react to a tough match, or a bad call. Here, too, I don't always react the way I should or set an entirely positive example, but I'm working on it. I've gotten better at walking with pride and dignity out there, no matter how things are going in a match. People are always asking me why I don't go crazy over bad calls, or get all emotional when a match tilts the wrong way, and it's because I try to carry myself in a certain way. I don't want to give my religion a bad name—and I never lose sight of this when I'm out on the court.

That was a key for me during that difficult day at Indian Wells. Believe me, I thought of flipping off that hateful crowd and storming off the court, but I reached for prayer instead. I asked Jehovah for the strength and resolve to get through that match—not to win, but to see my way proudly to the other side. The winning would take care of itself. Or not, because in the end winning wasn't important. The real test was to hold my head high and power through, to set a positive example.

For years afterward, people who'd seen that match on television or read about it in the papers would ask me how I managed to lift myself to the other side of all that venom and vitriol. Always, I tell them that I didn't do anything.

It was all Him.

Florida.

For a tennis family, it shined as a place of great opportunity. True, there were some great tennis coaches and academies in California. Plus, the weather was mild, so we could play all year long, but after a while Daddy started to think we needed a change. Together, my parents talked about how we could get better competition, better schooling, better everything in Florida. The more they talked, the more it seemed that was where we were headed. I didn't pay too much attention to all the talk, but at the same time it was impossible to ignore. It started to sound like the palm trees in Florida were even better than the ones we had at home.

Anyway, Venus and I were young, so we didn't really have such a strong opinion. We liked California well enough. We liked going to the Kingdom Hall. We liked playing on all these different public courts, and playing with our sisters, and entering local tournaments. We liked working on our game with our parents. It made for a tight family dynamic, I'll say that. But once everyone started talking about moving, it seemed like Florida was the Promised Land.

At first, my parents resisted the idea. They liked how things were. Mom cherished the Kingdom Hall where we went to meetings, and the community of friends she'd made there. She liked her job, and our house, and our school. Daddy liked the routine he'd set up for us girls. He liked the small network of hitting partners and tennis lifers he'd assembled to supplement our training. He liked the setup he had with his security business. We had a good, solid rhythm going as a family. Still, they were open to what Florida had to offer, because they were committed to providing us with the best training they could find to get us to the next level, so they agreed to visit with a few coaches who flew out to meet with us. They showed us pictures of their facilities, and there was no denying that they were nice. So many courts! So many brand-new tennis balls! So many kids wearing stylish tennis clothes! It would be a whole new environment for us, and if you looked up and down their rosters of former students, you could see a number of prominent names on the professional tour, so clearly these people knew their stuff. Some of these coaches were even offering to subsidize our training, so we had to think about that as well.

Of course, all of these coaches were interested in Venus. She was the big prize in the Williams package, because at that stage in our development she was the true rising star. These coaches wanted a chance to work with her and to grow their own reputations on the back of her success, because everyone could see she'd be a champion. With me, nobody could really see that just yet. Daddy could see it, I think. V could see it. I could see it. My mom could see it, too. But to the rest of the tennis world I was still just following in Venus's footsteps, playing in her shadow. It was like that reporter had said; the kid sister never makes it big, so why bother? Everyone made like they were interested in both of us—in Isha and Lyn, too!—but I could see it was all about Venus. Even at nine years old, I could see.

Absolutely, I minded all this on one level, but on another I didn't give it a focused thought. I was happy for Venus, that everybody wanted to work with her—really and truly happy. But at the same time I hated that all these people were writing me off before seeing what I could do. No, I wasn't physically imposing, like Venus was at that age. I played a much softer game because I was still so small. But that didn't take anything away from how competitive I was on the court. That didn't mean I couldn't make my shots. I was a good player! But nobody really noticed because Venus was so much better. The good news, I guess, is that nobody was saying anything negative about my game. It's just that I wasn't being touted as a rising superstar like Venus. In comparison to V, I was going nowhere.

Our older sisters didn't really want to go to Florida. Isha, in particular, was unhappy to leave her friends. I can't say I blamed her. I don't think I would have wanted to be uprooted like that if I had been in her situation. She was entering her senior year in high school, and that's a tough time to pull someone from her social swirl—a young girl, especially. In Isha's case it was particularly upsetting, because up until high school she really didn't have so many friends; all our time was spent playing tennis, and with each other, and now that she was finally making all these new relationships and moving around on her own she hated to have to give it up. It's like she'd been let out of a cage and allowed to run free, and now she was being coaxed back inside.

Tunde was already through with high school, but she didn't want to make the move, either. She said it didn't make sense for her to move clear across the country. She'd moved out of the house and started in on college and a life of her own, so why would she want to move? She was already into her own thing.

Lyn was younger, so she was more like me and V: she didn't have much of a voice either way. And yet for a while in there it was as if everyone had a different opinion. It wasn't just whether we should go—it was *where* we should go to. It was what our lives would be like once we got there, what our family would be like. I just listened in and worried what it would be like to split us all up, if that was what ended up happening. That was all I kept thinking about. I mean, Compton was all I knew. Maybe it wasn't the best or safest or most prosperous place in the world, but it was home.

Years later, my parents told me Compton itself was part of the problem. I didn't recognize their concerns at the time, but apparently there was a lot of gang-related violence, and drug use, and racial tensions. There were those gunshots ringing out while we played. We were protected from a lot of that as kids, because we were always together, always playing tennis, but that didn't mean it wasn't a problem. Tunde and Isha were starting to notice it, as they moved around town on their own. Some of their friends were in and out of trouble. Kids who didn't have a lot would sometimes take what wasn't theirs, like it was their due. People were struggling to get by and scrambling to stay safe, and after a while I guess this started to play in to my parents' thinking. They didn't want us to grow up in such an uncertain environment for any longer than we had to—and here it appeared we no longer had to.

More and more, it started to seem inevitable that we'd be moving to Florida. It seemed to be the natural next step in our progression as tennis players, and since this had been a full-on family affair going in, it would be a full-on family affair going forward.

Well . . . *almost* full-on. Tunde would stay behind in Los Angeles, but the rest of us would drive to Florida and start up in a new house, a new school, a new everything. We made a kind of exploratory trip, to check out a couple of these places before signing on to one in particular. We spent an afternoon at Nick Bollettieri's academy in Bradenton, Florida, where I thought everyone was just so nice. The kids, too! I really liked playing there, but that was not where we ended up. We ended up at a place called Grenelefe, which was run by a pro named Rick Macci.

Rick was one of those coaches who had come out to Compton to talk to my dad and watch us play. He'd worked with a lot of young players. He spent a lot of time with us, and Daddy really put him through the wringer. He asked Rick all kinds of questions. Daddy's thing was if he was going to entrust his girls to someone new, he should learn everything he could about that person. Not just everything about his tennis background and approach, but everything about everything. Daddy wanted to know his true character.

Of course, Daddy wasn't prepared to stop coaching us. That wasn't part of the deal. His plan was to work alongside these other coaches and to take advantage of the facilities they offered, and the stronger level of competition, and the new techniques and strategies they might impart. But he would still be our coach. That was never in question. He wouldn't be like those other parents who dropped their kids off at the academy after school each day and then went about their business. No, he'd be down on the court with us, racquet in hand, working to develop our game. He would direct our training. Looking back, I'm not so sure these pros were too anxious to have Daddy as a colleague—but we were a package plan.

There's a famous story that gets attached to Rick Macci's visit with us out in Compton, but I'm afraid it's been dressed up a bit over the years. Still, there's enough truth to it to make it worth telling. The story goes that Rick spent a bunch of time watching Venus hit. He was impressed, but not especially so. Remember, this was a guy who worked with tennis phenoms every day, so he was judging

Venus against this group. Remember, too, that Venus was only ten, and I guess it's hard to get all pumped about a ten-year-old athlete, no matter how much hype and hoopla she's managed to generate.

At one point, Venus asked for a break so she could go to the bathroom, and when Daddy said it was okay she dropped her racquet and walked part of the way across the court on her hands. Then she did a couple cartwheels and handsprings. This wasn't so unusual, because we took gymnastics and we were always doing cartwheels and handsprings. According to all these stories that have been written about us, Rick Macci looked at Venus's acrobatics and said, "Mr. Williams, it looks like you have the next Michael Jordan on your hands."

And Daddy—bless him!—looked over toward me and said, "No, Mr. Macci, we've got the next *two* Michael Jordans."

I remember this moment clearly, because it was another example of how Venus was the center of attention. Okay, so she probably didn't walk clear across the court on her hands, like it said in some of the articles. She didn't handspring all the way to the bathroom like a professional cheerleader at a half-time show. But she did do a cartwheel or two. And Rick Macci was probably impressed by her athleticism, because she was certainly athletic, and I guess you didn't see too many tennis players moving around while they were upside down, even for just a short distance, so he probably made a comment to that effect.

But Daddy's response was reported accurately. He made sure to call attention to me. I can still hear him singing my praises, like he always did. It's just that people didn't always listen, because Venus was the undefeated junior player and the toast of Southern California. She was the one they wrote all those articles about. She was the one with the great physical gifts. And she was the one all these famous coaches wanted to train at their academies. I remember thinking, *When is it going to be my turn? What about me?* And I remember sitting on the side of the court that afternoon, wondering if I'd get a chance to show the famous coach what I could do.

At just that moment, in my nine-year-old head, nothing was more important.

The yellow Volkswagen minibus with the white roof didn't make the trek to Florida. Daddy had actually painted the side panels red a couple years earlier, fooling us into thinking we got a new car, but we finally had to retire it one afternoon by the side of the road, when it wouldn't start. For this cross-country adventure, then, we piled our worldly possessions into a Winnebago and headed east. (Mercifully, Isha wasn't allowed to drive!) What was most memorable about that trip was that it was the longest stretch of time we'd gone without playing tennis. This was a concern, as I recall. Wasn't really a concern to me and my sisters, but my parents were thinking about it, that's for sure. They were looking for public courts along the way, but we weren't on too many side roads, and I guess we didn't find any. I do remember swinging our racquets in a bunch of rest stop parking lots, though. And we did some running and fitness work, too. We must have made an odd picture, stumbling out of that trailer, four girls of various shapes and sizes, swinging our racquets, playing air tennis at all those rest stops, but nothing could keep us from our game.

That all changed, as soon as we settled in Haines City, Florida, not far from the Grenelefe resort. It was kind of a backwater place in the middle of the state. Wasn't a whole lot to do but play tennis, so we played. All the time. Every day after school, for about four or five hours. Venus and I were on an accelerated school schedule, which meant we were out on the court by one in the afternoon. Our teachers overloaded us with homework to make up for the time lost in class. We'd play until about five or six, after which we'd usually go to dance or karate or some other activity. On Tuesdays and Thursdays, we'd go to the Kingdom Hall. Saturdays, we'd play all morning. Sundays were for rest and schoolwork—and Kingdom Hall, of course.

There wasn't exactly a whole lot of time to twiddle our thumbs, although we were still just kids, so we found all kinds of ways to amuse ourselves at home. There's another Greatest Hits–type family story that still gets kicked around among us sisters, and it took place here in Haines City. There was this pizza place called Hungry Howie's, not far from the Grenelefe facility. In the summer, when we were playing tennis all day, the people at the academy used to order pizza for all the kids, and that was a great treat. They also had this special bread that came along with the pizza, which we all called Hungry Howie Bread. I don't know what they called it at the restaurant, but that was how we knew it in our house. They made it with garlic and butter, and it was just so, so good. Man, we all loved that Hungry Howie Bread—all of us except Venus, that is. For some reason, it just wasn't her thing.

One day, Isha ended up bringing all this Hungry Howie Bread home, and we were pinching from our supply all day long. It was like we'd won the lottery. I'd go into the kitchen and grab a piece, and then I'd go back for another, and another. At some point, I started to realize that Isha and Lyn would be digging into the bread bag before long, so I took what was left and found a hiding place for it. A little while later, Isha went into the kitchen looking for some Hungry Howie Bread, and the cupboard was bare. She screamed, "Who stole the Hungry Howie Bread?" You could hear her all over the neighborhood, I bet.

I tried to play it cool. I was about ten—and long past the point where being the cute little sister would get me off the hook. Isha wouldn't let it go, though. There was just too much bread for one person to eat, so she knew something was up. We ended up having this big mock trial, and Isha started interrogating us. Lyn and I were the only two witnesses, and the only two suspects, because we all knew Venus had nothing to do with it. I had to have an alibi for this and an alibi for that—basically, to account for every move I'd made since we'd gotten home from Grenelefe. It was wild. But Isha was such a good lawyer, even then, that she wore me down, and I had to admit that I'd pinched the last few pieces of Hungry Howie Bread.

The surprise, though, was that I hadn't acted alone. All along, I'd thought I was the main culprit, but it turned out that Lyn had already stolen a bunch of bread before I'd even gotten to it, and here she'd been thinking that she was the one about to get caught. Isha wore her down, too. I had no idea about Lyn, and Lyn had no idea about me, but Isha busted us both, and to this day we talk about the Hungry Howie Bread trial. Someone will mention The Case of the Missing Hungry Howie Bread, and we'll bust up laughing.

I didn't like my new school. Back home in California, I used to look forward to all my classes, because I loved to learn. Put me in a classroom with a good teacher and bright, motivated students, and I was all over it. Here in Florida, I still loved to learn, but I didn't have a whole lot of friends. I didn't have a whole lot of friends in California, either, but at least it was familiar. Here in Florida, I did have one good BFF-type friend, but that was about it. I didn't have the best teachers in the world, or the most interested classmates, so that was a giant negative. Mostly, though, I didn't like the way I looked, so that made it hard for me to feel good about myself in the kind of way you needed to if you meant to reach out and meet new people. Little girls can be so mean to each other, only here it wasn't like they were especially mean to me. Instead, I was guarding against that meanness every day. I was waiting for it and waiting for it. I thought it was only a matter of time before these kids started picking on me because of the way I looked, so I didn't say much during the school day. I'd raise my hand in class from time to time, but that was about it.

Venus was still looking out for me. We were in different grades, so our lunch periods were at different times. I usually sat by myself. Eventually, she started to have some friends. People were always drawn to V, but not to me, so every time we were in the hallways or at recess I went looking for her. She was like a safe haven.

One day, I realized just before lunch that I didn't have any money. The way it worked at this particular school was if you didn't have any money for lunch you'd stand in this special line and they'd give you a peanut butter and jelly sandwich. It was always so embarrassing to have to stand in that line, but at least you got to eat. And we did have money for lunch; money was tight, but not that tight, but I had already spent my money on something else. Or maybe I'd lost it. On this day, though, they were serving fried chicken, and I loved fried chicken! (I still do, as you can sometimes see from my hips and thighs!) The thought of missing out on all that fried chicken, and having to eat a peanut butter and jelly sandwich instead, was just too upsetting, so of course I went looking for Venus.

I told Venus the deal, and what did she do? She reached into her pocket and handed me her lunch money. She didn't even think about it. She just said, "I'll have the peanut butter and jelly sandwich. I like peanut butter and jelly."

See what I mean when I say Venus is a special person? She never thought about herself when we were kids, at least not when it came to me. Whatever it was, a gold trophy or a fried chicken lunch in the school cafeteria, she hated to see me disappointed. And *I* hated to see me disappointed, too, so I took her money. You might think that by fifth or sixth grade I would have developed a little more self-respect than to have my hand out all the time, reaching for the kindness and indulgence of my big sisters, but the princess in me didn't see why I had to do without if someone else was perfectly willing to do without instead of me.

(Goodness, I was just *horrible*.)

For the most part, though, we adjusted to our new situation soon enough. Tennis was the constant. Kingdom Hall, too. Whatever else was going on in our little lives, whatever sense of upheaval and displacement we were feeling about our move to Florida, it all fell away when we were on the court or at one of our meetings. That's the great thing about keeping some kind of faith—it layers in a strong foundation for everything else. It becomes what you know.

On the court, we could lose ourselves in the rhythm of the game, in the familiarity of our routines. There, I could start to feel a little more sure of myself. Even at ten or eleven years old, I got very good at tuning everything else out while I was playing. I don't think I concentrated as intently or single-mindedly on anything else in my life, but when it came to tennis I was all over it.

It wasn't just tennis. At Grenelefe, they had us doing this intense fitness training, like hill running and strength work and other conditioning exercises. This was a big change for us. Daddy always appreciated the importance of fitness in our overall game, but back in California he'd built all these sprinting and fitness and strength measures into our basic drills, so we never really noticed that he had us working on our conditioning, but here there was no mistaking it for anything else. Here it was just flat-out running and hill work and even some weight room stuff, and I hated it. What little kid wants to be out there running every day? Or working out in a gym? Not me, I'll say that.

The move to Florida presented two major shifts in my training. First, it meant I was almost always hitting with boys, because Daddy believed that in order for me and Venus to develop as players we needed to learn to play faster, harder, stronger. I guess Rick Macci signed on to this view, because that was what he had us doing, even though at the time this was looked on as a fairly radical approach. I don't get the controversy, because it always seemed so logical to me. I still can't understand why nobody really approached girls' training in just this way. I mean, if there's faster, harder, stronger competition out there to help you fire up your game, you should absolutely take advantage of it. Boys, girls, it shouldn't matter. How you swing the racquet, how hard you play, how you push your opposite number on the other side of the net, that's what matters.

Second, it meant I played more and more with my dad. The way it worked at Grenelefe was Venus would be off on one court, working with these various coaches, while Daddy and I were usually on the next court, doing our own thing. For me, that was one of the great benefits of being on the second string, in terms of everyone's expectations: I finally had my dad to myself.

Isha and Lyn would come to the facility after their full days at school, and start playing on one of the perimeter courts, and I remember looking on at their drills and feeling a little jealous, because they got to be together, and they were doing all these drills with all these kids and having so much fun. On my court, it was just me and Daddy, or me and some other coach, and it was hard. We hit a ton of balls, over and over, and then when we'd pick them all up, we'd hit the same ton all over again. On Venus's court, too. They had us working, working, working. From time to time, we'd get to share the court and make a game of it.

This is a good spot to talk a little more about the influence my mom had on my game, because not a lot of people recognize it. When we were kids, it was mostly just me and my mom. She was working a lot, that's true, but almost all of my one-on-one training was with her. She's a lot different from my dad in her approach. She's tough—a real no-nonsense lady. It was all about the drill with her, and I remember thinking it was really boring on her court. Over on Daddy's court, Venus seemed to be having a lot more fun. Well, maybe *fun* isn't the right word, but her workouts seemed easier, more spirited. With my mom, it was a little more intense. She was always barking out instructions, telling me to move up on the ball or to pay attention to my footwork, reminding me of the purpose of each little exercise. Daddy had a more gentle demeanor. He'd tell you something once and wait for you to incorporate it into your game. Then, if he didn't see you making the effort, he'd calmly remind you what you should be working on. He liked it best when we figured things out for ourselves.

Once we got to Florida, though, that all started to change. Mom wasn't out there hitting with me every day. Now it was me and Daddy, while Venus worked mostly with Rick and the other coaches. She was their priority. All that time back in California, I looked over at Daddy's court and wanted to be working with him,

but now that I'd finally gotten what I wanted I found myself looking over at Venus's court and wanting to work with all these other
coaches. I wanted to be their priority, too, but of course that wasn't
how it was going to be just yet. I still had to grow into that priority
status.

Venus used to hit with this guy named Scott. For a long stretch,
my hitting partner was a guy named Jim. They were older guys, in
their twenties, but that was how my dad and Rick Macci matched
us up. Scott was the stronger player, but I couldn't touch either of
them. Venus could, though. She could really take it to Jim, and with
Scott she was fifty-fifty. Sometimes she beat him; sometimes he beat
her, but it was always close. Sometimes, for fun, we'd split into teams,
and Venus would always pick me to be on her team. We'd play to
21. First I'd play Jim, and Venus would play Scott. Jim would almost
always beat me badly. That was always the benefit of playing these
guys—they never let up. That's what made them such great hitting partners. Jim would beat me, say, 21–2. Venus would play Scott
pretty even. Then we'd switch it up. Usually, Venus would beat up
on Jim, and Scott would just trounce me, probably 21–0. Then we'd
add up the scores to see who won.

I could never understand why Venus always picked me for her
team, other than the fact that she was just being nice. But the truth
is, she was pushing herself in whatever ways she could. And pushing
me, too. She had to work really hard against Jim, to give us enough
of a cushion to make up for the points I'd lose, and I had to focus on
my game so I wouldn't be such a drag on our overall score. Really, I
could keep up with Jim, to a certain point. I could match him shot
for shot, but he was of course a much smarter player, a much more
experienced player, so these games would force me to anticipate his
next move.

Our lives in Florida shifted just a couple years after we arrived,
when we moved to Pompano Beach. Our move coincided with Rick

Macci's move from Grenelefe, but Daddy thought it was a good time for a change. Together with Rick and the other coaches, they'd made the decision to keep Venus and me off of the junior tournament circuit, and if you go back and look at some of the press coverage we'd started to get back then you can see this got a lot of people talking—a lot of tennis people, anyway. People in tennis seem to like it when things go a certain way, and here was this tall, proud black man from California, who'd never played tennis himself, raising up a real prospect and her kid sister, who might just turn out to be a real prospect as well, and going against the way things were done. He seemed to be thumbing his nose at the tennis establishment, but of course it wasn't like that. Anyone who took the time to talk to Daddy could see that, but it became too easy for people to seize on these negative first impressions and let them take hold. But Daddy just thought we didn't need the pressures of the junior tournament circuit, and he was right about that. He didn't like the way parents and coaches were all over their junior players, bouncing around from tournament to tournament. He wanted us to have a normal life. He didn't want to be one of those parents pushing and pushing his kids down a path they might not necessarily have chosen for themselves. Plus, he thought we could get better competition, just hitting with these pros and coaches and working on our fundamentals.

I've always thought this was a genius move, ever since I was old enough to fully realize how things went, but Daddy just shrugs it off. He makes it sound like a happy accident that things worked out this way. He says, "Meeka, there wasn't any point in traveling all around the country to watch you and V beat up on all those little girls."

In truth, the reality of our situation rests somewhere between the admiration and appreciation I have for Daddy's instincts, to hold us back from the circuit until we were emotionally ready to deal with it on our own, and Daddy's own casual take. It turned out to the good, because it's one of the real reasons Venus and I are still playing and still going strong. It kept us from burning out on tennis at an early age, and it allowed us to develop our games in an exciting new way. And it helped to build up all this anticipation about how we might finally perform once we started competing, which of course got people talking about us, in and around tennis. But that was just how it worked out, I guess. Absolutely, Daddy had a kind of master plan, but here he was just going by sense and feel, and making it up as he went along.

In any case, we stayed in Florida, now in Pompano Beach, once again under Daddy's watchful eye. We didn't have a whole lot of money, and for the first time in my life I was starting to be aware of that. I have one specific memory of a yard sale we held in front of our new house in Pompano Beach, where we made a lot of money selling all this old tennis gear we'd been given over the years, from various sponsors and academies. At the end of the day, we counted up the money and grew rich in our heads. The moment stands out because it offered a brief respite from the rigors of tennis—although, we did train on that day, as I recall, only not so much—but also for the way we were knitted together as a family, through tennis.

In many ways, the tennis part of our lives was a lot like it had been back in California. There were courts in the community just down the street from where we lived, so that was where we played. From time to time, we'd run over to Nick Bollettieri's, to work on a particular aspect of our games. Or maybe Nick would come to us. But Daddy was very clear on how things should go, and part of that clarity was keeping us off the tournament circuit until he thought we were ready. Until *we* thought we were ready.

A lot of times, when people hear how I grew up, and how much time and focus we spent on tennis, they ask me if I ever felt any pressure. I tell them no, and they're always surprised by my answer. But that's the truth. You can see it right here in Daddy's decision to keep us from the particular pressures of the junior circuit. You can also see it in the relaxed way we were nurtured in the game. Really, there was never any pressure placed on me—not by my parents, and not by any of these other coaches. In fact, I went through a period when I didn't really want to play at all, and nobody pushed me. This happened soon after we'd moved to Pompano Beach. I was lazy, for whatever reason. I wasn't motivated. I was bored running around on those courts. We still did ballet and gymnastics and karate, but I didn't have any real outside interests. And yet all during that time, I never felt like I had to get back out there and redouble my intensity, or anything like that. For my parents, if I never made it as a tennis player, they'd be proud and happy for me, as long as I was doing something that made me proud and happy. If I'd just gone to college and played tennis there, that would have been fine. Even if I stopped playing altogether, that would have been fine. They only wanted to give us this giant opportunity—after that, it was up to us to make of it what we wanted.

I remember growing to hate the courts where we played, because they were so close to our house. Up until this time, we'd get into the car to go to wherever we were playing. But now the courts were basically right outside our door. I think that proximity contributed to this weird funk I fell into regarding tennis. No, my parents didn't put any pressure on me to play, but those courts in Pompano Beach certainly did. They were so *right there*. They were in my face. There was no getting away from them. And they weren't the nicest courts, either. After playing in a resortlike setting at Grenelefe for all those years, it was like we were back in Compton, hustling for time on the public courts.

All in all, it was a tough adjustment. It wasn't just the courts that had me dragging. I didn't really like my new school. I'm not big on change, I guess. And my self-image still wasn't that great. I was still feeling awkward and in-between and that wasn't exactly the most empowering mind-set to take to a new middle school. Here again, my parents lived outside the lines a bit in how they responded to this, because Venus and I ended up being home-schooled. For me, it covered the second half of seventh grade and all of eighth grade—pretty much the balance of my middle school career.

My mom used to be a teacher, so she was in charge of all our lesson plans. She'd let her nursing work slide once we got to Florida, and I suppose that was one of the reasons money was so tight. But the silver lining was she had the time and the right skill set to teach a middle-school curriculum. You had to follow the approved course of study from your home-school district, so they sent over all this material. Mom was pretty diligent about making us do the work, but even so we just breezed right through it. The idea was it would free up some extra time for us to be out on the court, but it freed up so much extra time I ended up watching a lot of television that year. *Golden Girls*, mostly. I don't know why, but I just loved that show. Remember, this was back before TiVo and all this great digital technology, so maybe I just watched that show into the ground because they happened to show back-to-back episodes at the same time each day, when I had nothing else to do.

The routine in those days was to start out each day with tennis. We'd play for a couple hours in the morning at the courts around the corner from our house. Then we'd break for lunch, and our lessons. That just took a couple hours, so we were back on the courts again before school let out for all the other kids.

It was hard to get motivated under this type of setup. At least, it was hard for me. I don't think Venus struggled with it the way I did. In fact, I know she didn't. I'd always loved the classroom part of going to school. The sitting in classes and learning. It was all that stuff that went on in the hallways and the cafeteria that gave me trouble. Here at home, though, it was hard to get excited about learning. About tennis. About anything. Nothing against my mom, who did a good job with our lesson plans, but we got through them in no time at all, and then there was the whole rest of our day unfolding out in front of us. Wasn't a whole lot of structure to that time, so maybe that was why I found it tough to pick up my racquet each day. Plus, there was no escaping those courts, right outside our front door.

A couple years later, when Venus and I were building our first house, after we'd had our first tastes of success on the tour, we made a clear decision *not* to put a court in our backyard. We certainly had the room. We certainly had the money. But I think we looked subconsciously to build some distance into our lives between home and tennis. We didn't really talk about it in just this way, but that was clearly going on. For me, it went back to how I used to feel, living right by those community courts in Pompano Beach. They were always calling to me, and calling to me, only not in a good way.

Instead of lifting me up, they were dragging me down.

Jehovah is your strength. U R strong. As you walk through the deepest shadows, you fear nothing. You move from strength to strength. God Jehovah is with you.

—MATCH BOOK ENTRY

SIX

Going It Alone

Here's a curious admission: I've never been able to pinpoint when I realized what we were playing for—or when it dawned on me that in order to compete at an elite level, I would have to do so on my own terms, on my own impulse . . . on my own everything.

I've thought about this a lot over the years, about when it became clear that our parents were training us to be tennis *champions* and not just tennis *players*, and I can never quite put my finger on it. About the best I can figure is it was always out there, this idea of being the best of the best, but at the same time it was kept from us until we could understand it and use it to our advantage. Or, maybe we just couldn't spot it until we were a little bit older.

In the very beginning, tennis was about being together as a family and having fun. I wanted to be like my sisters, to do the same things they were doing and to do them just as well, so I set my personal bar at their level. At the same time, I wanted the praise and admiration of my parents and to have them recognize my extra efforts. That's all it was at first, but then at some point it became about pushing ourselves to being the very best we could be—which of course made some of our practice sessions a whole lot less fun!

This much is clear, but what I've never been able to figure out is when each of those shifts took place. Mind you, they weren't sudden shifts. We transitioned from one phase to the next without us kids really noticing anything different, and I have to think that was part of Daddy's handiwork. I've talked to V about this, and she's like me; she can't say for sure when the goal to be the number one player in the world came about. I wish I could say when that switched on for us, but I can't. To listen to my parents, that was the goal all along, but when we started out it wasn't a very realistic goal, any more than it's realistic to expect your baby daughter to become the first female president of the United States, so there must have been a switch for them, too.

Still, nobody in my family can say for sure when the idea that one of us Williams sisters might become the number one tennis player in the world seemed within reach. When it went from a faint hope or an impossible dream to an attainable goal. When Venus and I were tearing it up on the 10-and-under and 12-and-under circuits in California? I guess you could say we had it in mind to be champions by then. When we moved to Florida? Absolutely. That was the endgame scenario, and the whole point of our cross-country move. Keep in mind, though, that a lot of people in tennis didn't necessarily see our careers unfolding in just this way, because of Daddy's decision to keep us from playing junior tournaments, but we didn't pay much attention to people in tennis. That said, there were certain people in tennis who, like it or not, had a lot of influence on us— namely, the powers that be at the Women's Tennis Association, the governing body of the professional tour for female players. See, it's not like you can just enter a couple tournaments here and there, and put together your own schedule, and do whatever you want and hope for a good result. No, you've got to play by the WTA rules, and those rules kept changing. (They're still changing!) A lot of times the changes are to the good; a lot of times they're just annoying.

One of the biggest changes about to take place when we were kids was the age-eligibility rule. This was a big topic in our house. It used to be that you could play in tournaments when you were fourteen, but starting in 1996 that was going to change to sixteen. The thinking was that young players were not fully developed emotionally and could not really withstand the pressures of being on the tour. There had been some famous examples of young players who'd had flashes of success at thirteen, fourteen, fifteen years old, and then flamed out early on. In some cases, their lives off the court spiraled a little bit, or their bodies started to break down, or they became estranged from their parents or coaches . . . all because of the demands of the game.

This was a good change, a long time coming, and it made sense for a lot of players, but we were used to doing things our own way. As a family, we felt we had a good handle on our own situation. If we wanted to play tournaments at thirteen, fourteen, fifteen years old, we wanted to be able to make that decision for ourselves. We didn't want some governing body telling us what was right for the Williams sisters—even though Daddy had no thought to enter either one of us in professional tournaments when we were that young. He was sticking to his game plan. He used to say, "You'll be ready when you're ready."

It turned out that Venus actually thought she was ready before Daddy did, and she pushed for him to allow her to play. Venus can be pretty forceful when she sets her mind to something, and here she was just that. Daddy had no choice but to cave, and Venus entered a professional tournament in Oakland, California, in November 1994, just a couple months after her fourteenth birthday. The Bank of the West Classic. I remember it as such an exciting moment, such an exciting time. We didn't have enough money for all of us to travel from Florida, but I went as Venus's hitting partner. Lyn came, too. What a thrill! To be down on those courts with all those great players! Oh my goodness, I was so pumped! Daddy told me to hit as hard as I could when I was working with Venus, and I imagined that I was playing in the tournament and that Venus was the top seed and that all these people were watching us and cheering for us.

Actually, my imagination wasn't that far off, because our game was a whole lot different than that of most of the top female players at the time. The convention was to play a baseline rally game. There were just a few players who could hit with real power, but for the most part the girls on the pro circuit seemed to rely on shot placement and consistency—and here we were, two little black girls just crushing the ball on the outer courts. I guess we did turn a few heads! And Venus really was a star by then. She hadn't played a single point as a professional, but everyone knew who she was. She'd been written up in all the tennis magazines and in a lot of major newspapers. The fans were three or four deep on the practice courts, that's how anxious they were to see her play.

My mom made Venus a special skirt in honor of the occasion. I look back and think it's ironic, that Venus and I would become known for our head-turning tennis outfits and for working with all these outstanding, cutting-edge designers, and here she made her debut in a homemade skirt. It was a pretty skirt, too. My mom could sew!

Venus drew an American player named Shaun Stafford in the first round—and she beat her! I can't even tell you how happy I was for V. I was over the moon and back again. It was crazy! Stafford was ranked 58th, and the win earned Venus a whopping $5,350 in prize money—which was just about a fortune to her at the time. Daddy's idea was to let us keep *all* the money we earned, and to learn to be responsible for it right away, so Venus started to look really, really rich in my eyes, and I was only too happy to let her spoil me.

That first win also earned Venus the right to face the top seed, Aranxta Sanchez-Vicario, the number-two-ranked player on the tour. We were all so happy, Venus almost as much as Daddy, and Daddy almost as much as me. Going in, he didn't think Venus was ready for the pro tour, but this was something she really, really wanted, so he stepped back and let it happen. Now that she'd won her first match he was in her ear, convincing her she had the stuff to keep it going. It was like that time I'd snuck into my first tournament. I thought Daddy would be mad, but once he saw I had a chance to win he was all over it. Here in Oakland, once the championship was within reach, he helped with the reaching.

Venus didn't exactly need a lot of help, or a lot of convincing. She was an extremely confident player even then. She wasn't afraid to go up against a top player like Sanchez-Vicario. She just wanted to see what she could do, and she came out like a demon in her second-round match, taking the first set and wowing the crowd. Other than that one hateful time at Indian Wells, and I suppose on a few other rare occasions, tennis fans don't really root *against* a certain player so much as they might be pulling *for* a particular favorite. They tend to applaud and appreciate good play. But here everyone seemed to be pulling for V. It wasn't like they had anything against Aranxta Sanchez-Vicario, but Venus was the Cinderella story of the tournament, even though it was just the second round, and here she was off to a killer start against the number one seed. She even went up 3–0 in the second set, but then Sanchez-Vicario recovered and Venus didn't win another game, which kind of quieted the crowd. And *me*. Oh, I was devastated for Venus, once the match got away from her. She didn't mind that she'd lost, but I did. She was just happy she'd gotten to play, manage to win her first match, and throw a scare into a top player.

Still, as brief, shining moments go, this was way up there. No, it wasn't *my* brief, shining moment, but I soaked it up like it was—all the time knowing, hoping, praying that my moment would come soon enough, and that when it did I would pounce on it the way Venus had pounced on hers.

After Oakland, we went back to Pompano Beach and resumed our routines. Nothing really changed, except that Venus had turned pro, but it's not like she played this one tournament and then started traveling the world on the pro circuit. Not at all. In fact, this was in November 1994, and Venus didn't play again until the following August, as a wild-card entrant in Los Angeles. This time, she lost in the first round. And this time, it wasn't enough for me to just sit on the sidelines and soak up what was left of the attention being showered on my sister. This time, I was just a couple weeks shy of my own fourteenth birthday, so I wanted to be out there playing, making some noise of my own. I wanted what Venus had, and I didn't want to wait for it to be my turn. I wanted it right away.

True to form—and true to his cautious, disciplined approach— Daddy didn't think I was ready, but I talked him into it. (We're Daddy's girls at heart—we get what we want!) I'd learned all about the changes to the age-eligibility rule, and used that as an argument in my favor. The way it worked was, if I turned fourteen in 1995 before the new rule took effect, and if I played in a tournament that year, I'd be grandfathered in under the old age restrictions. If I didn't, I'd have to wait until I was sixteen to start playing—another two years! And even then, at sixteen, there would be all kinds of restrictions on the number of tournaments I could play. The new rule would kick in and I'd be chasing the calendar, so it made sense for me to play at least once in 1995, to establish my eligibility. After that, we could take our time and decide for ourselves when I was *really* ready.

Once again, Daddy finally caved, and he signed me up for a professional tournament in Quebec City. It was November 1995, and I drew a hardly ranked player named Anne Miller. It wasn't nearly as exciting as Venus's debut, but it was mine. For one thing, it was a much smaller tournament; for another, I was only playing in the qualifying round, to start. For some reason, the thing I remember best about that first tournament was that I was so ugly! Forget how miserably I played, what's stayed with me is how I looked. Thank God there was no digital video back then, because I'm sure I would have wound up on YouTube or some site, embarrassing myself. I joke about it now, but at the time I *hated* the way I looked, especially when I stood next to one of my sisters. They were so beautiful, so tall, so graceful, so perfect.

Thinking back, I've often wondered if my poor self-image had something to do with my poor performance that day in Quebec. Over the years, I've come to spend a lot of time on my appearance.

I want to look good while I'm out there, sweating and grunting. That's become my thing. Wasn't always my thing, but it is now, and as a stylin' tour veteran I have to think my self-image had *something* to do with my disappointing debut. I mean, it only follows that if you want to be at your best you have to look your best, right? How the world looks back at you has everything to do with how you look out at the world, and here I didn't like how I looked. Not one bit.

For whatever reason, I didn't play very well. Anne Miller beat me 6–1, 6–1, and the scoreboard didn't really tell the full story. Nothing against Anne Miller, but it wasn't like she was a dominant player. She wasn't running me around on the court. She wasn't dictating the points. I wasn't making my shots, that's all. On another day, under other circumstances, I could have beaten her, no question, but I think the moment was a little too big for my fourteen-year-old self. It messed with my head to be playing in front of a great, big crowd, underneath these great, big expectations.

Okay, so I wasn't ready. The powers that be at the WTA were right, I guess. Daddy was right, I guess. But I filed the experience away and vowed to learn from it. Even at fourteen, I knew there was an important takeaway inside this moment. For me it was that you can't take anything for granted. Playing in all those little-kid events out in California, I'd always expected to win—and I usually did. I think I lost just two or three matches in my little-kid career. Here, though, I could no longer expect to win. I'd have to earn it, fight for it. And I'd have to do it by myself. Daddy couldn't swing that racquet for me, and Venus couldn't tell me what to do, and my mom couldn't help me readjust my game if it turned out that my first plan of attack wasn't effective. No, when you're out there on the court in a tournament setting, for real, it's all on you.

I flashed back to how things were when we were just starting out on those public courts in Compton, when it was all of us together —on our own side of the net, even!—and I realized that from here on in I'd have the court all to myself.

*   *   *

Daddy saw to it that it wasn't *just* me out there on the court, all by myself, all the time. I didn't play another tournament until March 1997—at Indian Wells. In all that time, I stayed in Florida and went to high school and kept up with my training and conditioning every day. I was a professional in name only, because of that one appearance in Quebec, but in every other respect I was back to where I was. I was still just a kid, going through the motions and waiting for my opportunity. When it finally came, Daddy made sure that Venus and I played in separate tournaments, because we didn't want to have to face each other if we could avoid it. At some point, if things worked out the way we all hoped, there'd be no avoiding each other on the circuit, but here, when we were still picking our spots, we could stay out of each other's path.

Now, the part about it not *just* being me out there, all by my lonesome, is this: Venus and I started playing doubles. We'd always played doubles, so it seemed like a natural extension for us, but the side benefit to our playing together in my first few tournaments was that I had my sister at my side, *on my side of the net,* as I took some of these first steps as a professional. In some ways, it was just like crawling into Venus's bed in the middle of the night, because I didn't want to sleep alone. That was the kind of comfort I drew from having her near. Even on the court.

And so, in my second "debut" appearance, at Indian Wells, I was once again chased in the first round of the women's singles bracket in straight sets, this time by a French player named Alexia Dechaume-Balleret (6–4, 6–0), but the silver lining was that V and I were also entered in the doubles tournament. Playing singles, I was a little bit beyond my comfort zone; playing doubles, I felt more sure of myself, more like I belonged. Venus must have felt the same way, because we made it all the way to the quarterfinals before losing to Lindsay Davenport and Natasha Zvereva 6–3, 6–0. Venus was such a great source of strength and comfort that just having her near helped me to relax and lift my game to where it needed to be for us to compete. This was something. Remember, I was still only

Me and V in Los Angeles, with our childhood tennis pal Alexandra Stevenson, who'd go on to a pro career of her own. (family photo)

Just chillin' . . . Isha took this shot of me when I was eleven in Bradenton, Florida. (family photo)

Goofing around with Lyn. Check out my eyes! (family photo)

With Tunde. I always wanted to be just like her. (family photo)

With Venus. When we weren't playing tennis, we were usually reading. (family photo)

With Venus at a Pam Shriver exhibition event in Baltimore. That's Jimmy Connors on the far left, next to Jim Courier, Cal Ripken Jr., Venus, me, Pam Shriver, and Billy Ripken. Look how little I am, standing next to these great athletes! (family photo)

Me and V, sharpening our driving skills at a video arcade. (family photo)

With Venus, on our first trip to China, 1999. (family photo)

In 1998. One of my favorite pictures. (family photo)

Celebrating my very first tournament win in Paris, 1999. The champagne was just for show. At seventeen, I was still too young to drink! (family photo)

I love this shot. Posing with my mom the day after I won my first U.S. Open in 1999. (family photo)

Here I am catching my breath on a changeover, early on in my career. Even then you can see all the Post-it notes to myself on my racquet bag! (family photo)

Three cheers for the red, white, and blue! At the 2000 Olympic games in Sydney. (family photo)

Hanging out with V and my dad in 2004. (family photo)

With my mom. We look like sisters! (family photo)

I cherish this photo of Yetunde. I love the way it captures her personality, always enjoying life. (family photo)

Looking good, with Lyn, Isha, and Tunde in 2001. (family photo)

With Tunde and her kids. That's the world's best auntie on the right, in the bucket hat! (family photo)

All dressed up with Venus in Monte Carlo for the 2003 "Female Athlete of the Year" presentation, an honor I won that year. (Ron Angle)

With Venus, Lyn, and Isha at the launch of V's clothing line. (family photo)

Hanging in the pool with Jackie and Laurelai, my best friends in the world! (family photo)

One of my signature outfits. The latest in biker-tennis chic. (Ron Angle)

The famous "catsuit"—another trademark look. (Ron Angle)

Miami, 2007. An example of how much fun I like to have fashion-wise on the tennis court. (Ron Angle)

Triumph! Celebrating my 2002 French Open championship beneath the Arc de Triomphe in Paris—the first leg of my "Serena Slam." (Ron Angle)

Wimbledon, 2002. The second leg of my "Serena Slam." (Ron Angle)

Congratulating Jennifer Capriati after my disappointing and controversial loss in the quarterfinals of the 2004 U.S. Open. (Ron Angle)

Here I am celebrating after winning the 2007 Australian Open, where I was ranked 81st in the world at the start of play. I had to get past six seeded players! (Ron Angle)

In 2008, cutting the ribbon to officially open the Serena Williams Secondary School in the Kenyan village of Matooni. One of the proudest, most fulfilling moments of my life. (Sean Riordan of Build African Schools)

It's never too early to learn the game. With a cute little boy at one of the clinics we gave on my 2008 Africa trip. (Sean Riordan of Build African Schools)

Writing out my name on the blackboard. Hearing those kids pronounce it was such sweet music. (Sean Riordan of Build African Schools)

Bling! With V, showing off our gold medals at the Beijing Olympics in 2008. (Ron Angle)

No matter how hard we fight out on the court, we're still sisters. After our thrilling quarterfinal match at the 2008 U.S. Open. (Ron Angle)

Jumping for joy after winning the 2008 U.S. Open. That title put me back in the number one spot in the world rankings. (Ron Angle)

Stopping traffic in a killer red dress in New York's Times Square, just after winning the 2008 U.S. Open. (Ron Angle)

Back in the top spot after winning the 2009 Australian Open. (Ron Angle)

fifteen years old, with no real tournament experience, so I took my strength and comfort wherever I could find it, and hoped that it would spill over into my singles game as well.

Eventually, that's just what happened, but it took a while for *eventually* to find me. Indeed, my very first tour championship came in doubles—at Oklahoma City the following year, in 1998 when I was sixteen years old. Venus was seventeen, and she had already made it to Wimbledon, the French Open, the Australian Open, and all the way to the U.S. Open finals (with a 66 ranking!), before losing to Martina Hingis in straight sets. She was really getting it together, in a big-time way, but she still hadn't won anything until Oklahoma City. It was our fifth doubles tournament, and by this point we were starting to figure things out. Still, we were terribly young and inexperienced, as you could tell from our doubles ranking going into the tournament—192.

Daddy always told us it wasn't about winning, just yet, as much as it was about improving. That was our focus. The idea was to get our footing, to get a little better each time out, to start feeling like we belonged. Of course, if we could figure out a way to improve *and* win, so much the better. That's what happened here in Oklahoma, and it was such a rush to come away with the title. (For Venus, it was a double rush, because she ended up taking the singles title, too—her first!) Our championship run included an unexpected quarterfinal win over Katrina Adams, a great African-American doubles player, and her partner Debbie Graham, who had been the WTA's Newcomer of the Year a couple years earlier. They were the #1 seed in the tournament, and once we got past them we started to think we had a shot. (We were up 6–4, 4–3 when they "retired," but I've always counted it as a straight-sets victory!)

After that, we powered through the rest of the field without losing a set, and the great kicker was it was one of those tournaments where they present the winners with a giant check after the final match. We've all seen those checks, right? The kind they use for photo opportunities when someone wins a contest? I hadn't really thought of the prize money before we ended up winning, and I still don't really think about the prize money. I play to win. Even today, tournament directors sometimes have to come after me to get me to collect the purse. I'll leave the site without remembering to pick up my money. They end up mailing me the check. Not because I've got so much money in the bank that there's no room for any more. (Yeah, right.) No, because the money has never been the motivating force. That's not why I play, so I don't really think about it. For me, it's about the competition, the trophy, the title. Everything else is just gravy.

Back in Oklahoma City in 1998, winning was brand-new, but even then it was more about the accomplishment than the money. That sounds like a line, but it's the God's honest truth. And yet, that first time I won, I wanted all the stuff that came with winning. The ceremony at center court. The giant check. The photo op and the press conference and the article in the paper the next day. I wanted it all. I'd grown up watching all these great players accept their giant checks at center court, and it never occurred to me that one day I'd get a giant check of my own. It's such a silly prop, really, but when you're on the receiving end of a big old check with your big old name on it, posing for pictures and waving to the crowd, it's such a heady feeling. I hadn't really realized that was what I wanted, but now that it was happening it seemed like I'd wanted it all along. The check itself was for $4,500—a lot of money, absolutely, but hardly enough to justify all that paperboard for the fake check. And yet when they presented it to me and V it felt like we'd won a million dollars.

It was all the money in the world and a little bit more besides.

We still have that check, by the way. (No, you can't actually endorse it and take it to the bank—not that we tried!) Every time I look at it I think back to that first professional win, to how it felt to come out on top with my sister at my side. Of course, true greatness would only come once I started winning singles tournaments. Even at sixteen, I knew that full well, but for the time being this taste of half-greatness (with V tasting the other half) was just fine with me.

*   *   *

Very quickly, I went from being alone and untethered out on the court to feeling empowered when I was playing singles. I went from being a little overwhelmed and out of place to believing I was untouchable, unstoppable . . . all in the space of just a few tournaments. I had a lot of growing up to do in that time. I had to grow my game, that was part of it, but I also had to grow my mind-set to where it could withstand the pressures of tournament play.

Pressure comes in all shapes and sizes. It means different things for different people. For a lot of tennis players growing up on the junior circuit, it means pleasing their parents and coaches, and justifying the time and expense of flying all over the place just so they can compete. For others, it means worrying constantly about what they're eating, how hard they're training, what they're giving up by focusing so single-mindedly on their game. For me, it's been about the never-ending pursuit of perfection, and making room for the realization that I might never get my game *exactly* where I want it to be—meaning I'd never be firing on all cylinders at precisely the right time.

I never really worried about the component parts of my game. I'd always had the shots, and the killer instinct, and the fiery competitive streak, but I'd never had to put all those aspects of my personality together on such a public stage, so it took a couple stops and starts. Also, it took some time for me to grow into my body and reinvent my approach. Remember, I had always been on the tiny side, and my style of play reflected that. As I've written, I was all about lobs and volleys and shot placement when I was a kid, but at around sixteen I had this monster growth spurt, which gifted me a whole other aspect to my game. All of a sudden, I could hit with power, and I developed a range to rival my sister's. And my serve! My goodness, it became such a weapon!

It fell mostly to me to incorporate all these changes into the way I played. Emotionally, physically, it was on me. Daddy was a tremendous coach, but it takes being out there a time or two to really *feel* your way. My mom, too, tried to help me make sense of my various growing pains and plusses, but here again it was on me. It takes a certain measure of independence that's hard to come by when you're growing up in such a tight family, when you're used to doing everything together. (And I do mean *everything*!) It can be very isolating, very lonely, competing at a high level in an individual sport. There are no teammates to pick you up or cover your back. There's no one who can know *exactly* what you're seeing, thinking, feeling. It's on you. You can have all the support in the world—God knows I had a ton!—but in the end it's just you.

But I got there, before long. On my own. And then, one crazy-weird day in 1999, about a year after my first professional win, my parents told us they were getting a divorce. It threw me, I'll say that, but I was pretty much an adult by this point. Venus and I were building a house and planning to move in together, so a divorce wasn't going to change *our* lives all that much. My parents' lives, sure. That's the whole point of getting a divorce, to find a way to be happy apart if you can't find a way to be happy together. But our lives? Not so much. And yet, the change still did its own little number on me, because for years and years we had two great sources of strength and power running through our house; we had our faith, and we had each other. Our God, Jehovah, and our family itself. It was central. And so in this way, at least, my parents' announcement seemed to tear at the very fabric of our lives.

My first thought was, *How will we keep going as a family after something like this?* But then I realized that we were all grown and independent and doing our own thing. It wasn't like we were all living under the same roof and our lives would never be the same. It was more like: *Okay, if they're not meant to be together, they're not meant to be together; if they don't make each other happy, they should move on.* And if we sisters had a hard time dealing with our parents' breakup, we just had to get over it.

My parents are strong, opinionated people. I loved them dearly. We all did. That wasn't about to change. And we all knew they loved us right back. That wasn't going to change, either. If together they came to the decision that they should get divorced, then they should get divorced.

My take didn't much matter, but here it is anyway: I always saw my mother as the backbone of our family, the spine. My dad, he was the rest of the body. Together, they made up the whole. They kept our family working. At some point, their relationship wasn't working anymore, but they kept at it for a while. And then they split and I started to think: you can't live without the spine, can you? You can't live without all those other moving parts. For a while there, we were all worried how the spine would work without the rest of the body. We worried where we'd find our direction. I thought about it, and I thought about it. Venus and I, we talked and talked about it. We talked about it in terms of tennis, and in terms of everything else. I talked about it with *all* my sisters. I talked about it with my parents.

And guess what? In the end, it was all just talk, because you can't know a thing until you're in its middle. You've got to try it on for a while and see how it fits. Doesn't matter if it's the first baby steps you take on the professional tour or the first night you go to sleep knowing your parents are getting a divorce. It weirds you out at first, but then you wake up the next morning and realize your life looks a whole lot like it did the day before. The people who love you still love you. The opportunities you've been reaching for your whole life are still there for the taking.

It's up to you to get on with it, that's all.

Fear will hold U back. Champions fear nothing. Only fear God and give Him glory. Fear no man (woman). Use those legs. God gave them to U for a reason. Put your gifts to work. Take the ball on the rise. Attack the short ball—it's waiting for U!!! Show no emotion. U R black and U can endure anything. Endure. Persevere. Stand tall.

—MATCH BOOK ENTRY

SEVEN

Fashion Statements

I like to look my best on the court. I believe it's important. It goes to self-esteem, and at the same time it ignites an all-important spark for some of that silent fuel I like to talk about. It also gets me thinking how we sometimes draw strength in areas we never think to look. In my case, I'm an athlete; I'm meant to draw strength from the weight room, from my iron will, from the sheer force of my game. But here I am, fussing over how I look, thinking that this, too, will make a difference.

Face it, if you carry a positive picture of yourself you'll present a positive picture to everyone else. If you put your best effort into how you look, you'll put your best effort into whatever it is you do. Personally, I always felt that when there was an edge to how I looked, there was an edge to my game. That's why I tune it out when people give me flak for spending so much time on my appearance. They say I'm an athlete, not a fashionista. They say that if I'm doing my job, I'll be out there sweating and grimacing and trying to be competitive. I'll look a mess. And they're right. Once a match is underway, there's no getting away from that—and there shouldn't be. In fact, when I'm in the middle of a tough match, I wear all that sweat and effort like a badge. The nastier I look, the nastier I feel on the court, but why shouldn't I dress myself up and pay attention to how I look before I start playing? And after? Why shouldn't I put on a fun pair of earrings or a gorgeous bracelet or a killer outfit?

Like it or not, I live in the public eye. People are looking at me wherever I go. Most of the time, people see me on the court. They don't see me when I'm on the town, or shopping, or goofing around at the beach. Well, of course they *do* see me, moving about in my normal, mundane way, but only a relative few catch me up close, nowhere near as many as when I'm playing tennis, when all eyes are on me and my opponent. Think back to all the great tennis champions in recent years, and you'll see they all made an effort to look good on the court: Steffi Graf, Monica Seles, Martina Hingis. (And—she'll never let me hear the end of it if I don't include her in this group—Venus Williams, of course!)

Remember Fernando, Billy Crystal's *Saturday Night Live* character? The Fernando Lamas–inspired "You look mahvelous!" guy? The joke was that it's better to look good than to feel good, but underneath it was a hint of truth. Appearances *do* count. I firmly believe this. No, appearances aren't everything, but they're definitely part of the equation. That's why I spend so much time on mine.

I always considered myself kind of plain. When I look back at pictures of myself as a little kid, I'm put back in mind of how awkward and ugly I used to feel. Mind you, I didn't feel this way all the time. For the most part, I was just doing my thing, hardly giving my appearance much thought. I was just me. When I was in high school, I tried to wear whatever the other girls were wearing. Don't forget, I'd been out of the social loop for a bit, with those years I spent being home-schooled. Now that I was back among my peers I wanted desperately to fit in, so I didn't really have my own sense of style. And yet, instead of trying to call attention to myself with my clothes, I guess I looked to deflect it. I liked to shop, and I liked to wear nice things, but most of my stuff was basic, simple. Tunde would help me pick out a couple stylish, versatile outfits at the beginning of the school year on our shopping trips to Mervyns. I wore a lot of solid colors, as I recall. Nothing loud. And certainly nothing that would stand out.

That all changed soon enough. One morning I woke up and just started wearing different things. Whatever suited my mood at that particular time. It was like a light switched on for me. I started looking at fashion magazines and developing a sense of what I liked and what I didn't like. What might look good on me and what I shouldn't even think of wearing. I still didn't have my own sense of style, but at least I was a little more adventurous, a little more curious. At least I was open to what was out there.

Now, take that frame of mind and bare-bones fashion sense and layer it on top of the role I filled with my four big sisters. They were always dressing me up, and fussing with my hair, and basically putting me to work like a model or mannequin to try out all these different looks they were considering for themselves. They were a fashion-forward bunch, especially as they got older. When Tunde and Isha were in high school, they were looking in the mirror all the time! And, when they weren't looking in the mirror, they were working out their new looks on us! Lyn and V, too, in a sliding-scale kind of way, started dressing me up and working it out. I loved all the fuss and attention, and on some level I guess I filed it all away for later, for when I finally had the money and the opportunity— and the *stage*—to really strut my stuff.

Eccentric. Daring. Adventurous. Fun. Call it whatever you want, but very quickly I developed my own flair, which in turn was helped along by a couple of welcome developments off the court. The first was a sponsorship deal with Puma, which gave me license to be out there and bold and really, really distinctive in what I wore when I played; after Puma, there was Nike, another sportswear company that was willing to push the envelope and let my personality shine through in what I wore. The second was a course of study I started taking at the Art Institute of Fort Lauderdale in design and fashion. I'll hit the sponsorship deal first, because that's how it unfolded for me as well.

Coming up on the tour, I always wanted what Venus had. I repeat myself, I know, but it's one of the great themes of my life and career: Venus cut the path I meant to follow, so when she signed a big sponsorship deal with Reebok I came away thinking I wanted a sponsor of my own. I was still a long way from having any kind of real business sense, so my desire wasn't about money or financial security or any of those pragmatic things. No, it was about matching V and getting my own. Only trouble with this was that I didn't have the profile Venus had when I first joined the tour. This was back when V was the Next Big Thing and I was still just the Next Big Thing's Kid Sister, so it's not like all these sportswear companies were lining up to give me a deal. Plus, it was a time in the sport when there weren't a whole lot of sponsorship deals to be had beyond the very top-ranked players. About the best you could hope for as a middle-of-the-pack pro or an up-and-coming rookie was to get your gear for free, from companies like Wilson or Nike or Head or Reebok. You'd wear their stuff, they'd slap their logo on the sleeve, and it was a good deal all around.

Somehow, Daddy was able to negotiate this tremendous Reebok deal for V, but after that it seemed nobody was really interested in me. I guess there wasn't enough hype to lift two sisters to such heights, so I was grounded. I *got* that, but at the same time I resented it, and yet the harsh reality of big-time tennis was that there wasn't much of a market for a teenage player who hadn't really done much on the tour just yet. I understand that now, but I was really upset about it back then. There was a brief period in there when Nike expressed an interest, but it never went anywhere. I wore their clothes for a while, but then just after I had a great, deep run at a tournament in Chicago in 1997, that interest fell away. I'd just played my sixth-ever tournament and reached all the way to the semifinals. Along the way, I'd beaten Mary Pierce, the number seven player in the world, and Monica Seles, the number four player, before losing to the number five player, Lindsay Davenport, in the semis. For the first time, it felt to me like I was on my way, bound for some tennis glory of my own, but then I was left hanging—with only a couple complimentary Nike outfits to show for it.

I was only sixteen years old, and still I was left thinking, *What does a girl have to do to get a sponsorship deal around here?*

It was around this time that Daddy hooked up with a man named Arnon Milchon—a real mover-and-shaker out in Los Angeles. Over the years, Arnon has become a great friend and mentor. When I met him, he was a successful Hollywood producer and a real risk taker. He also owned a stake in Puma, which was how we got together. He was a huge tennis fan and one of the few people outside my family who saw my potential—at least in endorsement terms. He thought I had a big future in tennis, and that while I was at it I could help lift the Puma brand, so it looked like there'd be a good fit all around.

Arnon came along at just the right time. In my head, I was back to thinking no one believed in me, just like that newspaper reporter, or anyone else in tennis. This wasn't about tennis, not really, but at the same time it was. No one could see past the fact that I was Venus's sister. No one thought I'd be a force in my own right, even after Chicago. That is, no one until Arnon. He's been an unbelievable person in my life from the day we met. One of my dreams, outside of tennis, was to be an actress, so he was helpful to me in that arena as well. He set me up on a bunch of screen tests and auditions, and introduced me to casting people and acting coaches. Whenever people ask me what I would have done if I couldn't play tennis, I tell them I would have been an actress. Okay, so I probably would have been a struggling actress, but I would have given it a shot—and Arnon helped me reach for that as well. I used to tease him that he was like my adopted stepfather.

Arnon had faith in me, and he convinced his team at Puma to have faith as well. Daddy and I flew out to Los Angeles to meet with them. Arnon's daughter Alexandra was involved in the business, so she was there, too. It was the longest meeting. We got started around lunchtime and we were still going at mid-

night. It was one of those negotiations where everyone was getting along, and we were all determined to get a deal done, no
matter how long it took. At some point, I put my head down on
this big conference table where we were sitting and fell asleep.
The holdup seemed to be between Arnon and his partner, Jochen
Zeitz. Arnon was a bit more of a risk taker than Jochen, and at
first it was kind of funny to watch them go back and forth about
whether they should do a deal, and at what level, but after a while
it wasn't so funny. I didn't care so much about the deal terms.
All I cared about, really, was the deal itself. I wanted a sponsor.
I wanted someone to believe in me. That was my bottom line. I
wanted to be able to shake hands with these people, deposit the
good faith they had in me, and then step out on a court and show
the world that there was this great company behind me, Puma.
It would be like a seal of approval, at a time in my life when I
desperately needed a seal of approval.

Alexandra Milchon was so nice, so attentive. When I fell asleep,
she came over, gently shook me awake, and asked me if I'd be more
comfortable lying down. Daddy told her I was fine just where I
was. He wanted me to be at the table, even if I couldn't keep my
eyes open. I was just a kid, but he thought it was important that I
be in on this. And it was—as long as I could stay awake!

The key message here was that it wasn't just Puma taking a
chance on an upstart like me. It was me taking a chance on Puma.
It cut both ways. Daddy helped me recognize that. Usually, in a
successful partnership, both sides have as much at stake. That's
how it shook out here. Puma hadn't really sponsored anyone in
tennis before. They were big in soccer and other sports like track
and field, but not tennis. In fact, they didn't even have a line of
tennis shoes, like Reebok or Nike, so it was a big risk for me, too,
throwing in with them. The idea was they were going to create a
whole new tennis line with me in mind, which was kind of exciting, but at the same time it was kind of uncertain, so each side
was taking a leap. At sixteen, I didn't have the most sophisticated

business sense, but even I could see that with great risk comes great reward, and happily that's just how it turned out.

When we finally shook hands on a deal, all I wanted was a bed. I was still operating on Florida time, so I was wiped. But at the same time, underneath this allover exhaustion, I had this tremendous feeling of validation. Again, I didn't care about the money. I cared about the handshake. I cared about the vote of confidence, that these Puma people believed in me enough to cut a deal and get behind me in this big-time way. That was everything.

Well, not quite everything. There was also the matter of the clothes! Fast-forward another week or so. I was home in Florida, back to my routine of school and practice and school and practice, when this huge box arrived from Puma. I couldn't wait to see what was inside. They still didn't have a tennis line, but they were a European company, and they had all this great gear. Extremely cool stuff. Out-there stuff. Exciting stuff. Sportswear, mostly. I tried it all on, and it was such a thrilling moment, because I knew at the other end someone or some group of someones had collected all this stuff hoping I would like it. They put this box together with me in mind. Me! Forget all the little tastes of success I was having on the court. Forget that thrilling run to the semis in Chicago, past all those top-ranked players. It was this moment, going through this giant box of Puma gear that all fit perfectly, where I felt I'd finally arrived as a player.

Before I hit another tennis ball, I knew I'd grown my game.

For the first couple tournaments after I'd signed my deal, Puma still didn't have a pure tennis line, so they threw together something appropriate for me to wear. One of the first things I got to wear for them was this adorable neon blue shirt, with the Puma cat in the middle. It was my very favorite shirt, then we highlighted it with a cute white skirt—and I felt like such a princess when I took to the court in my thrown-together outfit—a powerful, purposeful princess. I had my own hopes and dreams on my racquet, along with the hopes and dreams of this great company.

From the very beginning, Puma wanted me to work with them on their designs. By that point, I guess I'd developed a kind of trademark look on the court, so they sought my input. That made me so happy! We used to sit together with a design pad and work out these different ideas, like the one we came up with for the famous catsuit I wore at the 2002 U.S. Open. Man, that outfit turned a lot of heads and caused a lot of controversy, but what most people didn't realize was it was so comfortable! Of course, that catsuit was so hot I would have worn it even if it was the most uncomfortable thing in the world, but it was designed with performance in mind.

They had me wearing all kinds of outrageous outfits. It got to where people started to wonder what I'd wear at the start of each tournament. I became known for my outfits as much as for my aggressive, relentless style of play. Spandex. Polyester. Lycra. Denim—later on, when I signed with Nike. Best I could tell, no one had ever worn denim on the tour, other than Andre Agassi on the men's side, so that was our inspiration, to try something a little different, and here it was a sport denim so there was some give to it. Whatever the designers could put together in an exciting, cutting-edge sort of way, I'd try it on or maybe give it my own spin or flourish. And then we'd accessorize, with big hoop earrings, or a bold new hairstyle.

Sometimes, if I was uncertain about a particular look or outfit, I'd run it by V, who also had a flair for what she wore on the court. Her advice was always the same. "Looks like fun, Serena," she'd say. "If you don't wear it, I will."

And that was usually that.

The second development on the fashion front came with a gentle push from Venus. Actually, it was more like a shove. I was sitting at home at the house we now shared in Florida, twiddling my thumbs, not doing much of anything beyond tennis. I'd graduated a year early from high school and never really saw the need to continue with my education. I thought I knew what I needed to know—and what I didn't know, I could learn soon enough.

But Venus had taken a different approach. After high school, she signed up for college. It wasn't a full-time deal because of the demands of the tour, but once our season began to wind down in late fall she'd sign up for a couple courses at the Art Institute and use her time productively until the season started again in January. The way she worked it out, it was just enough time to complete the winter semester.

V was on me all the time to join her at school, but I couldn't be bothered. She insisted it would be fun, but I was too busy doing nothing. I was back into *Golden Girls* mode, the way I'd been during that stretch when I was home-schooled in seventh and eighth grade. I was watching television, hanging out, playing tennis, watching television, hanging out, playing tennis . . . I'd sit down on the couch in front of the set, and I couldn't get up if I tried. V would burst in after another one of her busy days and say, "You're wasting your life, Serena."

Oh my goodness, she was on me. And she had a point. I was such a slug! One day, she got so fed up with me she just signed me up for classes, without even discussing it. She came home that afternoon and said, "That's it. I'm tired of watching you waste your time like this. You're going to college."

So that's what I did, all on the back of V's gentle shove, and it was a good thing, too, because I really was just wasting away in front of the television. Leave it to my big sister to know what was best for me. School was a blast. It was so much work, but at the same time it was so much fun. Most nights, we were there until eight or nine o'clock, working on some project or other. I studied design and fashion, so most of my courses had me sewing and drawing, learning the construction of a garment, considering which fabrics might work on which designs. I also took a sampling of liberal arts courses—math, science, and history—but most of my efforts were in the fashion curriculum, and I developed a real appreciation for design. In one class, we had to learn about more than one hundred different fabrics, so I came away with a great understanding of the manufacturing end of the business, and at the other end I really knew my stuff when I sat down with those Puma designers to develop a new line.

The school year was broken into quarters, and because of our wall-to-wall tennis schedules we could only attend during the fall-winter quarter. Normally, it's a two-and-a-half-year haul for an associate's degree, so on our slow-track schedule it would have taken just short of forever for us to complete the degree, but we stuck with it. In the end, Venus stuck with it a whole lot longer than me. But it was a great experience and a fantastic introduction into the fashion industry. Without those courses as a foundation, I don't think I ever would have been confident enough to start designing my own clothes, my own jewelry, or my own handbag collection—all of which came soon enough.

Somewhere along the way, I developed this obsession with Vera Wang. I started to think if things didn't work out for me in tennis, I could always design wedding dresses for a living. I have piles and piles of sketch pads at home, with pages and pages of designs. That's how I passed the time on those long plane rides back and forth to tournaments, or those long, lazy afternoons stuck in my hotel rooms, with nothing to do between matches but hit and work out and watch what I ate. I sketched and sketched, and dreamed of the day when I could finally launch my own line.

Gradually, I moved off wedding dresses and into evening wear, which I thought would be a whole lot less stressful. I thought, *Who wants to spend her days designing fashions for all these anxious brides?* Plus, it's such a limited market. With evening wear, I encouraged myself to think in all different styles, from formal to informal. Gowns. Cocktail dresses. Tops. Accessories. Even tennis and athletic wear. I was all over the place, and before I knew it I'd developed an entire line, which I started to call Aneres—*Serena*, backward. I thought that was fitting—a backward name, for a fashion-forward line. It took a while, though, for these designs to see their way into any kind of finished product, because by this point Arnon Milchon had sold his stake in Puma, and Daddy had negotiated a new sponsorship package with Nike, only here the terms didn't really allow me to pursue my own line. In the end, I had to put a lot of my designs on hold. That was cool, because I was finally in business with the top sportswear company on the planet. It was where I felt I should have been all along. Nike was open to some of my sportswear designs, which was great, and we put together some memorable, head-turning looks for me that helped to reinforce my burgeoning persona as a true tennis diva.

Best piece of advice I got on my fashion career? It came from my dad, of all people. I found myself running into so many dead ends trying to get my clothing line off the ground, and I started to get frustrated. One day, I threw up my hands and announced I wasn't going to launch my own line after all. I was going to put my energy into something else. Daddy heard this and sat me down for a talking-to. He said, "Serena, you don't drown by falling *into* the water. You drown by letting yourself *stay* there."

He was right. I'd fallen into the water and wouldn't let myself swim to shore. I was drowning, and taking my dreams down with me—hearing no the first time and leaving it at that. But I would never let myself hear no on the tennis court, so why was I so quick to back down in this endeavor?

As I write this, in January 2009, I'm looking ahead to the launch of my Aneres line on the Home Shopping Network, where we'll offer fun, everyday dresses at reasonable prices, along with tops and bags and jewelry—the kind of clothing and accessories I wish I'd had access to when I first started paying attention to my appearance. There'll be some high-end stuff, too, but not so high that most people won't be able to reach for it.

Here again, it's such a tremendous validation to be in business with people who value your contribution, to know you're not just lending your name to the endeavor but your creativity as well. In the fashion industry, it's like each item carries a little piece of you into the marketplace, and with every purchase you're making a powerful, personal connection with your customer. It's such an intimate transaction. You're out there as a designer, exposed, vulnerable, and if people respond to your creations there's such a gratifying feeling of accomplishment that comes your way as a result. It's unlike any sense of accomplishment I've ever felt on the tennis court, and at the same time I imagine it helps me play a stronger, more confident game.

Here's how I see it: when people invest in one of your designs, they're investing in you. They're putting it out that they believe in you and they like what you stand for. They're standing with you, behind you, alongside you. It's an endorsement, just like when I lend my name and enthusiasm to Puma or Nike or Hewlett-Packard. In success, it fills you with all kinds of empowering, uplifting thoughts and transports you to a place where you start to feel like everyone's rooting for you to do well. It puts you in a kind of zone—and, while you're there, to draw strength from a place most athletes never think to look.

Think. U have been writing these notes for years. Just do it. U want/NEED to win. Nothing is too hard for U. Nothing is too tough for U. It's U and only U!!! U R part of the strongest people alive. Nothing is worse than what your grandparents and great-grandparents went through. Nothing is more difficult. Nothing. Get up, get out and make yourself/ your people happy and proud!

—MATCH BOOK ENTRY

EIGHT

The So-and-So Slam

Sometimes, it takes a setback to get you jump-started and on your way; you'll need to turn adversity to advantage if you mean to compete over the long haul. I suppose I always knew this on some level—it's human nature in full force!—but it never really came up in all that time on the court. You'd think a thing like this would be drilled into young players, but it's not something that can be taught or coached or anticipated. It takes a bad patch to get you to realize it for yourself. When you find yourself in the middle of some defining difficulty, you've got to roll with it, and figure it out on your own.

It's like a scene from *The Wizard of Oz*. Dorothy learns that her ruby slippers always held the magical power to return her home, but she never knew to put that power to use until she realized that home was where she was meant to be, after all. It's the same with me and tennis. When I was just starting out, my parents emphasized skill and fitness and strategy. When I was older, playing with different coaches for the first time, repetition and muscle memory were key. But tennis is a mental game. It has everything to do with the mind-set you take to the court and the personality you carry off of it—the mental toughness that gets talked about into the ground. Technique, fitness, muscle memory . . . those are a given at the professional level, but it's what you do with your particular skill set and how you respond to the bad patches and regain your footing that sets you apart.

I didn't know any of this going in, although if I had I don't know that the front end of my career would have gone any differently. I mean, when I finally put two and two together here it's not like I could click my ruby heels whenever I wanted and start winning tournament after tournament. If that's how it worked, we'd all be trading deuce and ad points late into the night, and no player would ever grab or keep an edge because her opponent would have equal access to the very same edge. No, it's an epiphany athletes must reach on their own terms, in their own time, and even then it's unclear what they'll make of it.

My first piece of personal adversity was set against our nation's adversity—September 11, 2001. I had no special claim on the tragic events of that day, but I was in its middle. Recall that the attacks on the World Trade Center and the Pentagon took place first thing on a Tuesday morning. Recall, too, that the U.S. Open ended the previous weekend, with me on the short-end of a 6–2, 6–4 loss to Venus in the finals.

A little setup is needed: it had been a decent enough year to that point, despite three straight quarterfinal losses to Jennifer Capriati, who seemed to have my number that season, and six quarterfinal losses overall, but for the most part I was treading water. Not great; not bad; just somewhere in between. I was still only nineteen years old, but in just a few years I'd become a real factor on the tour. Here in 2001 I'd won a couple tournaments, including that controversial Indian Wells win over Kim Clijsters, but I struggled in the majors leading up to Flushing Meadows. I'd started the year as the 6th-ranked player in the world, and by the time the Open rolled around I had dropped to 10th—not exactly the direction I meant to be headed. And then, to lose to Venus like that, in our first-ever matchup in a major final . . . well, I went from thinking I'd clawed my way back to a respectable showing to thinking I'd slipped.

The silver lining to my nothing-special season was that I was in love. At least, I *thought* I was in love. Anyway, I was dating a guy I'll now refer to only as So-and-So. Why? One of my girl-friends told me that the way you get past a bad breakup is to refuse to speak your ex's name, so I'm going with that.

Some further setup: following that loss in the Open finals to V, a group of us went out to see Michael Jackson and his brothers in a reunion concert in New York City. It was the hottest ticket in town. Just the day before, a ticket to the Williams sisters final had been the second-hottest ticket, but now our moment had passed and the big-city spotlight was on the Jackson brothers. A group of us decided to go to let off some steam, only Venus stayed back. She was such a dweeb. (Sorry, V!) All these major artists and special guests were going to be there, like Justin Timberlake, Whitney Houston, and Britney Spears. Venus had just won the U.S. Open, but she insisted she needed her rest. If it was me, and I'd just won the Open, I'd have made my way onto that stage and danced my little head off, but that's the difference between me and V. She's disciplined, and a little nerdy; I'm up for any excuse to cut loose and have a good time.

Okay, so that's the backstory. The frontstory was this: on the morning of September 11, most of my family was up in the air. Literally. We'd come together for the Open in New York, and we'd gotten through the emotional big deal of our first all-Williams major final, and now we were dispersing. Lyn was on a flight to Los Angeles. V was headed home to Florida. I was on my way home to Florida as well, but my plane never got there; we were rerouted to the Washington, D.C., area, not far from where So-and-So lived, so he drove out to pick me up. Meanwhile, Isha was grounded in New York with my mom. Daddy had left town a day or two before—he never did stick around too long after a tournament—and Tunde was at home in California.

I was so allover tired that I didn't sleep the night before, but that just meant I'd sleep on the plane. I was on an early flight from

LaGuardia. No big thing. But then, just after eight thirty in the morning, I awoke with a start. My heart was racing. I'd always had a keen intuitive sense, and here I had this strange, uneasy feeling. Right there on the plane, the world felt a little *off*. I couldn't explain it, and it was only later that I pieced together that this was right around the time the first plane crashed into the World Trade Center. We landed soon after, just before all U.S. flights were grounded or rerouted for security measures. As I made my way through the terminal and began to pick up on what was happening, I was scared out of my mind. I didn't know where I was at first, but then I figured out that So-and-So was nearby, so he drove out to meet me.

My first thought was for the rest of my family, because a lot of us were flying, but I couldn't reach anyone on their cell phones. The circuits were down or overloaded, and so for an agonizing stretch I didn't know where anyone was or what was going on. I was all alone. I looked around the airport, and I could see everyone was desperate to plug back in to their families. There were huge lines at the few airport pay phones, but I could tell from the way everyone was slamming the phone back in its cradle that they weren't having much luck, either. It was such a surreal and sad and spooky morning, and I wasn't near a television set for the first while, so I was a little unfocused. Frankly, I don't remember a lot of what happened next, but I do remember sitting down and praying—for my family, of course, but also for everyone who was trapped in those burning buildings, the passengers on that hijacked plane, the frightened people on the pay phones, and anyone else caught in the crossfire of this horrible act of terrorism.

As the picture became clear, I kept thinking, *Oh my God, those poor people!* All this time later, I still can't get the anguish of that moment out of my mind. I close my eyes, and there it is. And yet, slowly, the situation with my family began to resolve; it took a couple hours, but V was eventually rerouted to Jacksonville. My mom and Isha were stuck in their hotel room in midtown Manhattan.

For the longest time, no one could reach Lyn and we were all so frightened, because she had flown out of JFK early that morning on an American Airlines flight to Los Angeles, and at just that time the thinking was that those cross-country flights were vulnerable. That's what they kept saying on CNN. Soon we learned with a great sigh of relief that Lyn's plane had been safely rerouted to Kansas City—she was stuck there for a whole week—and after that we were left to grieve for our nation and all these innocent victims and their families, along with everyone else.

Our family was intact, but our country wasn't.

A lot of people don't fully remember what things were like in the days immediately following those attacks. We've blocked it out because it was such a painful time, but there was a lot of anxiety and tension in the air, especially in New York and Washington. Confusion, uncertainty, fear . . . it was all around.

I spent the time holed up at So-and-So's mother's house outside D.C. We couldn't really go anywhere in the aftermath of those attacks. There was this huge military presence all over the city. So-and-So came over with his brother, and we played video games to pass the time. We watched a lot of television. I could have driven down to Florida, I suppose, but I chose to stay put, and part of that decision had to do with the special connection I felt with So-and-So and his family. I really liked this guy, and it was starting to feel like he really liked me, too.

I should have seen that he wasn't the guy for me. The signs were all there. Even the way we met was such a cliché: we were introduced during an ESPN shoot, but then he called my agent and asked her to give me his number so I could call if I was interested. That's not the way a real guy should go about asking a girl out—man, it was weak!—but I didn't see it. I called. Like an idiot, I called. To this day, I don't know why. I was bored, I guess. I thought he was cute, I guess. I wanted someone to talk to, I guess.

I was barely nineteen, so what the heck did I know? It wasn't that I was necessarily attracted to him, because I wasn't usually drawn to cute guys. I was drawn to power—that, to me, was attractive. But So-and-So was a professional football player, so he had that power thing working in his favor.

For whatever reason, I called. He didn't answer, but he called back a short while later. He said, "Hey, this is So-and-So."

I said, "Hey."

He said, "I wanted to let you know that I really enjoyed meeting you the other day. You put out such a positive energy."

I said, "Thanks."

Not exactly the most romantic opening exchange in the history of opening exchanges, but we kept talking. At the other end he said, "If you're ever in town, maybe we can get together. I'd really like to get to know you a little better, and I'm hoping you feel the same way."

As it happened, I was in D.C. just a couple weeks later, visiting Isha. I called So-and-So to tell him I was in town. We went out to lunch. We talked. We promised to get together again. And we did. We went back and forth like that for the next few months, every time I came through town, until finally he suggested we move things along on a more serious path. I resisted at first, but he wore me down. We had a lot of fun together. We went to King's Dominion, which is like the D.C. version of Magic Mountain. We went on all the rides. Isha came with us, and she liked him well enough. She didn't come back to me later and say, "Serena, you can do better." He seemed fine.

And that's how it went for the next while. So-and-So didn't come down to Florida that often—maybe once or twice—but when his football schedule allowed he did travel to meet up with me wherever I was playing. In fact, he was at Indian Wells that day the crowd turned on me and my family, and he told me afterward how much respect he had for the way I handled myself. He said, "I wouldn't have been able to keep playing, if people were yelling at me like that." He said, "I already knew you were an incredible athlete, but this tells me you're an incredible person."

I thought that was really sweet.

Next thing I knew, I was in love. Or, I thought I was in love. (I just *hate* that word, don't you?) Let's just say I was hooked, so it felt good and right and comfortable to be squirreled away with him during those tense few days right after September 11. The world was going crazy, but we could just shut the door and wish the world away.

And then he got sick. Really, really sick. Out-of-nowhere sick. So I dug in and took care of him. That's what you do, right? I made him soup. I changed his sheets. I brought him cool compresses and everything else you're supposed to do when you're taking care of someone in a relationship. To this day, I still don't know what was wrong with him—some killer flu bug or virus or something. Whatever it was, it finally got to where I had to take him to the hospital, and they hooked him up to an IV because he was superdehydrated, so I kept visiting him there for another couple days.

When he was better, and back on his feet, I made plans to leave. The airports were open again, and people were returning to their lives, and I had to get back and start training for my next tournament, so we said our good-byes and that was that. I figured I'd talk to him later that day, to tell him I arrived home safely, or maybe the next morning—you know, whatever you do when you're part of a couple.

But that was *really* that, it turned out, and things went from sweet to sour in a foolish hurry because I never heard from So-and-So again.

Can you imagine? I called and called, but he never picked up. It was right before my birthday, so I thought surely he would call. I convinced myself that maybe he'd lost his phone or something to explain his sudden silence, but he never did. I left him message after message. I said, "This is Serena. Your *girlfriend*." I said it like it was in quotes, like I was asking if that was really what I was to him.

For the life of me, I couldn't figure what had happened to set this guy off, but I wouldn't let it rest. I couldn't. It was clear he was avoiding me, but I kept calling and calling. Once, I blocked my number so he couldn't see that it was me on his caller ID, but I didn't say anything when he answered. I just hung up.

I didn't know what to do. I'd just turned twenty years old. This was my first serious relationship. I had no road map to follow, to tell me how to respond when someone you thought you loved wouldn't even return your phone calls. For no apparent reason. After you'd just dropped everything to nurse him back to health. In the middle of one of the most difficult, uncertain times in our nation's history. Everything seemed upside down—another cliché, I know, but it seems to fit those tentative times.

It's superfunny to me now, because I'm past it, but this guy tore my heart in half. Then he ripped up those pieces and stepped on them and backed his car up over them. And the worst part was he left me thinking it was on me. He left me thinking I was ugly, that I didn't deserve to be in a loving relationship. Heck, I didn't even love me anymore, after So-and-So got done with me. So what did I do? I went to Germany to play in a tournament. I wasn't planning to go, but I went. Tennis would be my salvation, I decided. Tennis would see me through. I would not be beaten down by this guy, I vowed. In the little match book I keep, I put his name in the margins. It reminded me I had something to prove to him. To myself. From there I just kept winning. I won that tournament in Germany, and it led right up to those four majors I won in a row. The Serena Slam, they called it, but I've always thought of it as my So-and-So Slam, for the way it came on the back of this bad breakup. I wanted So-and-So to regret how he treated me. I wanted him to see me everywhere, doing well. That became my focus. Nothing was more important.

It seems fair to note that it wasn't such a deep or talented field at that tournament in Germany, but I did beat Justine Henin in the quarterfinals. That was something. And I was all set to face Lindsay Davenport in the finals, but she withdrew at the last moment, so I won in a walkover. That was something, too. Personally, I never minded too terribly much when my opponent withdrew. I always feel bad for the other girl, that she doesn't get a chance to do her thing, but then my competitive streak kicks in and I start to think, Hey, I still get the points. I still win the tournament. I still get the money. And I don't have to work as hard. I know a lot of players don't feel the same way—they'd rather win a match outright—but I'm not like most players. My goal is to come out on top. Doesn't really matter to me how I get there, as long as I get there. That sounds a little cold and unsportsmanlike, I know, but that's what I get to thinking when this kind of thing happens. I think, *That's okay, Serena. You can use the rest. And, there'll be more in the tank for the next match.*

After that first taste of So-and-So revenge, I looked ahead to the start of the 2002 season with great anticipation. I was still determined to stay in this guy's face, to be a constant reminder of what we had, to rise above his shabby treatment and stand as tall as I possibly could. That tournament in Germany was just a start, I told myself, and after that I was off to Sydney the first week of January 2002, for an all-important tune-up for the Australian Open. The plan was to keep my perverse revenge mojo going at full tilt.

I got off to a good start, dusting Anna Kournikova and Amelie Mauresmo on my way to a semifinal showdown against Meghann Shaughnessy, but then the wheels fell off my plan. I was up 5–4 in the first set when I had to retire with an injury to my right ankle. Now it was Meghann Shaughnessy's chance to get some extra rest and fuel up before *her* next match. I hadn't counted on that—and it was especially disappointing because it felt to me like I had so much to prove. To So-and-So. In my head, it had gotten to where it was all about him, about lifting myself from the dirt he left me lying in after the way he treated me.

Looking back, I have to think I was playing for all the wrong reasons—but what did I care, if all the wrong reasons ended up taking me to the same place as all the right ones? Remember, the goal was to come out on top, no matter what, only here my bum ankle cost me some of my payback momentum. Not a lot, but some. I rehabbed like a demon, and I was back at it soon enough, winning my next tournament in Scottsdale, Arizona, and finally getting the measure of Jennifer Capriati in the finals. I took it to her again the following month, in the finals at Miami, and then again the month after that, in the semifinals in Rome, on clay, before beating Justine Henin in the finals.

Each victory helped me climb a little further from the hole I'd allowed this guy to dig for me, but I wasn't done yet. Dang, I was just getting started. From Rome, it was on to Paris and yet another run-in with Jennifer Capriati, this time in the semifinals of the French Open. Once again, I prevailed. And, once again, So-and-So loomed in the shadows, egging me on. He didn't know it, but I was playing for him. Despite him. *To* spite him.

That semifinal win at the 2002 French Open was significant because it put all the right reasons for competing back in play. All along, back as far as I could remember, Daddy used to talk about how he was raising the two best tennis players in the world in me and Venus. It was drummed into us from the very beginning, like it was our shared destiny, and Venus had just reached the number one spot for the first time. This was huge, of course. Huge for Venus. Huge for our family. Just plain huge. But underneath the sheer *bigness* of the moment was some more of that silent fuel that's kept me going throughout my career. I'd always wanted what Venus had, so right away it set in motion this whole other piece of motivation, which ran alongside this weird, revenge-mojo piece regarding So-and-So. I wanted desperately to taste what Venus now had. Once again, she was first and foremost in our family. First to the top. First among equals. First, first, first. Once again, I was the little sister, clipping at Venus's heels. You better believe it, Venus's success was a powerful motivator for me—certainly as powerful as anything that was going on with me and my ex-boyfriend.

The way it shook out, after I got past Capriati at Roland Garros and earned a spot in the finals against Venus, was I would climb to the number two spot in the rankings, no matter what happened. Venus would hold on to her number one ranking, no matter what happened, so here we were on the cusp of a great, historic achievement for my family. It was such a long time coming. Daddy was always telling reporters and anyone else who'd listen that someday we'd be number one and number two in the world. He believed this deeply, with all his heart—that Venus and I would dominate the game—and I remember feeling so happy for him when it finally played out just as he'd foretold. We'd all prayed for this day, and worked hard for it, and now that it was upon us it was such a rich, purposeful, validating moment. We were all so proud. Of course, I would have much preferred that it was me in the number one spot and Venus in the runner-up position, but I wasn't about to quibble.

Honestly, at just that moment, I didn't care if I won the championship, because the true victory, the family victory, was already at hand. We'd come so far from those run-down courts in Compton to become the two best tennis players in the world, and nothing else seemed to matter. Not the French Open title. Not So-and-So. No, the moment was bigger than any of that. It was about making history.

As it played out, I managed a straight-sets victory over Venus to win the tournament 7–5, 6–3. I wish I could focus here on the mixed emotions I surely felt in beating my sister in a major final, but the triumph wasn't about that at the time. It really wasn't. It was about cementing our legacy as a family. It was a win-win, for all of us. Venus was still number one, so she got to feel like the true champion she was. And I won the French Open, so *I* got to feel like a champion, too. (Pretty great, huh?) I still remember Venus taking pictures of me holding the French Open trophy. It was such a Williams family moment—so much so that I nearly forgot all about So-and-So and the way he'd treated me. But *nearly* doesn't quite get you all the way there, does it? Deep down, I guess I was still in revenge mode, still fixed on showing this guy what he'd missed and reminding him how badly he'd treated me.

No, it's not the healthiest approach to the game—but in fairness to me, it was layered in with this other, more positive take, and now that I look back on it I think, *Hey, whatever works, right?* Healthy or not, my twisted little payback mind-set was certainly working. And it kept on working. It worked in Wimbledon, where I beat Venus again in the finals and earned my first number one ranking—which I held for a thrilling fifty-seven weeks! (That win knocked Venus into my number two spot, so the Williams sisters were still on top, only the other way around!) It worked at the U.S. Open, back in New York, where as fate would have it I powered past Venus again in a final round rematch. And it worked in Melbourne the following January, more than a year after this guy dumped me and sent me on this career-stamping momentum run. Once again, it took beating Venus in the finals. (And, once again, I'm *so, so, so* sorry, V! Really, really, really!)

Four Grand Slam tournament titles in a row. Each on the back of an unfortunate piece of rejection and dejection—and each a reminder that it's in the picking ourselves up and dusting ourselves off and pushing ourselves forward that we find our will, our drive, our purpose.

Tell me "No" and I'll show U I can! Tell me "No" <u>because</u> I can! Tell me "No." Go ahead, tell me. Just tell me I can't win. Just tell me it's out of reach. Come on, I'll prove U wrong! Just tell me "No" and watch what happens.

—MATCH BOOK ENTRY

NINE

Tunde

Yetunde Hawanya Tara Price. My big, big, big, big sister. (That's four *bigs*, because she was the oldest of the five of us, and I was the youngest.) She was almost like a mom to me, Venus, and Lyn. She was closer in age to Isha, so they didn't have the same caretaking, mentoring relationship—but her little sisters all looked up to Tunde. She was so perfect. She was so slim, so pretty. I remember she used to wear this one miniskirt all the time, and we always admired it. We wanted one just like it, but of course they didn't make miniskirts like that in little-kid sizes.

Tunde had a giant heart. She used to call me her kid. There was such a big age difference between us—almost nine years—that she did kind of take on that role. She even took us back-to-school shopping when we were little. With her own money. That's pretty unusual, don't you think? This was when she was still in high school. She used to work at Mervyns, the department store chain, and I guess she had some type of employee discount, but she knew how important it was to us to have new clothes to start out the school year. Just a couple nice outfits, nothing crazy.

One of the running jokes between us was that my hair would never grow. As a little kid of four or five, I was in the bad habit of pulling my hair out in the back, so my hair was always long in the front and short in the back, and Tunde probably knew full well that

I was pulling on it but she made a joke out of it. She said there was something wrong with my hair because it never grew back there, so I finally decided to break that bad habit and let my hair grow. I thought, *I'm tired of looking like this. I'm tired of getting teased by my sisters.* So for weeks and weeks, probably months and months, I was very careful to keep from pulling on it, and gradually I could see my hair start to grow back there.

I was so proud of my new head of hair. I wanted everyone to notice, and soon everybody did. Even Tunde took special note. I felt like such a princess with my beautiful long hair, and finally Tunde said, "Meeka, we're gonna have to cut it soon, to even everything out." She said it was getting all wild, and I guess it was, so one day she said she would cut my hair. This alone wasn't so unusual, because she always cut my hair. I was like a little doll to my big sisters. They used to dress me up and set my hair and put makeup on me, and of course I loved all the fuss and attention. I loved that they tried all their new looks out on me.

This one time, though, Tunde's teasing pushed the wrong button. She took out her scissors while I was sleeping in her bed and started snipping, snipping, snipping, all the time telling me how nice I was going to look. I didn't really know what she was doing back there, but she was my big sister and I trusted her completely. Then she pretended to be surprised and really apologetic. She really poured it on. She said, "Oh my God, Meek. I think I've cut off all your hair in back." Of course, she hadn't *cut* anything; she was just playing with me, trying to get me going. She was laughing when she said this. My other sisters were up in their beds and laughing, too. But I wasn't laughing. I thought, *My hair! My precious hair!* I was too little to know that I could hold a hand mirror behind my head, to see for myself what my hair looked like back there. I just heard my sisters laughing and laughing, and I thought I must look a mess! I was so upset! And angry!

I didn't say anything, though, because I didn't want my sisters

to know I was so mad. As close as we were, I wasn't above retaliat-
ing, in my own little-kid way. Oh my goodness, I was so vindictive! I waited until Tunde and all the others fell asleep, and then
I reached for Tunde's scissors and cut her hair . . . *for real!* Tunde
must have been fifteen or sixteen, and at that age your hair is all-
important. It's all about the look, right? She had this nice ponytail, and I just snipped it right off. It was a lot of hair, and I guess I
was pulling on it some because she woke up, and when she figured
out what I'd done she started laughing. That made me feel so bad,
because she was such a kind soul that she could laugh about something like this. Remember, in our sisterly dynamic, Tunde was the
forgiver, and here she earned her role. If it was me, I would have
been crazy mad. Actually, I'd thought it *was* me, and I *was* crazy
mad, which was why I went back at Tunde like this. But Tunde
just laughed and gave me a hug and went back to sleep. She didn't
even reach for a mirror to see how bad I'd butchered her hair. She
just shrugged it off like nothing at all.

That night with the scissors is one of my favorite memories of
Tunde, because it characterized our relationship so perfectly. She
looked after me. She teased me. She let me get away with everything. I felt so awful about what I'd done, because she was such a
forgiving soul. I don't think I was able to sleep for the rest of the
night, that's how upset I was over what I'd done to my wonderful
teenage sister.

One of the reasons the move to Florida was so upsetting and
unsettling to me was because Tunde stayed behind. She had a life
of her own by that point. She was in college studying to be a nurse,
just like my mom. She was the least athletic of all of us, but she was
our role model just the same. I missed her desperately, and because
we didn't really have any money she never made it to Florida to
visit. That was what we all promised each other, when we packed
up to move, that she'd be back and forth for visits, but it didn't
really work out like that. It wasn't just the money, of course. Tunde
was working, and going to school, and dating some guy, and all of

a sudden we looked up and realized all this time had passed and everyone had moved on.

Years later, when things started to happen for us on the tour, we'd see each other more often, but all through my middle school years we were apart, and it was like a piece of me was missing. I don't mean to overstate, but that's how the separation left me feeling. A couple years later, when Tunde started a family of her own, I felt it all the more. Her oldest, Jeffrey, was born when we were still in Haines City, and I remember looking at pictures and thinking, *When did* that *happen?* Oh, I was so excited to be an auntie, but underneath that excitement, I guess, I was also mourning the end of our special sisterly dynamic. It hadn't been the five of us all together in one bedroom for quite some time, but at ten or twelve years old you tell yourself that things will get back to how they were before too terribly long. You have this snapshot in your mind that shows how things really are in your family—not quite realizing it's a picture of how things *were* instead of how things *are.*

Now I look back and it feels to me like my nephew Jeffrey has always been a part of my life, but it wasn't like that at the time. Not for me, anyway. For me, it meant that Tunde had moved on. I was overjoyed for Tunde, really and truly, and I loved my little nephew before I even had a chance to hold him in my arms, also really and truly, but for the first time I realized in my selfish adolescent head that Tunde had moved on.

Over the years, Tunde and I developed a more adult relationship, which was a great and welcome thing. When she left the house, I was just nine years old, so we only talked about certain subjects. As I got older, though, we talked about everything. Boys. Careers. Faith. All that good stuff. She'd give me advice on whatever it was that was weighing on me at the time, and she'd even ask me for advice, which always made me feel like I'd arrived in our little sisterhood. Me, the baby sister, giving advice to my picture-perfect role model.

After Jeffrey, Tunde had my niece Justus, and then my nephew Jair, who was born soon after I started having some real success on the tour. One of the things I looked forward to early on in my career was being out in Los Angeles and going with Tunde and her kids to Magic Mountain, because it reminded me of some of the special adventures we used to have as a family. That was one of our big treats, when we were little—going to Magic Mountain on Saturdays. For a time, it felt to me like we went every week, although I talk to my parents and sisters about it now and they tell me it wasn't that often. Still, it was a constant, until I got lost one Saturday and ruined it for everyone. I was too little to go on some of the rides. I wasn't scared or timid or anything like that, but I just wasn't tall enough.

Tunde and Isha were tall enough to go on every ride. The biggest was Free Fall. Oh, I was desperate to go on Free Fall with them, but of course I couldn't. I was so jealous! Invariably, we'd split up, because some of us wanted to go in one direction and some of us in another, and I was supposed to stay where I was, with one or two of my sisters, until everyone got back together. That was the deal, only I didn't pay attention to such things. I saw my parents wander off in one direction and decided I would follow them. I think I even called after them—"Wait up, I'm gonna come too!"—but it turned out they didn't hear me. Anyway, it wouldn't have mattered if they had, because I was immediately distracted by a waterfall, and I stopped to play in the water.

That place could get so crowded on a Saturday afternoon, there's no way my parents could have found me in such a sea of people. That is, if they were even looking, but at first they didn't know I'd gone missing. My sisters didn't know I was alone, either, because they'd seen me take off after my parents. So there I was, splashing around in the water for a while, happy as could be, until at one point I looked up and realized I was lost. So what did I do? I refocused and decided I'd try to find everyone, so I ran off in a direction that seemed to make sense, but after I ran around for a while I started to cry. I was about five years old, so of course I cried. It's amazing to me now that I didn't burst into tears straightaway, but I was a tough kid—even though *tough* only took me so far on this one.

After a while, these two really nice guys came over and asked me what was wrong. I remember thinking they would take me away, but they were so nice, so I went with them to Lost and Found. There were a couple kids in there when I arrived, coloring with crayons off in the corner, but I just kept crying and crying. Eventually, I stopped crying and started coloring, but I was still so frightened. Someone gave me an ice cream cone, I think, but that didn't stop the tears. Finally, my parents turned up, and we left the park right after that, and on the ride home my sisters were angry with me for getting lost and cutting our adventure short. For the longest time, they were mad, because we stopped going to Magic Mountain after that— probably because tennis was becoming more and more of a priority and Daddy didn't think we could afford to take so much time away from our game, but I always felt like it was because of me.

Tunde wasn't mad, though. Or maybe she was for a beat or two, but she forgave me soon enough. She always forgave me soon enough. And she'd tease me about it for years and years. Even as adults, on these visits to Magic Mountain with her own children, she'd say, "You tall enough to go on Free Fall yet, Meek?" Or, if we went off in different directions: "You sure you won't get lost?"

I cherished the time we got to spend together in California, although I hated that she lived so far out of Los Angeles, all the way out in Corona. I used to complain every time I came to town. She'd try to get me to come out to the house for a proper visit, but I'd whine and fuss and usually get my baby-sister way. Sometimes, she'd bring all three kids with her into town, and we'd make a day of it. One visit stands out, for a conversation we shared during some quiet moment or another. The kids were down for a nap, and we got to talking about tennis, about what Venus and I were accomplishing on the tour. It was such a powerful conversation. Tunde started telling me how proud she was of us. Actually, she wasn't just proud, she said; she was "honored." That was the word she used. How great is that? To hear from your big, big, big, big sister that she's *honored* by the life you're living? That you've lived up to whatever impossibly high expectations and hopes and dreams she'd set out for you when you were little?

Curiously, we'd never talked this way before—not about tennis. But here it all came out. She said she was jealous that Venus and I had this special talent, and also that we had the focus and determination to see it through. She remembered all the times we would go out to the tennis court and practice, practice, practice. And train, train, train. "I really respected you for that," she said.

"It was all of us, Tunde," I said, not feeling like Venus and I should be set apart simply because we kept it up the longest. "You were out there, too."

"Yes," she said, "but we were out there for you. Couldn't you tell?"

No, in fact, I couldn't. But then, when I considered Tunde's perspective, I guessed I could. We were all there for each other in the beginning. And then, I guess it did become about me and Venus. It was still about us as a family, but on top of that, or maybe alongside, it was now about me and V as powerful, purposeful young women.

I got that from Tunde. Her take on life and love and tennis became so important to me as a young adult that it was one of the main reasons I eventually took an apartment in Los Angeles. Another big reason was the tug and pull of Hollywood, because I really wanted to be an actress, and I thought if I was stationed in town I'd be better positioned for auditions and classes. But being closer to Tunde was right up there in the plus column. Tunde even worked as my personal assistant for a while, helping to coordinate my schedule and track my appearances and correspondence, so while that was going on we spent *a lot* of time together. We talked pretty much every day. This alone wasn't so unusual, because I pretty much talk to everyone in my family at least once each day, but when Tunde was working with me we knew each other's schedules, each other's habits; we were a part of each other's life once more.

I still hated going all the way out to Corona, but I liked being around Tunde. She had this really massive house, with a whole bunch of bedrooms. When she decorated, she pushed another wrong button, because her decorating style didn't exactly mesh with my tastes. She painted one room yellow, one room red, one room green. All these different colors, sometimes even in the same room! I said, "Tunde, you can't do that!" I told her she needed to reach for more neutral colors, like brown and beige, but she just laughed me off. She didn't care what I thought. She liked all the colors. She *really* liked orange. There was orange everywhere. And in her closet! It was like walking into an orange grove in there.

We used to make so much fun of her, with all her orange clothes and furnishings, but now it's my favorite color, too. Now, whenever I see a nice, bright orange, it puts me in mind of Tunde. It's such a bright, happy color, don't you think?

September 14, 2003. I was in Toronto, shooting a television show. Lyn was along for the ride, staying with me in my hotel room. Isha was out in San Francisco, visiting friends. Venus was at the house we shared in Florida, with my mom nearby at her house. Daddy was in Florida, too. It had been a long, long time since all seven of us had lived under the same roof—and yet during that same long, long time, I continued to picture us as a family. That was my family snap-shot. Yeah, we'd each moved on (my parents, too!), but I could close my eyes and remember those days like they were with me still.

I'd been on the set all day, filming. I'd had to withdraw from the U.S. Open that year because of a knee injury, and I figured I'd fill in some of the downtime with an acting gig. In fact, I hadn't played since winning Wimbledon that July, beating Venus for the fifth straight time in a major final. (Sorry, V!) I'd been playing great tennis, but then I busted up my knee and ended up having to have surgery. That was a giant disappointment, to be sure, but I chose to see the positives in it. For one thing, it helped me reconnect with Tunde. She visited me almost every day when I was in the hospital, and after that she came to the apartment when I was stuck there.

For another, the long layoff allowed me to pursue some other career opportunities. On the professional tour, there's not a whole lot of downtime, so if I wanted to try on this acting thing I figured I had to grab whatever time came my way—even if it meant I'd have to do it on one good knee. Lyn came up to join me and make an adventure out of it, and we loved hanging out on the set, pretending like we were real movie stars. It was so exciting! We went to bed each night exhausted because we were out and about all day, and on top of whatever they had me doing for the show I was also rehabbing my knee, so sleep was a welcome thing.

When the phone rang at about four o'clock in the morning, it was like a bad dream. It was my mom, calling from Florida. Her voice was calm but confused. She said, "Have you heard from Tunde? I can't reach her. I think maybe something's happened. Maybe she's been involved in a car accident, or a shooting."

The call didn't make a whole lot of sense. It wasn't *that* late out in California. Tunde had a sitter at home for the kids—that I knew. My first thought was that maybe she'd put the kids to bed and gone out to a late dinner or something, or maybe out with some friends. I didn't get how my mom made the leap from not being able to reach Tunde to thinking she'd been involved in an accident or a shooting, so I shrugged her off. I said, "Mom, I've got a shoot tomorrow morning. I'm sure Tunde's fine. Get some sleep."

Of course, I couldn't fall back asleep after that. It wasn't that I was too terribly worried, but there was something about my mom's incongruous thinking that kept me awake. I learned later that someone had called my mom and suggested she check in with Tunde, so that was what had her on edge. I guess that's how it goes sometimes, when someone close to you (but not quite close enough!) wants to alert you that something terrible has happened but doesn't want to be the one to actually deliver the news. Of course, I didn't know this at the time, so I just thought Mom was being a little dramatic.

Still, I couldn't help thinking that something was going on. Lyn was asleep in the bed next to mine, but I didn't want to wake her over this, so I called Tunde's house. One of my cousins answered the phone. I thought, *That's strange*. But at the same time I didn't really think anything of it, so I just said, "Hey, it's Serena, is Tunde around?"

That's when I heard. That she'd been involved in an accident. That she'd been shot. My cousin wasn't really making a whole lot of sense, and of course it was late and I was tired and probably half-asleep. Everything just sort of half-registered, but all those halves added up soon enough, and then the whole dark truth took shape in my head. Finally, I heard the words I'd been subconsciously dreading since my mom put out all those negative thoughts: "She's gone, Serena. I'm so sorry."

I thought, *Gone? Tunde?* It didn't make sense. I'd just spoken to her earlier in the day. She was so excited about this show I was working on, and the progress I was making on my knee, how well Venus had played that summer, how beautifully her children were growing, and on and on. She'd just opened her own beauty salon and was finally starting to do well with it. She was only thirty-one years old, and I know it's a cliché but she really did have her whole life ahead of her. Gone? My sister? There was just no way. It was too crazy. Too impossible. Too sad. Her children needed her. Her parents needed her. Her sisters needed her. Her baby baby baby baby sister needed her.

I pushed the thought right out of my head. I said, "What do you mean, gone? Is she out or something? Did I just miss her?"

"No, Serena," my cousin said. "There's been a terrible accident. Tunde's been shot. I'm afraid she's passed."

By this point, Lyn was wide awake, after listening to my end of the phone call, and we were screaming and crying and consoling each other. Underneath all that screaming and crying, though, we were also confused. I remember saying to my cousin, "For real?" Over and over. "For real?" Like someone would really joke about something like this.

"For real? For real?"

At some point, I just dropped the phone. I couldn't think what to do with my hands. It was awful, just awful. All that time in Kingdom Hall, all that time praying to Jehovah and trying to live a good, purposeful life, and there are no words of comfort, no pieces of scripture, no amount of faith that can swallow up the hurt of something like this, no comfort to help you absorb the news. You just don't see it coming, and when it hits you it doesn't fully register. It's like a glancing blow. You feel it, and you don't; you understand it on one level, and on another it's just impossible to comprehend. For the next day or two, even, a part of me thought there must have been a horrible mistake, that Tunde hadn't passed, after all. Maybe they'd gotten her mixed up with someone else. Or maybe by some miracle she rallied and was okay. Something. Anything but this awful, lurking, dark truth.

Lyn was just a wreck. She had been superclose to Tunde. Like me, Lyn had also recently moved back to California, only she didn't have to do all the traveling I did on the tour, so they were together constantly. Lyn babysat Tunde's kids all the time, or just came around to hang out. She was shaking when I dropped the phone, and she crawled onto the bed and leaned into me and wanted me to tell her what had happened, but I didn't know anything. I just said, "Something's happened to Tunde. It's bad. I think she's been shot."

What happened was Tunde had been out for a late dinner with friends, just like I thought. But then she drove over to Compton, our old neighborhood, with this guy she'd just started seeing. It was just after midnight, and some kind of argument or confrontation took place. I can't imagine Tunde arguing with anyone over anything, so I'm guessing the guy she was with was doing the talking. Anyway, somebody pulled out a gun, and shots were fired into the

SUV Tunde was riding in. According to the police report, Tunde was hit by the shots that were meant for her boyfriend.

Just like that, she was gone. Just like that, my great, big sister was taken from us—just when we needed her the most. Her three young children needed her most of all, this was true, but her baby sister needed her, too. And just then, I didn't see how I could ever step down from that bed in my Toronto hotel room and do whatever needed doing.

For real.

Somehow, Lyn and I shifted into emotional autopilot and started making phone calls. I think some of the strength and willpower I needed to push my game to such a high level was also at play here. That strength you develop as a serious athlete isn't just physical; it's emotional, and it courses through you like a giant force. Without even thinking about it, I must have put on that superhero cape I'd fashioned for myself on the court, and here it helped me through these next agonizing paces. God knows, I couldn't have made it through on my own.

First call I made was to my mom. She picked up the phone and before I could even say anything she said, "My baby's gone, isn't she?"

The calls just got harder after that.

And the flight back to Los Angeles the next morning? Man, that had to be the worst flight ever—and the longest! We were so upset! The whole way, Lyn and I were in this weird state of denial. They say that's the first stage of grieving, and here we were, right in the middle of it. When you're up in the air like that, literally, you allow yourself to think all kinds of illogical thoughts. You think, deep down, maybe you'll land at the airport and learn this wasn't what really happened. Maybe the guy who was driving the car was the one who was shot, and Tunde was just grazed in the crossfire. Maybe they did some kind of operation, and because we were on the plane and away from a phone nobody'd been able to contact us to tell us Tunde was going to be okay. Maybe,

maybe, maybe. It's a whole lot of maybes, and you hang your every last hope on each and every one of them and hope *something* catches.

But, of course, *maybe* doesn't help. You touch down and the truth takes hold and doesn't let go.

The next days and weeks were a blur, and I didn't want to bother my parents or sisters to help jog my memory on this because it was such a private, painful time. By the grace of our God, Jehovah, we managed to slog through it. We held on to each other for dear life.

Tennis was about the last thing on my mind, just then. Forget that I wasn't physically ready to pick up a racquet. It just didn't seem all that important. A lot of people ask me if maybe tennis would have been a good way to power through all this grieving, but that never occurred to me. When I get angry or hurt or frustrated, I don't go out and play tennis. I reach for my family, for my friends, for whatever love and support I can find, and here I had all of that going on in a big-time way. That's what helped me power through. I had my sisters. I had my friends. I even had a long, meaningful visit with So-and-So, who came out to offer whatever comfort he could—so I guess maybe he wasn't such a terrible guy, after all.

The most difficult piece was helping Tunde's kids. My mom took the lead on this one. She moved right in to Tunde's house and set about raising those kids as her own. Wasn't any discussion about this, as I recall. Wasn't ever an issue. It was just what happened next—only here, too, I have no real memory of this new setup taking hold. I looked up one day, and there it was.

One specific memory comes back to me, though, from those first days and weeks after Tunde's death. We played a lot of UNO, just like we used to do when we were kids. Me, V, Lyn, and Isha. Jeffrey and Justus, too. It turned out Justus was really good at it. She was smart, like her mom. And fearless. For hours and hours, we'd play UNO. At Tunde's house. At my apartment, or Lyn's.

Wherever we happened to be—and for the most part, we happened to be together. None of us could sleep, so it was a way to pass the time, a way to keep Tunde close, a way to refocus that picture we all carried of our time together as little girls, sharing that one small bedroom in our house in Compton, talking all night about anything and everything. Here we didn't talk all that much, but we were together, going through the same motions we did as kids. Late at night, in the middle of the afternoon . . . whenever. Yeah, there was a piece of us missing, but in some ways we were still whole.

I look back now and catch the symbolism in the game itself. I mean, UNO is all about being number one, being the first to announce yourself and claim the top spot, and as kids it served to reinforce the competitive streak our parents hoped to instill in us on the tennis court. Here, it seemed to mean something else. Tunde was the oldest, our number one. She was the first to announce herself, and spread her wings, and move on toward a life of her own. No, she wasn't a gifted athlete, but she was strong, focused, driven. We all cheered her on, same as she cheered us on. And now she was gone, and the four of us would have to take turns in her number one spot, filling the spaces where she had been.

Your destiny has just begun. Remember your people. Remember your sister. I'm proud of U. Your people are proud of U. Tunde is proud of U. Always, always, always. Keep it up. Play for the moment. Play for yourself. Play for your people. Play for Tunde. U are capable of anything.

—MATCH BOOK ENTRY

TEN

Change It Up

Like I said, tennis was about the last thing on my mind after Tunde died—although to be honest it wasn't exactly front and center before she died, either. Keep in mind, I'd hurt my left knee just after that great Grand Slam tournament run that started in 2002. I hurt it in a foolish way, and I'll offer those details here, to help me make the all-important point that sometimes a rash or stupid act can derail your plans in a big-time way. All that sweat and effort I put in on the court went out the door right after I beat Venus to win the 2003 Wimbledon title. It was the last tournament I played that year, because I was such a dancing fool. That's what it came down to: a dancing injury. The first major injury of my career, and it happened on the dance floor.

I was out at a club in Los Angeles, dancing and partying and having a grand old time, but the foolish part was that I was doing it in heels. Everything had been going so well on the court, so there was every reason to celebrate, but then at some point I went into this little spin move out there on the floor and I could feel something go in my knee. I did my move and thought, *Oh, no, Serena. This can't be good.*

It turned out my left quad had partially detached from my knee, and I would need surgery. I hated being sidelined for such a frivolous reason. It was embarrassing—so much so that I couldn't bring myself to tell anyone how it happened. At first I thought I could play through it. I'd been ranked 1st for an incredible stretch, and won all those majors, and I wasn't ready to step away from all that, I guess. A part of me thought it was expected of me to power through. That's what champions do, right? They suck it up and press on. In the back of my mind, I kept thinking how it took Zina Garrison five years to get a clothing contract after turning pro, and how my Puma deal was almost up, and I didn't want any potential new sponsors to have second thoughts about getting into business with me. It was hard enough for an African-American woman to make some noise on the tour in success; I wasn't about to make it any harder in struggle.

Also, I knew that my parents and sisters had put all this effort into my career, and that in some ways Venus and I carried the hopes and dreams of our entire family, and I didn't want to let any of them down, especially after we'd been riding so high. That's why I didn't tell anyone what had really happened. I made up some story about how I hurt my knee while I was practicing, so nobody would be disappointed in me. It was silly, I see that now, but at the time it made complete sense. I could put off the surgery, I supposed, but I'd risk further damage. The only thing to do, really, was shut it down.

Anyway, that's what led me directly to those long months of rehab and recovery at home in Los Angeles, and the precious gift of all that time with Tunde, but then after Tunde died I was adrift for a while. We all were. I went through the motions of rehabbing and keeping in shape, because that's just what you do when you've spent your entire life around the game, but my heart wasn't in it and my head wasn't even close. It's like I was on autopilot.

Frankly, I don't know what I would have done if I hadn't had that knee surgery to hide behind. It was an easy excuse to stay on the sidelines, because God knows I wasn't ready to get back out there and play tennis, but at the same time I didn't think I could go on *not* playing, if I was physically able. Venus actually went back for the 2004 Australian Open in January, and I remember feeling a little jealous that she could step on the court and maybe forget for a few hours the anguish and agony of losing Tunde, but at the same time I didn't think I was emotionally strong enough to start playing again even if I had been healthy. And so for me the injury doubled as a silver lining *and* a black cloud.

My rehab continued for several months, and yet in all that time I don't think I fully allowed myself to grieve for Tunde. Oh, I went through the motions of grieving, but I was still too numb and raw to *really* grieve. I cried, but the tears didn't really take me anywhere. I prayed—about how we might repair our lives and become whole once again—but in many ways it was a surface kind of prayer. I thought about Tunde and her kids constantly—but here, too, I'm afraid I made room for only surface memories, and surface hopes and dreams, because anything below the surface or too deeply personal was just too painful to consider.

I didn't realize it quite this way at the time, but with perspective I see I was keeping myself at arm's length from what was *really* going on inside, and here again I think I hid behind my knee. It offered a convenient scapegoat, and a misplaced focus, and in this way I allowed my injury and my recovery to become more important to me than they actually were, which in turn made them less important than they might have been under less trying circumstances. I don't know if that makes sense, but that's how I've come to see it; my knee became my main focus, when really I was too unfocused to have a main focus. And so, just as I was going through the motions of grieving, I was going through the motions of healing as well.

I was such a mess! Yet everywhere I turned I was encouraged to suck it up and press on, so that's what I did. I plowed through my grief. I plowed through my physical therapy. I did all my exercises. I worked my butt off and made myself physically whole. And the good news was I put my new knee to work with positive results—at first. My very first tournament back was in Miami in April 2004, and I won it in convincing fashion, with a 6–1, 6–1 victory over Elena Dementieva in the final. After that, I was knocked out early in my next few tournaments, including a quarterfinal loss to Jennifer Capriati at the French Open—a back-to-back disappointment, it turned out, as Jennifer had just chased me from the semifinals in Rome a couple weeks earlier.

Next, I somehow got it together to reach the final round at Wimbledon before falling to Maria Sharapova in straight sets (6–1, 6–4).

It was a progression, to be sure, but I wouldn't exactly call it progress. If anything, it was a "one step forward, two steps back" kind of progress. Whatever edge I'd given myself following that dispiriting breakup with So-and-So was by now long gone, and for the first time in a long while I dropped out of the Top 10 rankings. This was a disappointment, but not a major disappointment. I mean, it's unreasonable to expect to play at such a high level indefinitely, wouldn't you agree? It'd be nice, don't get me wrong, but you can't count on it. And with Tunde gone, it wasn't really important to me just then. Playing was important, because it offered a compelling distraction to what was going on at home, with my family. Working hard was important, because it gave me a place to put my bottled-up energy and frustration. And winning was certainly better than losing, but in the end it was just a game. My drive, my sense of mission and purpose, my desire to be the best in the world . . . all these things had fallen away without me fully realizing it, and it wasn't clear if I'd ever get them back.

It took a frustrating (make that *maddening*!) loss to Jennifer Capriati in the quarterfinals of the 2004 U.S. Open to relight the fire in my game. What's interesting to me here is that once I realized the outcome of this match was out of my hands, it was like a switch flipped. I was pushed to accept the fact that I could never be *completely* in control—of my life, my game, whatever. All I could do was put myself in position to succeed and then hope for the best.

The match itself has become kind of famous in tennis circles. For one thing, I had a great outfit that year, so people remember it because of these killer shiny-black warm-up boots I wore over my sneakers, the short denim skirt, the studded black sport tank that gave the outfit an in-your-face, hip-hop feel. It was a real signature look for me—and it made an impression, I'll say that. Mostly, though, the match is still talked about for the ton of missed calls that seemed to tilt the outcome in Capriati's favor. This, too, made an impression—a far more lasting one than my head-turning outfit. In fact, people in tennis look to this match as the catalyst for the player challenge system that was adopted soon after— and all I can think in response to this is: It was about time.

Look, I never like to blame the officiating for deciding a match, because the incorrect calls tend to even out, but here on this night, before a packed house at Arthur Ashe Stadium, on the healing end of a personal and professional turmoil, there was a plague of incorrect calls—almost all of them against me. Even a call that shouldn't have been a call went against me. It was just so ridiculous.

In the very first set, there was a terrible call in the third game that might have signaled what was to come. I didn't give it much thought because I was up a break and ahead 40–15. I hit an apparent baseline winner that was called long. I questioned the call, but not too force-fully. The ball was clearly in, but the umpire failed to overrule the line judge and the call was allowed to stand. I was more annoyed than rattled, especially when Jennifer won the next point to bring the game to deuce, but I managed to hold serve and push the score to 3–0 in the first, so I set the missed call aside.

It was nothing, I told myself—a hiccup. It would be awhile before I knew these hiccups were contagious.

I ended up dominating that first set, 6–2, but Jennifer fought back in the second. For some reason there were an unusual number of close calls throughout. At one point, when I was down a break in the second set, I hit a passing shot that caught the back of the baseline, but the crowd let out such a groan of disapproval that Jennifer approached the umpire to argue. She didn't say anything at first, but now she thought it was out. She didn't get anywhere with her complaint, but when you're on the other side of the net and your opponent approaches the chair to protest a call and take some of the air out of your energy, it's never a good thing. Even if the call is upheld and the point stands in your favor, it can be unnerving, and that's just what happened here. It got me thinking of that missed call in the first set, the one that turned out not to matter. It set it up in my head—and, for all I know, in Jennifer Capriati's head, too—that this was a match we couldn't trust to the officials.

Indeed, here and there for the balance of the match, a close call seemed to go against one of us, and if you look at the replay you can see the frustration on our faces. You can hear it in the groans of the crowd when they thought a call was missed. We were both playing so well, trying to use as much of the court as possible, so the lines came into play a lot more than usual, and that's a tough way to play when you're not sure you can trust the lines. It cheats you of some of your canvas. The real test, though, came after Jennifer forced a third set. She had a break point in my first service game of the third set, but I battled back to deuce. Then, with the score knotted, I hit a gorgeous passing shot that was completely inside the line—by about six inches! I mean, I was so happy with that shot! The ball was so clearly in, the line judge didn't even bother to make the call, but the umpire scored the point for Jennifer. I learned later that she didn't actually overrule the call, because there was no call; she simply put it in the Capriati column and instructed us to move on.

The same kind of thing had happened to Venus in Wimbledon earlier that summer, when an umpire mistakenly awarded a point to Venus's opponent during a tie-breaker. Venus ended up losing the match, largely because of that one scoring error, and I wasn't about to let that happen here, so I marched over to the umpire's chair. I said, "That ball was so in. What's going on here?"

I probably should have asked the umpire to check with the line judge, to confirm that the ball was in, but I didn't think of that at the time. Plus, it didn't even occur to me that the umpire had simply misread the score; I just assumed she was overruling and calling the ball out, so I merely complained, as forcefully and respectfully as I could—to no good result. The point went to Jennifer, giving her a second opportunity to break. However, I won the next point, bringing us back to deuce, and as I collected myself before my next serve I took time to think, *If it wasn't for that missed call, Serena, this game would be yours.*

The "lost" point messed with my head. It shouldn't have, but it did—and sure enough Jennifer ended up breaking me to go up 1–0 to start the third set.

I thought, *Isn't that how it goes, when a call goes against you?* It's never on a nothing, throwaway point; it's always meaningful, and it always comes back to bite you or set a negative tone for the rest of the match. I'd allowed that to happen here, so now I wasn't only frustrated with the umpire and the line judge; I was frustrated with myself as well. But that wasn't the end of it. Jennifer gave me back that break in the very next game—on a double fault, no less. It felt like a gift, but then I gave it right back, allowing Jennifer to take the lead with another break of her own. That made three straight service breaks to start the third set, which I guess meant we were each playing tight, like we were afraid to lose—never a good approach if you mean to make a statement win.

I was so rattled by this latest missed call that I actually said something to the umpire during the changeover. I said, "I can't believe you would sabotage me like that." It wasn't like me to mouth off to an official—but at the same time it wasn't like me to blindly accept an abuse of authority, either. That's how I saw it. Every official misses a call from time to time; but you're only supposed to miss the close ones, right? The rules of the game are the rules of the game; the boundaries of the court are the boundaries of the court; and we're meant to play by the rules, within the boundaries. Otherwise, what's the point?

Jennifer held serve in the next game to go up 3–1 in the deciding set, so I answered with four straight points to push it to 3–2. The next game was a real showcase, with one great point after another. It actually felt to me like I was controlling the pace of play. I was running Jennifer from sideline to sideline, but I couldn't put her away. She was tenacious, unyielding. Whatever I did, she had an answer. I earned a break point in the middle of a seesaw deuce battle, but Jennifer fought me off, until she finally held to go up 4–2.

Then I held serve, too, to climb back to 4–3.

Jennifer's next service game was another hard-fought duel. She had me on my heels. I continued to control the pace, but she kept winning points. I got off to a strong start, taking the first point on an approach to the net, and the second on a great return of serve, wide to Jennifer's backhand side. But then Jennifer clawed her way back into the game and won the next four points to hold serve yet again and push the score to 5–3.

Now I was really up against it, and this was where that switch seemed to flip for me—only not in the most positive way at first. It was more like a moment of despair than a moment of personal discovery. I was playing great tennis, and yet somehow I'd allowed a few incorrect calls to nearly chase me from the tournament. Nothing against Jennifer, who was also playing great tennis and showing a whole lot of grit and determination, but it felt to me like this was my match to win, and like it was being taken away from me in an arbitrary way.

I managed to hold with a convincing service game to keep things close. That still gave Jennifer, up 5–4, a chance to serve for the match, but she double-faulted on the very first point of her service game, and for a beat I thought she might unravel. In fact, I nearly helped with the unraveling, hitting a backhanded passing shot that caught a big chunk of baseline, but not enough to keep the line judge from calling it out. Here again, the replay confirmed that the ball was in, but I just couldn't get a call.

There would be two more calls against me in this final game—the first an apparent double fault at 30–30 on a second serve that was clearly long; the second an apparent winner at deuce that was somehow called wide to give the advantage to Jennifer. The replays later confirmed that each of these calls, too, should have gone my way, but both went to Jennifer during the run of play, and she finally put me away on her second match point to end the contest.

Three calls in the same game! A game I needed! A game I would have won, if the first two calls had gone the right way! A game that would have put the match back on my racquet, where I felt it belonged. But it was not to be.

Certainly, this was a tough loss, but it came at such a curious crossroads for me that I didn't quite know what to make of it. At first I kind of threw up my hands and thought, *I can make my shots and do every-thing right and still come up short.* I thought, *All I can do is all I can do.* But then I thought about it some more and started to see the power in these realizations. No, I couldn't control the umpires or the line judges any more than I could control my opponent. The only person I could control on the court was me.

To be honest and supercritical of myself, I don't think I did such a great job keeping my emotions in check that night. I kept flashing the umpire these cutting looks, as if those alone might set things right. But the thing to do when you're on the receiving end of adversity is to rise above it. Or at least to try. When you buy into the adversity and shout that things are going against you, then things have a way of going all the way against you. But when you set it aside and move on, you give yourself a fighting chance. As I reconsidered this Capriati match in my rearview mirror, I came to look on it as an opportunity for growth. I started to see all these points of connection between the match itself and what was going on in my personal life—struggling with the loss of my sister, battling back from an injury, trying to redis-cover my will and focus.

As such, this frustrating (and yes, maddening!) match presented me with a real turning-point moment. It would take awhile, though, for me to gain the perspective I'd need to let it turn me in the right direction.

I got it together to win my very next tournament, in Beijing, and I somehow reached the finals in the season-ending Tour Champion-ships, which were held that year in Los Angeles, before falling to Ma-ria Sharapova in three sets. I even started the 2005 season with a bang, winning my second Australian Open—this time, battling back from 2–6 to beat the top-ranked Lindsay Davenport 2–6, 6–3, 6–0.

But after that I lapsed into serious downhill mode. My knee was fine, as this recent minirun had demonstrated, but looking back I think my head wasn't in the game. By all outward appearances, things should have been looking up on the court, but it didn't seem that way to me. The lesson of that Capriati match had yet to take hold—and more than that, I couldn't quite rededicate myself to my game. I tried to play through whatever funk I was in, but the more I played the more I resented playing. I'd never felt this way, but suddenly it was harder and harder to get out and hit each day between tournaments. It was like every competitive bone in my body was broken—only I didn't have the self-awareness or strength of character to see that anything was wrong.

I didn't know it at the time, but I was slipping into a depression. I don't think it was what a psychologist would have called a *clinical* depression, but it was an aching sadness, an allover weariness, a sudden disinterest in the world around me—in tennis, above all. Call it what you will, although at first I didn't think to call it anything. I tried to either ignore it or power past it. I just kept playing and playing. And struggling and struggling. Underneath, I had my share of aches and pains. An ankle sprain. A shoulder pull. My results from that period tell the tale: after Melbourne, I made it past the quarterfinals only once the rest of the year—and even then, in Dubai, my shoulder forced me to retire before Jelena Jankovic could beat me in the quarters herself. Heck, in the final five events I played in 2005 (Rome, Wimbledon, Toronto, the U.S. Open, and Beijing), I didn't even make it *to* the quarterfinal round, so I was clearly hurting.

I wasn't honest with myself about how I was feeling, what I was thinking. In truth, I'd never been honest with myself about stuff like this—and that right there was the root of my troubles. People would ask me what was wrong and I'd shrug them off. I'd say everything was fine, but of course everything wasn't fine. *Nothing* was fine. Usually, I could talk to my mom about something like this, or my sisters, but I wouldn't let myself. Daddy, too, had always been a great sounding board, but I shut him out as well. I started seeing a therapist in Los Angeles during this period—weekly, at first, then a couple times a week—and I didn't even tell my mom about it; that's how closed off I was about whatever was going on with me. I wouldn't even leave my apartment, except to go to therapy.

In my therapy sessions, the more I talked, the more I started to realize that my gloomy funk had to do with making other people happy. It came up because of Tunde. It came up because of me not playing following my knee surgery. It came up because of me wanting to validate the faith the good people at Nike had just placed in me with a big new sponsorship deal I'd signed when I was rehabbing my knee. It came up because of all those weeks at number one, and the pressures I felt to get back there. It was all these things, mashed up together, but the main ingredient was me trying to please everyone else. That was the theme, just as it had been a theme reaching all the way to childhood. It was a lifetime of me on the tennis court, working hard to make other people happy—so it was inevitable that I would come to resent tennis at some point.

I've read that in times of stress and duress we start to resent what we love the most, and I suspect that's what happened here. It's like tennis had become a job for me, instead of a passion, a joy, a sweet release. At a time in my life when I needed something to lift me up and out of the fog that found me after my sister's passing, all I could do was keep playing tennis, which was all I could ever do. And now, for the first time, tennis couldn't solve anything for me. When I wasn't looking, it went from being the answer to the question. My whole life had been tennis, tennis, tennis, and here I desperately wanted something more.

Something else.

Something new.

It all came to a head in Australia in January 2006. My dismal 2005 season was still fresh in my mind—and in everyone else's, I feared. I'd thought I could put it past me and start fresh, but then I found myself in the middle of a third-round match against Daniela Hantuchova, a tall right-hander from Slovakia. She was wearing me out! And all I could think was that I *so* didn't want to be there, at just that moment. On the court. In Melbourne. Fighting for points I didn't really care about, in a match I didn't really care about. So what did I do? I cried. Right there on the court. I don't think anyone saw, because I was all sweaty to begin with, but tears were just streaming down my face. It started during one of the changeovers, but it continued when I went back out to play, and it was such a low, despairing, *desperate* moment for me. I don't know how I managed to keep playing, but I kept playing, because that's just what I did. I sucked it up and pressed on, but I was no competition for Daniela that day. She beat me in straight sets, and I still remember walking to the players' locker room after the match feeling so completely lost and beaten and confused.

I went back to Los Angeles as soon as I could, and I didn't pick up a racquet for months. Officially, I put it out there that I was hurt, but I wasn't hurting in any kind of tangible way. Nothing was physically wrong with me. I was depressed. Deeply and utterly and completely depressed. I didn't talk to anyone for weeks and weeks. I think I went about a month and a half without talking to my mom, which was so out of character for me because we usually spoke every day. It freaked her out, I'm sure. I didn't talk to my sisters, and it freaked them out, too. At one point, they came out to Los Angeles to shake me from my doldrums, in a kind of intervention, and after that I started seeing my therapist on a daily basis, so I guess it had a positive effect. I wasn't on any medication, although we talked about it in therapy, but I was leery of changing my moods or messing with my already fragile state of mind, so I resisted.

Eventually, I came to the realization that *I* was the problem. It wasn't Nike or the pressure to be number one or being an emblem of hope for my family, or any of that. It wasn't losing Tunde. These were all *contributing* factors, but ultimately it was on me. It was all this negative energy I'd allowed to build up around me, that's what was dragging me down. I couldn't even make myself happy, so of course there was no way I could make anyone else happy.

For the longest time, Venus and I used to marvel that all these girls on the tour would burn out from tennis, and we would just keep going. I'd never once felt any kind of pressure, or that I was anywhere close to burning out—that is, until Tunde died, and then all of a sudden I started to feel pressure. The pressure to get back to tennis. The pressure to heal. The pressure to fulfill the promise and responsibility Nike had placed in me. And on and on. All of a sudden, I looked up and felt like tennis didn't matter anymore—because it wasn't *about* tennis anymore. It was about playing, and going through the motions, and keeping all these people around me happy. I'd let the game get away from me.

And then a weird and wonderful thing happened. That switch I talked about, when I was describing that Capriati match? It finally flipped in a positive direction. It flipped to where I chose tennis. This was a first for me—and a real breakthrough. All along, going back to when I was a kid, I'd never made an active or conscious choice where tennis was concerned. It was always like tennis chose me. Don't get me wrong, I was honored to have been chosen, and I was blessed with a God-given gift, and I came to love the game—really and truly. But it had always been handed to me, and expected of me, and held out like a given. I came to it by default, and it took reaching for it here, when I was down and desperate and miserable, for me to fully embrace the game.

I chose tennis. At last.

It might seem like a small shift in my thinking, but to me it was all the difference in the world, and it tied in to those feelings of frustration and powerlessness I'd felt on that court at Arthur Ashe Stadium, when the umpire checked out on me. It signaled to me that my game was there for me whenever I was ready for it, on my terms. Yes, I might do everything I could to get it back and still come up short, but all I can do is all I can do, right? All I can do is reach for what I know, and know that in the reaching I might find my true self.

What would U do if U were not afraid?

—MATCH BOOK ENTRY

ELEVEN

Only the Strong Survive

Have you ever done something or been somewhere that left you feeling exactly right? For me, that feeling found me on the coast of West Africa, on a goodwill trip to Ghana and Senegal I made with Isha, Lyn, and my mom in November 2006. I went to Africa again, in November 2008, this time to South Africa, Kenya, and once more to Senegal—but I want to hit that earlier trip first, because it was really like a coming of age for me. Even better, a coming to terms, because it put me in full mind of my heritage and my responsibility to that heritage.

As a kind of bonus, it came at just the right time to shake me from the depression that had been dogging me since Tunde's death and the professional funk that went along with it. Somehow, that first trip to Africa lifted me from my doldrums and set me back down on a positive path, because since that trip I've been playing the best tennis of my career; I've been focused, determined, and boundlessly aware of how strong I am and how far I can go.

For the longest time, all through my childhood and at the beginning of my career, I felt like I belonged in Africa. There was a magnetic pull calling me to the continent. I carried myself like a proud African-American, but it's almost like I came to that self-image by default. I didn't really know my roots because I'd never been to Africa. Well, I knew my roots on one level, but I didn't really *know* them—and in that italicized word there was a whole lot of uncertainty. I wanted to go because I thought it would give weight and meaning and context to my life. It would authenticate the stories I carried about my family—where we came from, what we endured—but there was always one reason or another not to go. It's not the easiest thing, to travel halfway around the world when you don't really have any money, and then later on, when you finally do have a little bit of money, it's not easy to find the time. Until a couple years ago, the tour season ended late, and there wasn't a whole lot of time to travel all that way and still get back in time to start up again in January. And yet even though I never made it to Africa, I always meant to go. It felt in my heart like that was where I belonged, like I was missing something by not being there.

Finally, I decided to just go for it. I didn't care if I had to fly directly to Melbourne after the trip to get ready for the Australian Open in January. I didn't care if it took me a tournament or two to get my game back after such a long, difficult trip. It was time. I would not put it off any longer. Anyway, things hadn't been going all that great for me on the tennis front: I'd been struggling. I'd been hurt, depressed, burned out. It seemed like the perfect time to go, so I told my mom about it, and my sisters, and we set it up.

Actually, my mom and our friend Cora Masters Barry did most of the organizing. They even took an exploratory trip ahead of our visit to make sure everything would go smoothly on our tight schedule. The idea was to tour the region and the schools and maybe give some tennis clinics along the way. I'd heard that people followed tennis over there, so it made sense to pick up on that. We thought it would be a great door opener for us. We'd go for two or three weeks, and at the other end we'd have a better sense of who we were as a people, and who we were as a family. Happily, that was just how it happened, with the added windfall that I came to some kind of renewed sense of who I was as an athlete and a competitor.

Now, my family history is a little sketchy, going back a few generations. Most African-Americans around my age can't reach much past their grandparents' generation. That's what centuries of slavery and oppression can do to a family tree, and yet for some reason I always believed we came from West Africa. I've got no documents to back this up, and we've lost some key branches of our family tree over the years that might have offered up some confirmation, but a lot of the slaves who were sent across the Atlantic to North America were from West Africa. At least, that's where a lot of them were captured and tortured and sold before making the voyage. So that's where we went.

We built our schedule around these tennis clinics we'd set up for little kids in small towns and villages in Senegal and Ghana. I was amazed at how talented some of these kids were. Really, a lot of them were good! You'd think that in a country where there's so much poverty and illness and hardship there wouldn't be time for a joyful release like tennis, but most of the people we met knew who I was. And, incredibly, a lot of them played tennis. They didn't have the latest equipment, but they weren't exactly playing with wooden racquets, either. I was surprised. They had decent gear. They followed the game. Those who didn't know who I was knew that I played tennis, that's all. There were public courts, every here and there. The courts weren't in the best shape, but they reminded me of the courts I used to play on back in Compton, so I told the kids that I grew up playing on courts just like theirs. They seemed to like that. We had a translator with us. The kids seemed to like that, too, that we were making an extra effort to communicate. I told them that if they worked hard at it, like I did, they could become one of the best players in the world, even on a run-down public court.

We also spent some time giving out polio vaccines, malaria pills, and vitamin A supplements at area hospitals and clinics. And various types of mosquito netting. This was God's work, I thought—and a real highlight of the trip. It was impossible to visit these remote, impoverished villages and not be moved by the plight of the people there. It was such a gratifying feeling to know we were helping people who couldn't really help themselves. West African governments have always had a hard time keeping ahead of epidemics like polio and measles and malaria, and here we were, trying to stay out in front of this good fight—a truly rewarding experience, I'll say that.

Through UNICEF, we got involved in a program that distributed bed nets to help cut down on the spread of malaria. A lot of the people in these villages couldn't afford the vaccines, so programs like this one were essential. It's not like here in the States, where kids are required to get certain inoculations by certain ages. Over there, thousands and thousands of kids are dying because of these totally preventable diseases. It's a heartbreaking thing to see first-hand, and yet underneath the heartbreak there's an unimaginable sense of spirit and good cheer. I'll never forget the look on the face of this one young mother; she couldn't have been more than fifteen or sixteen years old, and her eyes just lit up when it was her turn in line. I thought back to how things were with me, when I was this woman's age. I'd just started playing professionally. I didn't want for much—except, maybe, for a couple close calls to go my way. Here this young mother—a child herself!—had the weight of the world on her small shoulders. She'd come to get vaccines for her infant twins, and the babies were no bigger than four pounds each, and the mother was so unabashedly grateful. Oh, she was simply beam-ing at her good fortune, to be at just that spot at just that time. She didn't mind that she had to wait in line, because it was like we were giving her children a chance. And I guess we were.

Here's something else I won't forget: It was just after Halloween. Candy was on sale and we'd gone out and bought plenty of it so I could walk around and give it to the kids. I was down to my last piece one afternoon, and I gave it to this little girl who must have been about five. Just then, she caught the eye of another little girl, and without even thinking about it she offered her the last piece of candy. The child without didn't even think to ask. The child with didn't even hesitate to offer. I came away thinking you don't see that type of generosity back home. This little girl had nothing to give, and yet she was giving. The other girl had so little, it would have never occurred to her to even ask for more. It was the most amazing, most heartening thing. I wondered how I could be more like that first little girl, how we could all be more like that first little girl.

In Senegal, I met with President Abdoulaye Wade, and I agreed to help him build a school that young children could attend for free. The schools over there are set up on a pay-as-you-go model. It costs about ten cents a day to send your child. You have to buy a little coupon book, which lasts for about a month at a time, so it comes to around two dollars, and a lot of people can't even afford that. If you've got several kids and you're hardly earning a subsistence wage, it can run to a lot of money. It's such a desperately poor place, so all over Senegal you see these little kids during the day doing these odd jobs because their parents can't afford to send them to school. Or maybe there are two or three siblings working just to make enough money to send another sibling to school. Here again, it reminded me in some small way of how we'd banded together as a family, back in Compton. We didn't have much, but we had each other. We picked each other up and carried each other forward. We rallied. I don't mean to reach for a clichéd tennis expression, but that's how it was for us, in nontennis terms. We spurred each other on and moved about on our shared momentum. Of course, the stakes here in Senegal were completely different from the stakes back home. At home, we were doing mostly okay, scrambling to get a leg up and improve our circumstance. Here, families were just trying to survive. It's so relentlessly difficult for these people just to meet their basic needs, so of course I was thrilled when President Wade laid out the project for me, and honored to help out. In fact, I couldn't wait to go back for the opening and see his commitment to free education for young people finally realized.

I came away from my meeting with President Wade thinking this was how you make a meaningful change, with small strokes. One child at a time. One village at a time. One school at a time. Anyway, it was a place to start. I was like that first little girl with that last piece of candy. What I had in plenty I was obliged to share.

Nobody had to ask.

*   *   *

Perhaps the most personally meaningful stops on that first African tour were our visits to the notorious "slave castles" on the coast of Ghana. There was one called Elmina Castle, and one called Cape Coast Castle. We also visited a castle on Goree Island, off the coastal city of Dakar in Senegal, but those castles in Ghana were the ones that kept me up a bunch of nights.

The Cape Coast Castle was built originally by the Swedes as a shipping facility for timber and gold, but it was eventually taken over by the British in the 1600s and used as a kind of depot for the transatlantic slave trade. It's this huge concrete building on a cliff overlooking the water—and, really, it's such a sad, sad structure, even after all these years. It just sits there by the ocean, reeking of sorrow and suffering. A lot of the slaves were captured in the interior of Africa and brought here, and if they survived the weeks-long warehousing and starvation that followed they were packed into waiting ships and sent off to North America. There was a point down by the water where the slave ships used to dock. Everyone called it the point of no return, because no prisoner ever came back from there. If they survived the slave castles, they were taken to the point and loaded onto the ships. After that, no one knew what would happen except that there would be no coming back.

There's also a "point of no return" doorway leading out to the water on Goree Island, and it's such a creepy, eerie sight, to look out through the opening and see nothing but ocean! It was such an emotional experience to tour those dark, dismal dungeons, where so many of our ancestors were kept and tortured centuries ago. People told me ahead of time that I might not be able to handle it, but going in I didn't think it would get to me. I didn't think I would cry. But of course I cried. How could you not cry over something like this? How could you help but realize that one of your own ancestors—someone with *your* blood!—survived these tortuous conditions so that you could stand in his or her place?

How could you not be changed?

I walked through those big, cavernous rooms, and I could *feel* all this trapped power, all this short-circuited energy, all these lives cut down by oppression. It was awful. There was no light, no ventilation. Incredibly, you could still smell excrement in some of the rooms, and where the women were kept there was a slightly stronger, almost sour smell, which our tour guide said was from their menstrual cycles. In some rooms, they put all the women together. They kept them there for up to three months. Infants and children were placed in a separate room. Their mothers were held in the room next door, and they could hear their children crying and crying on the other side of the concrete walls, until eventually they weren't crying anymore.

It's a wonder anyone survived, but a great many did, and for their troubles they were sold into slavery. Literally, only the strong survived. If you didn't die in the castles, you probably died on the slave ships from dysentery or some other disease. The slave traders didn't want any weak slaves. You had to be pretty strong just to make it across the ocean—and then, when you made it to North America, you had to be stronger still. The irony of the struggle was huge. I mean, to survive all that . . . for what? To be beaten into the ground on some other continent. To be further stripped of your dignity, your individuality, your freedom.

I came away thinking I was a part of the strongest race in human history. That was the takeaway lesson for me, and I looked on it as an uplifting one. Someone else might have been depressed by what I'd just seen, and it certainly was depressing, but I chose to find the power in it, to be lifted by it. After all, if we weren't strong, I wouldn't be here. My ancestors would have never made it to the United States. My grandparents wouldn't have had my parents. My parents wouldn't have raised five powerful young women. Because, let's face it, only the strong survive. A part of me knew as much going in, but it took walking through those castles for me to sign on fully to it. It took smelling it and feeling it and touching it in just this way for me to own it, and to know it in my bones.

Really, my entire mind-set changed as a result of that trip, and I hate to discuss something so deeply moving in terms of tennis, but the truth is my approach to the game was changed as well. The very next time I held a racquet in my hands I thought, *There's nothing that can break me. On the court. Off the court. Anywhere.*

It was an incredibly empowering experience, and an equally empowering realization. If you could see what I saw, feel what I felt, *smell* what I smelled in those slave castles, you would not be denied. Also, I was on my way to Australia right after that. I had a tennis tournament to win. It was a big deal. No, it wasn't any kind of big deal next to the centuries of oppression and degradation and persecution of my ancestors, but it was a big deal to me. I hadn't won a tournament since 2005, and here it was January 2007, and I was thinking, *I can do anything. There will be no stopping me. Nothing can break me.* And the moment I stepped onto my first practice court in Melbourne, I closed my eyes and imagined myself back in one of those dark, dank rooms of the slave castles, and I imagined my ancestors before me in those same dark, dank rooms. Then I drew a line that ran from Ghana to Michigan to California to Florida to Australia, and it was on that line that I hung my hopes and dreams, and the hopes and dreams of my parents, and their parents before them, and on and on.

No, I thought. *We will not be denied. I will not be denied. I can do anything.*

I went back to Africa in November 2008—this time to South Africa and Kenya, before returning again to Senegal. For this trip, I was in a completely different frame of mind: I was going to give something back, not to take something away. This time, it wasn't so much an escape from the pressures and difficulties of tennis, or a search for identity and purpose that might help me lift my game. This time it was more of a celebration, an affirmation. My thinking was, it had been such a gratifying year on the court, it seemed only

fitting to finish it off with a meaningful homecoming. Plus, logisti-
cally, it made a whole lot of sense. I was scheduled to be in Qatar,
on the Persian Gulf, competing in the season-ending WTA Tour
Championships in Doha. I figured since I was already going to be
halfway around the world, and since I'd have those few weeks of off-
season coming up, I might as well slot in this second African tour
before heading back to the States.

We went first to Johannesburg—or Jo-burg, as the locals call it.
This time around, only Isha and my mom were able to accompany
me, along with my friend and manager, Evan Levy. (For this second
trip, Isha did all the advance work for our group.) We'd arranged
through a local charity to visit with kids from an orphanage just
outside the city. Only it wasn't just any orphanage. All the kids
there had AIDS, and they lived together in this big house. There
were about thirty of them—teenagers, mostly, but some of them
were so frail and tiny they looked like they were eight or nine years
old. It was so incredibly sad—at least at first. We met at a nearby
country club, where they had a few tennis courts, and I started working with these kids. It wasn't a fancy country club, like we have here
in the States, but it was a whole lot nicer than the public courts I
used to play on as a kid, and certainly nicer than any facility these
kids were used to visiting.

For a moment, when we first started playing, I didn't get why
it was set up for me to do this clinic with these kids, because a
lot of them were so sick. Tennis was probably the last thing on
their minds. I would have thought it'd be a better use of our time
together to just hang out. But once we stepped out onto those
courts, there was an incredible transformation—in the expressions on the faces of these kids, in their body language. They were
sick, but they weren't so sick that they couldn't run around and
play, and once they started doing that it was night and day. I'd
never been around kids who didn't smile—and as we got things
going these kids didn't smile. They moved about with these blank
expressions. It was so upsetting to see all that pain on their faces.

And yet once they started moving around on those tennis courts, that all changed.

I got them to bounce the ball up and down on the faces of their racquets. It was basic, and they all managed just fine after a couple tries. Then, I got them moving, walking from the net to the fence just beyond the baseline and back, bouncing the ball the whole time. Then we tried the same thing with some pace. Eventually, we got around to hitting. And get this: a few of them could *really* hit. There was this one young man who'd never played before, but he managed to learn and fairly master an overhead after only a few tries.

The more we played, the more success these kids kept having, the more their demeanors changed, and I reminded myself all over again of the restorative, healing power of self-confidence. It's a beautiful, sustaining side effect, and it doesn't have to be about tennis or competitive sports. It doesn't have to be about a physical pursuit. It can be about anything; if you feel good about yourself and what you can do, it changes your whole outlook.

There was one girl in particular who seemed to smile ahead of the rest. Like the boy with the accomplished overhead, she had never held a tennis racquet in her life before our visit. She didn't even have shoes. I wasn't sure if she knew who I was, or what we were doing on a tennis court. But she was out there, running and working hard and trying to get it right. Soon, her smile turned into laughter, and it became infectious. Soon, all the other kids were smiling and laughing—and so were we. It was an astonishing thing to see, and I felt blessed to be a part of it.

I realize that our visit to this group of kids didn't change anything in any kind of lasting way. They still had AIDS. They were still without parents, and families. Their futures were still desperate and uncertain. But for a few hours at least, they had a kind of hope. For a few hours, they were lifted from the sadness of their day-to-day and taken on an adventure to this nice country club and allowed to run around like other kids and maybe set their troubles aside.

They had a chance to have fun. It was a small gift, to be sure, but I left praying it would have some real carryover benefit—because of course they didn't need me to take them out to a tennis court, or to take them outside their group home to experience something new. They just needed to make the effort, or for someone to make the effort on their behalf—and I came away thinking maybe this would happen for them going forward.

The other highlight from the South African part of our trip took our group by surprise. We were visiting a mall in Jo-burg, for an appearance arranged by my sponsors at Hewlett-Packard. There was an HP store in this particular shopping mall, so they set it up for me to come by and talk to everyone and sign some giveaway items. I do this kind of thing at home all the time, and it's always a lot of fun. It can get a little crazy, but it's the good kind of crazy. Plus, you don't have to ask me twice to go out to a mall, only here there was such a mob of people out for this event I didn't think there'd be much chance to do any actual shopping.

Just as I started waving hello to everyone and posing for pictures, we got an unexpected phone call. It was a representative from Nelson Mandela's office. We had been trying to arrange a meeting with President Mandela for weeks leading up to our trip, but there were so many demands on his time that it didn't look like it was going to happen. This was disappointing, of course, but I understood. He's a busy man. There's a lot on his calendar. He was on my MySpace page—the only person I listed under "People I Want to Meet"—and now we were being told there was a sudden opening in his schedule and he could meet with us immediately. It was such a welcome surprise, but the timing wasn't so hot. I mean, we were right in the middle of this mall appearance. All these people had come out for it. Still, we figured that since President Mandela's office was only a few minutes away from the shopping mall, and since we would only have a few minutes of his time, we could be there and back in about forty-five minutes. The HP folks in charge encouraged us to go, and the people who had gathered for the event didn't seem to mind, so we made our apologies and made a quick exit, promising to return as quickly as possible.

On the way, I tried to put myself in the right frame of mind to meet one of the great icons of our time. Keep in mind, I had just pulled an emotional all-nighter the week before, staying up in my hotel in Doha to watch the election returns from the United States and celebrating Barack Obama's historic victory. It wasn't the smartest move on my part; I was in the middle of an important tournament, and I certainly needed a good night's sleep before my match the next morning, but I couldn't help myself. I was swept up by the moment. As Jehovah's Witnesses, we don't vote in political elections, but that doesn't mean we can't take a rooting interest—and there I was, nine hours ahead, in the Persian Gulf, waiting for the polls to close back home and rooting, rooting, rooting.

It was such an exciting, momentous election I wanted to be a part of it, even though I was half a world away. (I actually cried when CNN declared Senator Obama the winner!) For African-Americans in particular, it was certainly a powerful, consequential symbol, to see a black man elected president of the United States, so all these thoughts of history and moment were very much on my mind. Now I found myself racing through the streets of Jo-burg to meet another powerful, consequential symbol—someone Barack Obama himself was said to admire. It was a little too much for me to take in at just that moment.

Why? Well, Nelson Mandela was a giant in the black community. His name was spoken with such reverence, such gratitude. For years and years, I'd looked up to him for the great and important stand he took in the struggle for apartheid, and for the steep price he paid for his convictions. From the moment I learned about him in school, he became a true hero to me—and it's not often you get to meet one of your true heroes. I caught myself wishing I'd had time to choose a more appropriate outfit, or to think of something appropriate to say, but there was nothing to do but move forward.

We arrived at President Mandela's office and were led inside. He was dressed casually in one of his trademark loose shirts, with the distinctive African prints and tribal colors. He looked distinguished and gentle. That was the first word that came to mind. *Gentle*. For someone with such a fighting spirit, I was impressed by his gentle soul. Everyone around him called him "Mandiba," but that seemed a little too familiar for our group so we just called him Mr. Mandela. He stood to greet us from behind his desk, although we encouraged him to remain seated. After all, the man had just turned ninety years old, and he actually looked about twenty years younger, but we didn't want him to overexert himself on our account. He insisted on standing. He said, "When you meet with such beautiful and talented women, you must stand."

How could we argue with *that*?

He couldn't have been more gracious, more welcoming. Personally, I was thrilled that he even knew who I was, but he said he had followed my career, and Venus's, and that he had wanted to meet us for some time. Then he said that we were important role models for so many young women. And finally he said he was so enormously proud of us and what we had accomplished.

I must confess, I'm usually terrible when I meet someone famous. (Ask my sisters, and they'll say that's the understatement of the century!) I get tongue-tied and awestruck and self-conscious; somehow, the thoughtful, witty, insightful comments I plan on making never quite manage to leave my lips. I panic every time, and I'm afraid that's what happened here. I had meant to tell Mr. Mandela what an honor it was to meet him, how much I admired him, how pleased we were to be in his country and in his company. But nothing came out. Luckily, my mother and sister are never at a loss for words, so they covered for me. I'm sure I said *something*, but for the life of me I can't remember what it was—and I'm almost certain it had nothing to do with what I'd wanted to say.

The meeting only lasted about fifteen minutes, and during the entire time I felt like pinching myself. To be in the presence of such a great man, at such a profound moment in black history the world over, was such a gift, such an honor. Such a surprise! I stepped outside myself for a moment, in a way that the visit seemed almost surreal. After all, here was this gentle, soft-spoken man, who was so unassuming, so genuine, so kind, it was easy to forget what he'd been through. He was on the tall side, but he wasn't what you'd call an imposing man. He was just a man—and a gentleman, at that. It didn't fit with this image I'd carried in my head all these years, of a kind of warrior-statesman, someone with the strength to endure over twenty years in prison for his beliefs. And yet there he was, in the flesh, making small talk with the three of us like we were old friends.

A part of me wanted to take a picture, but a bigger part didn't want to cheapen the moment by taking out my camera. Plus, I was afraid to ask if it was okay, so I started to think about sneaking one instead—but I never found the right moment!

During our brief visit, Mr. Mandela spoke admiringly and enthusiastically about Barack Obama. The election was just the week before, so it was very much on his mind, he said. We talked about the hope President-elect Obama represented for the United States, and where he might stand on the world stage. We talked about South Africa. He asked about the schools we were visiting, the clinics we were giving. He took a genuine interest—which of course was nothing up against *our* genuine interest. In meeting him—Nelson Mandela! The first democratically elected president of South Africa! A man who had come to stand for freedom and equality, all over the world!

Those fifteen minutes alone were worth the trip.

From Jo-burg, we flew to Nairobi, but not before we visited a lion zoo and a game preserve. A giraffe poked his head through our open car window. I held a white lion. Then, when we got to Kenya, we found some time to do more tourist-type things. We had dinner at this wonderful restaurant called Carnivore, where we sampled all kinds of exotic local meats. I don't eat red meat, but here I was encouraged to try crocodile and ostrich and all kinds of weird, wonderful delicacies. (I couldn't swallow, I was so scared!)

The most compelling part of this Kenyan leg of our tour was a dedication ceremony for a new secondary school. Prior to our trip, we had made a special point of connection with a group called Build African Schools. I had already gotten that new school off the ground in Senegal, and here I was hoping for more of the same. Just a few weeks before we left for Africa, my friend and business partner Satchiv Chahil, from Hewlett-Packard, had shown me pictures of these Kenyan children, bending over in the dirt and scratching out math problems with a stick. I couldn't believe it! They were so poor—literally, dirt-poor!—they couldn't afford pencils and paper.

Here again, it was sad upon sad upon sad. The people at Hewlett-Packard already had a relationship going with Build African Schools, and it was such an exciting, meaningful partnership I asked if I could be a part of it. Build African Schools is such an incredible foundation. They do some amazing work—and without a whole lot of money. For about $60,000 they can build and outfit an entire schoolhouse, solar-powered and good to go. It's nothing fancy, but it gets the job done. I thought, What better investment can I make with my money than in the shared futures of these desperately poor Kenyan children?

The generous executives at HP were all too eager to help. They'd kicked in a computer lab and other technology ahead of our trip, so by the time we arrived at the school site the facility was ready to be dedicated. The dedication itself was like the local equivalent of the Super Bowl. Our group took a forty-minute helicopter ride to the remote village of Matooni, and when we touched down there were thousands and thousands of villagers waiting to greet us. It's not every day a helicopter lands in the middle of nowhere, I guess, and so we were greeted accordingly. Most of the people had no idea who I was. Electricity wasn't widely available in the area. Computers were scarce. Nobody followed the comings and goings and strange doings of the professional tennis circuit. And yet here was this sea of people, out to greet us. It was the most astonishing thing. I'd never been at the center of so much attention. I felt like the fifth Beatle!

And that was just the beginning. There were even more people crowded around the school site—about eighteen thousand. Can you imagine? Some people had walked up to twenty miles just to be there. Each way!

Next, several local groups made various presentations. One tribe, the Masai, performed a special dance that someone told me was centuries old, but it struck me as so vibrant, so contemporary, so relevant. In all, the ceremony lasted about an hour, and there were songs, and dances, and poems. There were tributes. Everyone spoke English in Kenya, but they also spoke Swahili, and a lot of these songs were in Swahili. I couldn't understand a word, but every once in a while I could recognize my name: "Serena!"

I'd never heard it said in such a joyful way.

I thought back to when I was a kid and I'd learned to say "hello" in Swahili—*jambo*—and I wished I'd taken the time to learn more.

Finally, the ceremony was finished and we had a chance to tour the school—and, I must say, I was overwhelmed. Completely blown away. In just a few weeks, Build African Schools had completed this wonderful structure, using a professional construction crew from Nairobi and local workers from the surrounding villages. One of the crew chiefs told me with special pride that they paid their local workers $1.25 per day, even though the average local wage was less than 20 cents per day. It still seemed like an impossibly low number, but this guy assured me that it was generous. Besides, he said, if you pay too much, the locals won't trust you. It's better to overpay by just the right amount, and you'll get back loyalty, dedication, extra effort like you'd never find back home.

The school itself looked like it was in move-in condition. The computers were all wired. The plumbing was working. The desks and chairs and school supplies all in place. The teachers were ready to get started. They'd set up this wonderful ribbon-cutting ceremony out in front of the building, and I can't overstate what a thrill it was to inaugurate the Serena Williams Secondary School. By the end of our visit, with the school up and running, kids were downloading music and surfing the Internet. They were so smart, so quick to figure things out. They were dressed in special colors that corresponded to their ages, and they were all so unbelievably polite. I'd never seen such well-mannered, respectful kids, and I came away feeling like they deserved everything that was being provided for them—and more.

I started to think, Wow, now these kids have a chance. Their brothers and sisters were dying from malaria and all these other diseases, because they didn't have access to education and medication and all those good things, and here they were being presented with an opportunity to change all that. Building this one school, in this one village, was more meaningful to me than anything else I'd ever done. It was more gratifying, even, than that first school launch in Senegal, because here there was no language barrier. Here I could speak directly to these children and their families and hear in their own words what this school might mean to their future. And here I could actually *see* the school, up and running. *Their* school. My school. With all these good people around to celebrate the opening.

I'll say this: cutting that ribbon felt better than winning Wimbledon, better than winning an Olympic gold medal. Absolutely, those accomplishments are important to me—but it's just *me*. Here I'm helping an entire community, and hopefully changing all these young lives for the better. Here, I'm taking the many blessings I've received from my God, Jehovah, and from all my hard work and good fortune, and redeploying them on the other side of the planet, where they can contribute to meaningful change. And that meaningful change has spilled over into my life as well. The thrill and excitement of all these opportunities, unfolding for all these children and their families, lifts me up as well.

Obviously, I'd love to make that kind of contribution in the United States, but my money goes a lot further in Kenya. Here at home, I give out school grants for college kids, but $60,000 doesn't go that far. Even $600,000 or $6,000,000 won't make much of a dent. But Africa is my home as well. That's how I've come to look at it. These are my people, too. They turned out to greet us in such great, thrilling numbers—of course they are my people. Of course.

The dedication put me back in mind of that takeaway phrase from my first trip to Africa just a couple years earlier: *only the strong survive.* I started to realize it's not only about strength; it's also about opportunity. You need to be strong, but you also need a shot. Strength is nothing without an opportunity to put it to use. A dirt-poor kid scratching out math problems with a stick could have an iron will like you wouldn't believe, but without a firm foundation her children and her children's children would still be stooped over in the dirt. They'd never reach up and out; there'd be no way to exercise that strength or put it to productive use; and the cycle of hopelessness would just continue.

From Kenya, we moved on to Senegal, to check on the progress of my school initiative there, and to visit with more kids in more villages. It was such a wild, wonderful, whirlwind tour, and at every stop there was a reason to be uplifted. Of course, there was reason to despair as well, because we came across so much poverty and desperation on this trip, but we tried to counter this in what ways we could. We really did. And in a lot of ways we succeeded.

Once again, I chose to find the power in the struggle of these good people. Once again, I chose to be lifted by their perseverance, their resilience. Once again, their will became mine and I was strengthened.

U R a queen. U have been waiting for this moment. This moment has been waiting for U. For billions of years, this energy has been building up in U for this moment, this tournament. It all happens now!!! Release and go. U don't have to hit every ball hard. Just relax & focus. U don't have to be perfect. Just be strong, and brave. She's the one who should be scared. She's the one who isn't ready. "Lose control." (Beyoncé—again!!!)

—MATCH BOOK ENTRY

TWELVE

Up from Down Under

I played a couple tournaments before leaving on that first trip to Africa in November 2006, just to take my measure. I'd been away from the game for so long it felt a little like I was relaunching myself—Serena Williams, version 2.0. This version had a few glitches after all that time on the shelf, to go along with a few extra pounds.

As you might imagine, I ate a lot during that period in Los Angeles when I wasn't playing. There was a place called Stan's Donuts in Westwood, not far from where I lived; it's considered one of the best donut shops in the world, and it just about did me in. And, to make matters worse, I wasn't doing any fitness training (unless you happen to count shopping on Rodeo Drive as an aerobic activity), so those excess calories had nowhere to go but my hips and thighs.

I was in terrible shape, but I figured I could play myself back into form. Of course, it was naïve to think I could do so without any criticism or scrutiny from the tennis community, but I couldn't see any other approach if I meant to start playing again in any kind of timely fashion. If I waited until I was completely ready to resume my career in an all-out way, I might never get it going. I talked to my parents about this, and they agreed that the longer I was away from the game the harder it would be to return. Venus, too. The thing to do was jump right back in and figure out what I needed to work on from there.

My first tournament after the long layoff was in Cincinnati—in July, a full six months after my third-round loss at the 2006 Australian Open. I don't know what it was about that Cincinnati tournament, but it just popped out at me when I was looking over the calendar. It's like it was calling me to come play, and I guess I must have been ready to get back to it because I listened. Right around that time, a day or two before I signed myself up for the tournament, I ran into this adorable little black girl on the street in my neighborhood, who was just superexcited to see me. She hurried over to me and said, "You're Serena Williams!"

I must confess, she caught me a little off guard. I had my sunglasses on, and probably a hat, and I wasn't exactly looking my best. (Come to think of it, I might have been coming out of Stan's Donuts, so she caught me red-handed, too!) So I gathered myself and said, "That's me."

Well, this girl popped a smile so wide I could see her full set of teeth. She was so cute! She said, "I just love you so much, Serena. When I grow up I want to be just like you!"

It had been awhile since I'd gotten this kind of star treatment, but coming from this adorable little girl, with that bright, wide smile, it was just the push I needed to get back to my game. She told me how Venus and I were her role models, how she had a big sister and how they called themselves "Venus" and "Serena" when they played tennis. She said, "You're just so awesome."

I said, "You really think so?" Just then, I wasn't feeling so awesome, so it was good to hear.

We talked for a bit, along these same *you're so awesome* lines, but then this little girl completely surprised me. She said, "I know you haven't been playing a lot lately, but I hope you start playing again soon. If you're sick, I hope you feel better. I hope you come back because you're still a great player. I just know you'll come back and be better than ever."

Well, that just took my breath away. I thought, *If a little kid*—I'm guessing she was ten or twelve—*can look me in the eye and tell me*

I haven't played my best tennis yet, there must be something to it. So I gave her a hug, thanked her for her kind words, and raced home to look at some tapes of my past matches. I do that sometimes, when I'm not feeling sure of myself or confident of my next move. It's an amazing motivator and a powerful pick-me-up to pop in a video of one of your Grand Slam tournament victories and put yourself back in that championship frame of mind. Right away, it reminded me how much I used to enjoy playing, how much I used to enjoy winning. I looked at all this other footage, too, of these other girls winning their Grand Slam tournaments, and I started to think, *I can beat those girls. In my sleep, I can beat those girls.* That's what I always think when I see someone other than me or Venus holding that trophy—only here I hadn't looked at tennis in a while so it was a revelation, and it was all on the back of this uplifting encounter with this African-American girl.

She picked me up, this little girl, and she'd never know it but she set me right back down onto the career path I'd all but abandoned, because I signed up for that Cincinnati tournament the very next afternoon. Like I said, it had been nearly six months since I stepped away from the game, following that early exit in Melbourne. That's a long time to be away from an activity, even one you used to be really, really good at. I'd dropped to a rank of 139—the lowest I'd been since I was on my way up in 1997. You know, on the way down, it was a whole other perspective. Back when I was starting out, it felt like I was going places. Now, after all that time at the top, it felt like I was nowhere.

I didn't play all that badly in Cincinnati. I actually surprised myself—I surprised a lot of people, I think. Nobody was really expecting me to do all that much, so I caught my opponents unprepared. I beat the #2 seed in the first round—Anastasia Myskina of Russia, 6–2, 6–2. To this day, I'm sure I beat her mostly on muscle memory. That, and my big serve, which never left me—thank You, God! I remember making a conscious effort to win points as efficiently as possible, because it was ridiculously hot, and I didn't think I had the stamina to play too many long rallies. (As it was, I was huffing and puffing!) That meant going for a lot of winners, at a time in my career when I might have been more patient, but I didn't think I had that luxury here, so I just pounded away at this girl. At some point, probably after I hit my first winner, I thought, *Wow, this is so great to be playing again.* And it was. The tournament organizers were so gracious, so welcoming. The fans were extremely supportive and generous. It was just such an encouraging return, in every possible way. After that first match, I pushed past two American players in the next two rounds—Bethanie Mattek and Amy Frazier, also in a straight-sets hurry. Vera Zvonareva finally knocked me out in the semifinals, in a 6–2, 6–3 trouncing that more accurately reflected the quality of my game and my level of fitness.

Thinking back on that tournament, I believe I won those first few matches on shock and awe; players were a little in *shock* to see me out there, and a little in *awe* of my past accomplishments, so I managed to sneak past them into the later rounds. It felt good to be playing again, though. Good and right and welcome. In some ways, I found, high-level tennis is like riding a bicycle. Once you climb back on, you're good to go. Only in my case, with that overall lack of fitness and those few extra pounds, together with the fact that the players on the women's tour kept getting better and better, it's like I got back onto that bicycle on a steep uphill climb. I could move the pedals, but I couldn't really get anything going just yet.

Next, I earned a wild-card berth in Los Angeles a couple weeks later, which I thought would be a good tune-up for the U.S. Open. And here again, that's just what it was, for a stretch, until an up-and-coming Serbian player named Jelena Jankovic sent me packing, 6–4, 6–3. This was before Jelena had cracked the Top 20, but she really took it to me that day, that's for sure. She didn't really have much of a serve, but she could put her stamp on a game in every other aspect, and here she ran me around pretty good.

At the Open, I had to get past what the old me, Serena 1.0, might have seen as the indignity of having to qualify for the first time in my career. The new me tried to look at it as just another hurdle I'd have to take on the way to getting my game back. And that's all it was, really—an obstacle. My rank was back in the double digits, at 91, but that was hardly worth celebrating; I was still a long way from where I wanted to be, so I had that obstacle, too.

My plan was to mess with other people's tournaments. Wasn't really any kind of strategy, but I didn't have a lot of options. I knew the seeded players tended to look past their early-round opponents, thinking they'd draw low-ranked rookies and wouldn't have to worry too much about surviving their first few matches. I knew this because that used to be how I approached my early-round opponents. I took them for granted. Here at the U.S. Open, I knew these top players wouldn't be thrilled to face me in the first or second round, so I tried to play that to my advantage. And that worked well enough, taking me through the first three rounds with straight-sets victories over Lourdes Dominguez-Lino, Daniela Hantuchova, and a rising star named Ana Ivanovic, all in straight sets.

It was in Round 16, though, that I needed to ratchet up my game, and I'm afraid I fell woefully short. I was up against the top-ranked Amelie Mauresmo of France. We'd faced each other a bunch of times, going back to 1999, and she'd beaten me only once—in Rome, in 2003, at the end of my great run. Now, things were a little different. Amelie was the same dangerous player—big and strong and smart—and she'd been playing great tennis. Me, I was a wild card, in every sense of the term. No one knew what to expect from me, least of all myself. I'm sure Amelie wasn't too terribly happy about running into me so early in the tournament, but at the same time I wasn't too terribly happy about running into her, so in this one respect at least we were dead even.

She ended up beating me, but I made her sweat. I took the middle set 6–0, and that's always a powerful calling card, when you can break a top player three times in a single set and beat her 6–0. When you're coming back from nowhere at all, you take your accomplishments where you can find them, and here I took this one and held it close.

I figured I'd need it before long.

That first trip to Africa led directly to a career turnaround—another Godsend, I've come to believe. A lot of people bring back souvenirs when they travel: crafts, trinkets, art, clothes . . . Me, I brought back a renewed sense of purpose and a freshly charged personal battery. Unfortunately, I also brought back a few extra pounds—which, also unfortunately, I added to the few extra I'd started carrying during my long layoff.

The tennis press was only too happy to point this out when I turned up in Melbourne in January 2007 to prepare for the Australian Open. I went first to Hobart, Australia, to play in a tune-up tournament. The idea was to get another couple matches under my belt before the Open and to get my body clock adjusted to the sick time difference. I wasn't alone in this, of course. A lot of players spend some extra time Down Under ahead of the Australian Open to acclimate and get settled, especially because the tournament sits at the front end of the tour season and there's not a whole lot going on other than a couple of tune-up tournaments on the continent. It makes sense to settle in there and complete your off-season training regimen at some local facility so you can hit the ground running once the Open begins.

I was pumped and energized and ready to jump-start my career, but you wouldn't have known it to look at me. I was seriously out of shape and nowhere in the rankings—now back down to 94, headed into Hobart. In my head, I was thinking I was back in the mix and on top of my game, but that's not where the game was played. What counted was how I'd perform on the court. It's not like I was a little kid, tearing it up on the little-kid circuit in Los Angeles. I had to go out and get it done.

I was in a new phase in my thinking when it came to tennis.

Now that I'd rededicated myself to my game, the plan was to focus on Grand Slam tournaments. I would be all about the majors, I told myself. It used to be that every time I'd take the court, every tournament I'd play, I expected to win. Anything less than a championship was a disappointment, but that's a sure mind-set for burnout, don't you think? The better approach, I'd decided, the more *seasoned* approach, to put myself in position to do well when it counted and where it counted on the women's tour, were the majors and a couple of the Tier I events.

Beginning in 2009, the WTA tour changed how these events are classified. Now the old Tier I events are known as Premier Mandatory tournaments, and the lesser events are known as Premier 5 (or Premier) tournaments, but it all amounts to the same thing. There are big, meaningful tournaments, and small, less meaningful tournaments, and my idea was to focus on the big ones. Everything else was a tune-up. That was how I set it up in my head, and here in Hobart was one of my first opportunities to put this new approach to the test. It was a Tier IV event, so a lot of the top players wouldn't be in attendance, but the main objective was to get some more matches under my feet. The more I kept winning, the more matches I'd get to play.

Anyway, that was the plan, and it was working well enough. I won a couple of nothing-special matches to reach the quarterfinals, but then I ran into an Austrian named Sybille Bammer, who was ranked 56th at the time. What a frustrating match! I couldn't get out of my own way. I won the first set, but Sybille battled back to win 3–6, 7–5, 6–3, and I thought, *Man, this is bad, Serena. You can't even get past the quarterfinals in a Tier IV tournament.*

So much for my more seasoned mind-set, right?

I was so mad at myself for letting that match get away from me. I went out that night and started running, *Rocky*-style, just like in the movie. It's almost like I could hear that theme song in my head. The next morning, I got up before the sun and went out for another *Rocky* run. My mom was staying with me in my hotel room, but I didn't even tell her I was heading out. I just tiptoed from the room without waking her and hit the streets. I ran through all these different neighborhoods, up and down steps. I put myself through some serious paces. At one point, I found this huge park and started doing a series of sprints. I didn't tell anybody where I was going or where I'd been. I did it for me. I was tired of losing.

Who knows, maybe this was my way of catching up to the rest of the field.

We went to Melbourne that afternoon, thinking at least I'd have another day or two to settle in before the tournament. Unfortunately, there was a pile of negative energy that found me almost as soon as I unpacked my bags. The biggest drag on my positive frame of mind was the negative press I'd started to notice as soon as I hit town. I try not to pay attention to what media types are saying about me, but there's no avoiding it in Melbourne. The Australian Open is such a giant big deal when you're Down Under, it's tough to tune it out. I'd have to have been deaf and blind to miss all the criticism. The Australian press can be so mean, so petty. And so loud! The British press, too. The general consensus was that I was a big fat cow. That was what I kept hearing—in just those terms, too. All the talk in the sports pages was how the championship was a pipe dream for me because I was so out of shape. My best days on the tour were behind me, they said. I hadn't won a tournament since 2005. I was a lost soul who'd been away from the game for too long to get back to the top.

My first thought was, *Moo.*

I just had to laugh. It was either that or cry, and I wasn't about to let these people get to me, so I tried to smile and press on. On the body-image front, I'd always been comfortable as an adult with how I looked. I'm big and athletic, so I know I'm never going to have one of those rail-thin, supermodel-type bodies. I'm not some blond, blue-eyed thing. I have big boobs, and I have a big butt.

That's me—and I love it! But from time to time, like most women, I stress about my appearance. I don't want to, but I do. I know better, but I do. I look in the mirror and everything seems too big, too much, too fat . . . too, too, too! Most times, I see my reflection and what I get back is hot and sexy and all that good stuff, but I have my low moments, same as everyone else. I have my worry spots, and here in Australia, carrying all that extra weight, I had more than my share, so it wasn't as easy to laugh off these hurtful comments as it might have been at some other time in my career.

Of course, it wasn't how I looked that mattered. It was how I played, and I reminded myself that even though I'd always played to win I had to be realistic. I was coming off that long layoff, and the mean-spirited comments about my fitness and my game were rooted in truth. I *was* a little heavy—maybe twenty pounds heavier than I wanted to be at that point. And I wasn't *expecting* to win, not with the same confidence or certainty I usually brought to each tournament. Don't misunderstand, I wanted to win, but I wasn't counting on it. Rather, I was putting myself in position to win the next time out, or the time after that.

Even if I had been in top form, in top shape, the tournament draw was stacked against me. As an unseeded player, now ranked 81st in the world, I would have to face six seeded players on the way to a championship. No one had ever done that before, so there was that to consider. Actually, there was a lot to consider, and I went into my first match thinking it wasn't so easy, getting my head around this tournament. So many people were counting me out, the same way they had when I first came up.

All these negatives added up, and I remember lacing my sneakers in the players' lounge, going through all my last-minute preparations and thinking there was a lot of pressure on me to do well here. I'd meant to kind of sneak up on the tournament in a no-pressure sort of way, but that clearly hadn't happened. Of course, I was putting a lot of this pressure on myself, but some of it was external. And then, just to add insult to insult, I received an upsetting visit from a Nike representative, who told me in no uncertain terms that if I did not perform at my accustomed level the company might drop me from my sponsorship deal. This guy actually came right out and said, "You really have to do well here." In the players' lounge, right before my first match! To which I answered with something like, "Are you serious?" I couldn't believe it, that this was what this man was telling me, right when I was getting ready. So that was another distraction I really didn't need going in to a major tournament.

Understand, it's not that I shy from pressure. Throughout my career, I'd always responded well to pressure. In fact, I play some of my best tennis when I'm up against it. Plus, I was always putting pressure on myself—to be better, to do more, to win. My dad used to say, "The only pressure you feel is the pressure you put on yourself." But here it was coming at me from all sides. Here it was gaining on me.

In the back of my mind, I suppose I knew my sponsors could not have been too happy with the deals we'd made just a couple years earlier. I wasn't exactly returning big dividends for them on the court. For the past six months, I wasn't even playing. I could see how I'd put them in a difficult spot, but that didn't mean this one rep had to put it on me in just this way. At just this time. Now there was this anxiety that I was going to be dropped by my sponsors, and on top of that there was all this other anxiety that came from hearing about my weight, about my lack of focus, about really needing to have a good showing. What's a good showing? It depends. For my sponsors, for serious tennis fans, a good showing would have probably been making it to the quarterfinals, but for me, it was making it to the finals. Anything less, and I would have felt like I could have done more.

Despite all these misgivings, I didn't have too much trouble with my first-round opponent, a seeded Italian player named Mara Santangelo. I put her away, 6–2, 6–1. Then I faced a qualifier from Luxembourg named Anne Kremer, who pushed me to a tiebreaker in the first set, but I managed to power past her in straight sets anyway.

It's tricky, playing a qualifier in a major tournament, because the way it sets up is they have to be playing great tennis just to earn a spot in the draw. Anne Kremer had already won three qualifying matches before the main draw got underway, and she'd won her first-round match as well. She was clearly on a roll, playing like she had nothing to lose and everything to prove. That was my approach, too, only she was fitter, faster, and hungrier. That's what I was up against in that first set.

The welcome news here is that it didn't seem like the extra weight I was carrying would get in my way. No, I wasn't as quick on my feet as I usually was, but I was quick enough. And I wasn't fatigued. This last was key. That second-rounder was a difficult match, but I came out of it feeling fresh and strong. I'd been worried how I would hold up in a long, grueling battle, and here I'd passed my first test, so that was a good sign.

The one bad sign was a blister that very quickly developed on my foot. I hadn't seen that one coming, but I should have. See, one of the fallouts from all that time away from the game was that my feet weren't hard and calloused like they usually are when I'm on the court every day. This could have been a major problem, but thankfully my mom knew just what to do. It was such a nasty, massive blister, it's a wonder I played through it, but somehow I'd get to the end of each match and then start walking on my heels, so I wouldn't make it worse. It became a pattern for the balance of the tournament. I looked like a creature from *Night of the Living Dead* the way I shuffle-walked off the court. At first, one of the trainers tried to cut it open and drain it, but that only made it worse, so my mom took over. She put some zinc on it to dry it out, but that wasn't so effective. The only relief came when she had me soak my foot each night in a bucket of superhot water, which she filled with Epsom salts. It was excruciatingly painful, but I told myself it was just another hurdle to get past. Then she'd wrap it with these special pads, and I'd try to put it out of my mind until the next round was over.

My third-round match was pivotal. I was up against Nadia

Petrova, the #5 seed. As good fortune would have it, I owned a career 6-1 record against the Russian, including victories in our previous two meetings, but Petrova took the first set while I wasn't really paying attention. My blister was giving me some trouble, but that wasn't it. I was also fighting off a nasty cold. Every night, I'd stand over the stove, my face pressed down over a huge pot of boiling water. I hadn't been tested by a player of Petrova's ability in a good long while, and I wasn't exactly answering the call.

I'd talked to V before the match, and she reminded me to just look at the ball. "It's simple," Venus had said. "Just look at the ball, and it'll come, it'll come."

From the first point, I tried to do just what Venus said. I was looking at the ball, and looking at the ball, but it wasn't coming. I felt good. I felt strong, focused, whatever. But it still wasn't coming. That was why I lost the first set. In the second set, it still wasn't coming. I checked the scoreboard and realized I was two points from losing the match. I kept hearing Venus in my head telling me to just look at the ball, telling me it would come. And then, finally, it did. It's like the skies parted and there it was. There was this one point when I let out this unbelievable grunt. It was almost primal. You could hear it outside the stadium, someone told me later. It was just a release, for all that pressure I was feeling from the start of the tournament. The pressure I put on myself. The pressure from my sponsors, spoken and unspoken. The pressure from being away from the game for all this time. And it came. Just like Venus said it would. Everything came together after that.

I was still down a set, still two points from losing the match, but I knew it was mine.

The funny thing is, that blister gave me trouble the rest of the way—all the way to the finals. All the way past Jelena Jankovic, Shahar Peer, Nicole Vaidisova. Good players. Strong players. Players who certainly didn't expect an overweight, out-of-shape, has-been champion like me to give them a game. After each match, I'd limp into the locker room on the outer sides of my feet. People couldn't understand how I could walk, let alone compete against all these top players. But I hung in there. And I felt a little better about my chances each round.

By the time Maria Sharapova turned up as my opponent in the finals, I would not be denied. I went from thinking I just wanted to play well and get my footing, to thinking I wanted to play deep into the tournament to quiet my critics and sponsors, to thinking I could win this thing. Absolutely, I could win this thing. My cold was finally gone. And, for the first time since that second-round match against the qualifier, I wasn't feeling any pain in my foot. The blister was gone, too, and the raw baby skin at the bottom of my feet had finally had a chance to toughen up, so I was feeling like I could run all over the court if I had to—and against the top-seeded Sharapova, I told myself, I just might have to.

But it was more than just being pain free. It was more than finding my rhythm on the court and settling in to a comfortable groove. It was more than hearing Tracy Austin dismiss my chances on television by suggesting that I'd had a great tournament but my ride was over. She actually came right out and said in her tournament analysis that Maria would have no problem with me once the match got underway. I heard that and thought it was such a mean, unnecessary thing to say. After everything I'd been through. Being called fat in the press. Being asked before every match why I was so out of shape. Being told by my sponsors that they were going to cut me loose if I didn't perform. Being forced to defend my time away from the game. And on and on.

But that wasn't it. Okay, so maybe that was some of it, but not all of it. The real push came from taking all those negatives and mashing them together into a great big positive. I put it in my head that I would not be beaten down. By my critics. By my peers. By my sponsors. By my opponents. Together, it became my silent fuel, to power me through these next paces. I would not be dismissed.

I would dominate poor Maria Sharapova—and, indeed, that's just how it played out, with me on top by the convincing score of 6–1, 6–2. I would prove everyone wrong, and in so doing I would prove something to myself. That I was back where I belonged, playing tennis at a high level, fighting for Grand Slam tournament titles, making my mark. I was determined to win, but not for those jerks at the newspaper who called me a cow. Not for all the sportswriters who said I had no shot. Not for the sponsors who wanted nothing to do with me. No, I would do it for me. For the first time in my career, it hit me: *that's* why I was playing, after all.

Breathe. Remember, there are so many more important things.
This is so small.

—MATCH BOOK ENTRY

THIRTEEN

Play On, Serena!

Oh. My. Goodness. Winning the Australian Open like that, coming up from such a low ranking, being counted out before the tournament even started, dealing with all that extra weight and the negative press and the not-so-subtle pressures from my sponsors, struggling the whole way . . . it was so completely awesome, to overcome all of that. I didn't play my best tennis, not even close, but I played well enough in each round to get to the next round, and sometimes that's all you need, right?

Each time out, I got a little better, a little stronger, and a little more confident, so that by the final round, against Sharapova, I was at last in high gear. I was making my shots, dictating the pace. My fitness wasn't where I wanted it to be, especially compared to Sharapova, who was probably in top shape, so I tried to serve a little bigger and shorten points wherever I could. Happily, that worked out to the good. I even took the time during a couple changeovers to think, *Hey, it's been awhile, but it's good to be back.* And it was. Believe me, winning the whole thing was such an unexpected turn, but it wasn't as important to me just then as being back in the mix—and *that*, to me, was the best part of my surprising performance in Melbourne. It set me up for the next phase of my career. It was as if I was born again as a player, like I'd put myself in position once again to compete. No, I didn't play again for a couple months, until Miami in April, and after beating Justine Henin in the finals there, I couldn't get past the quarterfinals until I got to the finals at Moscow in October, where I lost to Elena Dementieva. But I was back in the Top 10, back in the discussion. Back in the game.

Understand, nothing came easy the whole rest of that year, but I told myself that was okay. This wasn't just an inner pep talk or a way to ease past a disappointment. It was really and truly okay. I knew the ultimate victory would come in the battle itself, and that by powering through to the other side of my long layoff I would be a champion once more. I didn't just *tell* myself these things; I believed them. This was never more apparent to me than in an impossibly difficult match against Daniela Hantuchova of Slovakia, in the Round of 16 at Wimbledon that summer. We'd played each other six times before, and the only time she'd ever beaten me was in 2006, in Melbourne, when I had that low, despairing moment and I *so* didn't want to be on that court. Other than that, though, I'd handled her pretty well. She's so tall—not quite as tall as Venus, but she hits the ball hard, behind a big, big serve. Plus, she's so pretty!

I'd been playing well early in the tournament that year, against some middle-of-the-pack-type players, but I was having some trouble with my left thumb. You wouldn't think a left thumb injury would be much of a bother to a right-handed player—but it affected my backhand, of course. It affected my toss on serve. Also my balance and rhythm. My game felt a whole lot less fluid to me, just because of that injury to my thumb.

There was a lot of rainfall that year, even for Wimbledon. The match was barely underway, 1–1 in the first set, when a storm came through and we had to suspend play. They're really quick to cover the court over there because it's on grass, of course, and you can't really play through a steady drizzle the way you might on a hard surface, so these kinds of delays come with the territory at Wimbledon. You learn to expect them, and to deal with them, and to shrug them off. But then, when we came back, we went through the same five-minute warm-up we take before the start of each match, and by the time we were ready to resume the skies opened up again. It was so frustrating! Not just for me, of course, but for Daniela as well. It can really mess with your routine, when that happens back-to-back. You don't know when or how much to eat, when or how much to drink, when or how much to stretch. You're all out of sorts. Before a match, there's a whole set of paces I put myself through, and here I had to hit restart on those paces not just once, after the first rain delay, but twice—and we didn't even start playing again that second time.

I tried to keep focused during the two delays, and to keep hydrating, but it was tough, not knowing when we'd get back underway. When we finally did, I came out strong. Daniela had held her serve in the first game of the match on four straight points, and here I answered in her second service game with four straight points of my own. I went up 0–40 with a pretty drive-volley on an approach to the net. Daniela seemed so stunned by this sudden turnabout that she double-faulted on the next point to give me the first break of the match.

I broke through in her next service game as well, also on a double fault, to end it, and once I had that double-break I started to feel untouchable. It's not that I was playing such a mighty brand of tennis, or that Daniela was struggling so mightily on her side, but it was a combination of the two. All during those two breaks, I kept telling myself the stoppage would work to my advantage. I kept telling myself and telling myself until finally I believed it. Of course, there's no reason the downtime should have worked in my favor, because we were each equally disadvantaged and inconvenienced, but I kept giving it this positive spin.

It was here with that double-break in hand that I went on a tidy run of love service games. I didn't give up a point in my next three service games, and by that time I was up a set (6–2) and we were on serve at 1–2 in the second. Already, I'd put the match in the win column—a dangerous mind game because so much can go wrong, which was what nearly happened here. I don't mean to come across as arrogant or full of myself, but it really felt like Daniela couldn't stay with me that day. My serve was working, my ground strokes were sharp, and I guess I let my head run away from me a little out there on the court.

Just then, my game started to follow. Daniela broke through to take a 3–1 lead in the second set. The turning point of the game was a terrific passing shot by Daniela at 15–30, when I approached the net and couldn't quite put the ball where I wanted it on my return. With that one shot, she poked some serious holes in my confidence. It was just one shot, and it doesn't seem like much in the retelling, but it's everything when you're out on the court. Well, maybe not *everything* . . . but it's meaningful, that's for sure. I still had a commanding lead. It still felt to me like I was in control. Only now I wasn't so sure.

Daniela kept the pressure on with a love service game of her own to go up 4–1, finishing it off with an ace. That's always one of my favorite psych-out moves on the court, to end one of my service games with a big serve on our way to a changeover, because then you get to start walking toward the umpire's chair while your opponent is still lunging for your serve. I think it messes with their head, to see you walking off in triumph like that while they're still a little bit on their heels—and here Daniela put me in just that spot. A part of me thought, *Hey, that's my move!* But then another part thought, *Okay, Serena. She's not going away so easily. Better get it into gear.*

I held serve (love, again!), but Daniela pushed back in the very next game—the key game in the match, to that point. I thought I'd have an opportunity to break and put the set back on serve. The first point of the game was a huge rally, and it felt to me like I was dictating the point. I had the chance to take one of Daniela's returns in the air and put the point away, but I played it off the bounce instead. To this day I don't know why, because it would have really marked this game for me, and as it turned out this would be my last real shot for the next while, but instead the rally went back to neutral and I ended up losing the point on an unforced error into the net. I didn't have time to get down on myself, though, because on the next point Daniela gave the momentum right back, when she mistimed a net cord shot and went long on her return.

Next, at 15-all, Daniela caught me with a neat touch when I was behind the baseline, and after that things seemed to bounce back in her direction.

At 30–15, I hit the net cord again, and Daniela was barely able to flick the ball over on her approach, leaving me with the entire court behind her, but I missed way wide with my lob. I was furious with myself, because I'd let such an easy chance get away. Like all great players, Daniela put the game away after that, icing it with another ace as she walked off for the changeover.

That's where the trouble began. All day long, after the second rain delay, the winds had been kicking up pretty fierce. They were swirling, gusting down on that court. My dress was flapping up during that whole match, like I was Marilyn Monroe standing over an air vent. And here, perhaps as a result of those chilling winds, I started to feel like I was cramping in my left calf. If you're an athlete, you'll know what I'm talking about when I say it felt like my calf muscles were about to go into spasm. You're on this strange precipice, where if you step the wrong way or make one wrong, sudden move, you just *know* the pain that's waiting for you on that wrong side. I was still okay, still able to play, but I could feel it coming, and I have to think now it had to do with the cold and the fact that those earlier layoffs had messed with my hydration in some way. I'd timed my fluid intake for a match that should have been over hours ago, and here I was still fighting it out in these wet, cold conditions, so maybe that explained it.

So what did I do? I called for a trainer. I told the umpire I was about to cramp, and asked for a trainer on the next changeover. I thought I could certainly make it through the next couple games, but now I had to play with a certain urgency—to put the game away before I started to spasm. I set it up in my head like a race against my own body, and as soon as I started to think in this way I wanted that last game back, because it would have put me in position to take the second set and end the match quickly.

The sense-of-urgency thing worked, because I came out like a demon. I hit this great backhand passing shot down the alley for the first point of my next service game, and it was such a killer shot I gave myself a little fist pump at the end of it, together with one of my trademark rallying cries: "Come on!"

I was so fired up!

It ended up another love service game, and on Daniela's serve I really started to push her around. At 0–15, I made a strong return on a second serve to go up 0–30, and I followed that with a big point at net to go up three break points, but I finished her off on the very next point and put us back on serve.

The trainer met me at the changeover, and I told her I felt a spasm coming on. I was concerned, but I wasn't frantic with worry or anything. It was just something to deal with, a trouble spot to get past. We talked for a bit, but there really wasn't anything she could do for me. I asked for some salt tablets, not fully realizing that nobody really believed in salt tablets anymore as a way to guard against cramping, but it was such an unusual spot because it had hardly ever happened to me, so I didn't really know the first thing about how to treat it. Together, we decided that the thing to do was for me to keep playing, and to hope that I could somehow hold off the cramps until the match was over and I could massage the area and get proper treatment. So I came out with the same hurry-up mind-set as before, thinking I'd do well to push ahead. That meant another love service game, to bring us to 5–5 in the second set, and here I started to think, *Okay, Serena. Break her here and you can serve for the match.*

That was the plan—but it didn't exactly work out that way.

The wind seemed to pick up as Daniela started to serve. She actually made a bad toss or two because of the ripping winds, and right after the third point of the game, with Daniela up 30–15, I started to spasm. I took a wrong step in just the wrong way at just the wrong moment, and I knotted up like you wouldn't believe. The first thing I did was bang the back of my calf a few times with my racquet, thinking this would help, but the next thing I knew I was down on that grass court, writhing and grimacing and screaming in pain.

Oh, I was in such agony!

I don't remember too much after that, but the trainer came out, and the umpire, and maybe another few people. Again, if you've ever experienced one of these spasms, you'll know what it's like—I wouldn't wish it on anybody! The pain was so excruciating, so intense, and underneath you start to think there's something you should be able to do to get some immediate relief, except of course there's nothing to do but ride it out and stretch it out and work it through with some deep massage. That, and time—only when you're in the middle of a match at Wimbledon you don't really have any time.

The way it works is, once the trainer makes an assessment of your injury you have three minutes to treat it before you have to resume play. Three minutes! That's nothing, but those are the rules on the tour. They're pretty clear-cut. If you're not ready to go after three minutes, you're done. It used to be that if the trainer even touched you during the run of play, without a proper time-out being granted by the officials, they could disqualify you just for that, but now they had this three-minute rule in place. I think I probably knew the rule at the time, but I wasn't exactly aware of it. All I could really think about was getting that spasm to pass. I wasn't even thinking about the match. The trainer was working on me by this point, so the clock was ticking. The good news was I started to feel a little relief. Not a lot, but some. I could stretch and lean a certain way and the pain would be manageable.

Just then, this giant storm cloud appeared over the stadium, and I realized that the only way I could get through this match was with another rain delay. Then I could get a proper massage, and take the time I needed for the spasm to fully pass, and even though the muscle would be sore and tender I could probably play on it. The longer the delay, the more time I'd have to recover, so as I was lying there I started praying for rain. Buckets and buckets of rain. I never like to pray to my God, Jehovah, for mundane-type things, like a competitive edge in a tennis match or a sudden rainstorm to put me back in the game. At least, I don't like to pray this way *for real*. But here I prayed in a wishing kind of way. I prayed and prayed. I wished and wished.

It would be storybook and fairy-tale to be able to write that the clouds burst at just that moment, and that the rains washed over me in sweet relief because I knew the match would now be suspended, but that's not exactly what happened. What happened, exactly, was nothing. The skies darkened, but that was about it, and when my three minutes were up the trainers and officials cleared the court and left me standing behind the baseline. I felt like a wounded warrior out there. I couldn't move. I could barely put pressure on my left foot.

I don't think I've ever felt so alone, so vulnerable.

Mercifully, I had the crowd behind me. My parents were standing in the players' box. Venus was there, too. Everyone was trying to be so supportive, so encouraging. Even Daniela Hantuchova, to her great credit, came over while I was down and struggling and wanted to let me know she was pulling for me. (I thought that was *really* nice of her!) All of that helped, but it was one of those times where nothing could have *really* helped. It was an impossible moment.

You know, it's funny, but all during that injury time-out it never once occurred to me to forfeit the match. It's not that I was trying to be tough, or that I was so determined to play through this agonizing pain. It's just that I didn't give quitting a thought. It wasn't an option, perhaps because when I step out on that court for a match I'm conditioned to stay there until the match is done. Win or lose, I mean to see it through, and that was my attitude here. Shutting it down just wasn't something I thought about, at just that moment. Not because I was particularly brave, or because I had any kind of superhuman ability to play through pain, but because it's what you do. You play on.

And so I played on. I stood in there while Daniela served out the game. I couldn't even move toward her next serve, which I guess went down as an ace, and at 40–15 she must have taken pity on me because she served it right at me, and all I could do was swat at the ball and watch it float weakly to the net.

I hobbled to the chair on the changeover and here the trainer was allowed to work on me briefly—as long as she did so in the time normally allotted on a change. Here, it was just enough time for another quick massage, and for her to wrap my calf with prewrap and tape; heck, she was barely done with her tape job when the umpire was motioning for me to hurry up and take my position, so they don't really cut you *any* slack.

Tour rules are pretty specific about this. After those initial three minutes of treatment, you're allowed two additional treatments for the same injury, as long as those treatments occur during a change-over. If there's a subsequent, unrelated injury, you can start the process over again, but for this one spasm I could get only one more visit from the trainer after this one.

I shuffled back out to the court thinking, *Serena, what are you going to do?* Again, quitting wasn't even an option, so it was just about sucking it up and playing on—only I knew I couldn't push off on my left leg with any kind of authority, so I wondered how I would even serve. Then, as I got into position, I felt a raindrop. Just one drop. And then another. I thought, *Come on, rain! Please, please, please!*

But the rain held off and sure enough, down 5–6, my first serve had absolutely nothing on it—although by some miracle Daniela returned it long, so I was up 15–0. Then I double-faulted into the ad court, but looking back I believe these two missed serves helped me figure a way to compensate and shift my weight so that I could get at least a little power on my serve. The adjustment allowed me to surprise Daniela on the next point with a big serve that she probably wasn't expecting, putting me up 30–15, and after that I took the next point, too, with a silly little drop-shot winner. I figured since I couldn't move, I'd use some touch to put a quick end to the point—and it worked!

Next, I hit another ball weakly into the net, so at 40–30 I thought another big serve might catch Daniela off guard. At the same time, I had a conflicting thought: I realized there was just no way I could expect to win a tiebreaker, so it occurred to me that maybe a better strategy would be to give up this game for lost and head directly to the third set. Then I thought maybe this wasn't such a good idea, either. Maybe the tiebreaker would stretch the clock in my favor, and even if I had no chance to win it would give the muscle more time to heal, and it might even give the weather more chance to do its thing and start raining.

There were all these thoughts rattling around in my head, at a time when I really wasn't thinking clearly to begin with, so I just set them all aside and went for it. I limped to the line and unleashed my eighth ace of the match, putting us at 6–6 in games and headed for that tiebreaker.

I thought, *Okay, Serena. That settles that. It's not in you to even try to lose a game, even if it might be your only shot at winning the match.*

Predictably, I dug myself a quick hole, giving away the first three points of the tiebreaker on two unforced errors and a double fault, and with Daniela serving up 3–0 I started to think I was doomed. By this point, the spasm had nearly dissipated, but my left calf was still ridiculously tender and sore. (Man, it hurts just writing about it!) I was still in a kind of midlevel agony. Most significant, I couldn't push off on my left leg, and I certainly couldn't run.

Down 0–4 in the tiebreaker, I got a bit lucky. I caught the net on a weak return of serve, and the ball deflected off in a funny way to give me the point. Then, with the serve back on my racquet, I an-

swered Daniela's return with an odd little slice that she misjudged
and hit wide.

Now I was down 2–4, and it was time for a much bigger break:
rain. Finally. And not just a drop or a drizzle but a real downpour.
The buckets and buckets I'd been praying for. I closed my eyes and
tilted my head toward the sky, and for the first time since I went
down with that spasm I saw a way through. I thought, *Somebody up
there likes me.*

At just that moment, the rain seemed heaven-sent. I could have
cried. In fact, I did—only they were tears of anguish mixed up with
tears of relief.

I got the treatment I needed during the delay, and I gradually
began to feel better, but it would be days before I could work those
muscles like they were at full strength. I still couldn't move all that
well, but at least I could move, and I knew that as I warmed up and
started playing again I might move even better. Time was now my
not-so-secret weapon. Before, when I first went down, the clock was
against me, but now I knew the longer it ticked the better off I'd be.
I knew that every additional minute would be precious to me and
my recovery, and all during our five-minute warm-up—our fourth
of the day—I worried how my body would respond once I really had
to test it, if I'd gathered enough of those precious minutes to allow
me to play at close to full strength.

I ended up losing that second-set tiebreaker—I'd dug myself too
deep a hole!—but that long delay put me back in the match. We
started the third set on my serve, and I was tentative at the outset. I
gave away the first two points because I didn't fully trust my left leg
just yet, but then I made a few adjustments and launched my fastest
serve of the match for an ace. I followed that with another ace (on
a second serve!), to bring the game to 30–30, and then I took the
next two points behind two more big serves.

Daniela could see I couldn't cover the court that well, and of
course she looked to take advantage. I would have done the same
thing. This was a competition, after all. Running at anything close

to full speed just wasn't about to happen for me, so Daniela moved me around a bit in this game and won it easily. She moved me around so much, I fell on my thumb! I tried to shake it off, but it started to bother me more and more as the match went on. I nearly gave Daniela a break in my next service game, missing an easy overhead and hitting another ball into the net. At one point, at 40–30, I thought I had the game won with an apparent ace, but as I started my triumphant walk-off to the chair Daniela signaled for a challenge, and the call was overturned. I'll tell you, it really knocked the air out of me to lose a close call like that, and I ended up double-faulting and letting the game slip to deuce. I was so mad at myself I slammed my racquet to the court in disgust, but then I took the next two points to hold serve.

From there we took turns holding, but in the back-and-forth I got a little stronger, a little more sure of myself on my feet. Those precious minutes started to pile up. I was moving better and better with each point, and whatever edge Daniela Hantuchova might have had after my injury had by now pretty much fallen away. If anything, it had tilted back to me, simply because she hadn't taken full advantage of the opening she'd received, and now that it was closing up on her it seemed she was chasing it, and chasing it, and finding it more and more out of reach.

At 3–2, I found an unlikely source of motivation when I asked to use the bathroom. I don't mean to be indelicate or less than lady-like, but I really, really had to pee! I'd taken in so many fluids by this point, I was about to burst, but the umpire wouldn't give me permission to leave the court. I couldn't understand it, and we argued about it for a while, and after a full minute or two of discussion I threw up my hands and said, "I could have been back already!"

As it happened, my bladder gave me a whole new sense of urgency, and I broke Daniela's serve in the very next game to go up 4–2, and that played out as just the opening I needed. I won the next two games, in convincing fashion, and at the end of the match I was reduced to tears yet again. It was such a purposeful, emotional moment for me. For my whole family, too. Even the fans, I heard later, were moved by the experience of watching that match. Everyone was crying and hugging each other and letting out these great big sighs of relief that you could practically hear, and I just let all that emotion rain down on me and fill me with a renewed sense of spirit and certainty.

I'd been good and gone for a good long while, but now I was good and back and raring to go—all on the shoulders of this unlikely, uplifting fourth-round match at Wimbledon. Absolutely, that win in Australia had set me right, but in so many ways it was this emotional win over Daniela Hantuchova that lit the fire that would take me the rest of the way.

Unfortunately, wherever the rest of the way would take me, I had to make a couple more detours before finding it. Isn't that how it goes, more times than not? You power past some adversity or other, and then you hit some brand-new but related adversity on the other side—only this time you're better prepared for it. Even if the adversity gets the better of you on the follow-up, you're still in good shape for the next bad patch. And the one after that.

That's kind of what happened to me here. I couldn't get past the top-ranked Justine Henin in the quarterfinals of that Wimbledon tournament, just as I hadn't been able to get past her in the quarters at the 2007 French Open, and as I wouldn't be able to get past her in the quarters two months later at the 2007 U.S. Open. She had my measure that year—and here at the All England Tennis Club in London she also had me reeling. My left calf was still impossibly sore after my marathon ordeal against Hantuchova. Against a top player like Henin, I simply couldn't keep up. On top of that, my left thumb started to give me more and more trouble as the match progressed, and I just didn't have it.

Still, I would not be deflated by these losses, and I look back and count that fourth-round match at Wimbledon as a great and telling and pivotal moment—one of the most important matches of my career. It was me at a real crisis point, powering through. Yes, the rest of the year was essentially a bust, but there was no letdown. Even when I struggled, there was no letdown. How could there be a letdown, when you were down as low as I had been to start the season? When you pick yourself up from the grass at Wimbledon (literally!) and find a way to win through the most terrible pain you've ever known?

And so I armed myself with all these fortifying, emboldening experiences from 2007, and I went into 2008 determined to finish what I'd started the year before, and even though I was bounced in the quarters in Melbourne by Jelena Jankovic, I got off to a solid start. I won my next three tournaments—a Tier II event in Bangalore, India, followed by Tier I championships in Miami and Charleston—and by the time the spring and summer Slam events turned up on the calendar I was once again positioned as a player to watch.

It's like I was back on the tennis map, all because of that surprising win in Australia the year before and that gritty, rain-delayed match at Wimbledon.

I was Serena Williams. Again. At last. And I would not be denied. I might beat myself from time to time, and I might run into a brick wall every here and there, but I would be a force, here on in.

As it turned out, Venus would be on the court with me for three of my highlight moments that year. She beat me in the finals at Wimbledon, in a match that quickly became legendary in tennis circles. Really, it was such a tremendous fight, on both sides, although to be honest I wasn't the most gracious loser in the world right after Venus won. See, I'd gotten off to a breakout start in that match, and I'd been having such a breakout season, that I guess I didn't have the strength of character to shoulder the loss the way I normally might. And yet, if a lowlight can stand as a highlight, this one certainly ranks. It was the first major disappointment of this second phase of my career, and at first I don't think I handled it too well (I sulked and grimaced all through the trophy ceremony at center court!), but I drew strength from it just the same. It was the first real brick wall of the season, but I came away determined to bounce off of it and dust myself off and play on.

Together, Venus and I reached another Wimbledon final that year—in women's doubles, beating Lisa Raymond of the United States and Samantha Stosur of Australia in the finals. After such a disappointing loss in the singles final, it was a little like earning the cherry on top but missing out on the ice cream sundae, but over time I was okay with just the cherry. A sweet victory is just that— sweet! There's no sense turning it bittersweet when you don't have to, right?

Anyway, Lisa had been a top doubles player for years and years, so it was always an especially satisfying win when we had to go through her, and here it put us in a good spot heading into the women's doubles event in the 2008 Olympics, in Beijing. We'd won a gold medal in doubles in 2000, and even after all this time on the tour that still stood out as one of the proudest, most fulfilling moments of our careers, so we really wanted to have a strong showing. We went in as the #2 seed, and our hope was to dominate all the way through. We stumbled a little out of the gate, though, losing the opening set of our first-round match to a Czech team before setting things right. We ended up losing another set, to another team of sisters—Alona and Kateryna Bondarenko, of Ukraine—but we got past them 4–6, 6–4, 6–1 to earn a spot in the finals against Anabel Medina Garrigues and Virginia Ruano Pascual of Spain.

It's a tremendous honor to represent your country in the Olympics—and when you do so alongside your sister, it's off the charts! Here it was even more tremendous than it had been in 2000. In the intervening years, the United States had undergone a kind of transformation on the world stage. We went from being an admired superpower to this much-maligned, much-resented nation all around the globe. You could hear it on the court, with fans so quick to boo or to judge just because we were Americans, so we were doubly determined to do well, and we came out like a firestorm against that Spanish team. We played unbelievably well, winning 6–2, 6–0, and we came away feeling so unbelievably proud and patriotic that I now place that gold medal right up there with any of my Grand Slam tournament wins. It's certainly my biggest doubles title, and it's side-by-side with all those others.

The final Venus-accompanied highlight of 2008, of course, was our quarterfinal showdown under the lights at the U.S. Open. It was such a tense, gripping match. It felt like I had my back to the wall the entire time. Venus was just relentless that night! But I hung in there. I look back and think, *Good for me! And good for Venus!* Somehow, I found a way to hold off ten set points and earn a 7–6 (6), 7–6 (7) win in a match that was delayed by more than an hour to start and took nearly two and a half hours to complete. It was exhausting and exhilarating, all at the same time.

I was heartbroken for Venus, though. I really was. It's one of the only times we've gone head-to-head where I felt badly for her afterward, because she played so well. She certainly played well enough to win—but then, I did, too. After she had me down that first break in the first set, I scrambled back. Then she had me 5–3, but I scrambled back again and pushed the first set to a tiebreaker.

Venus said later that it felt like she was in control of the entire match, and I can see her view. I mean, she *was* in control, but she couldn't put me away. I was like the Energizer Bunny on the other side of the net: I just kept going and going. She certainly did dictate most of the points, but then she should know better than anybody else that I don't like to be told what to do.

She had me 5–3 in the second set, too, but I wouldn't go away. Up 40–0! On her serve! But I fought off all those set points and managed to break. She had another set point when I was serving at 5–6, but I held to force the tiebreaker.

The point of the match? That's hard to say, there were so many of them, but a lot of people I talk to mention this one rally from the second tiebreaker. Venus was up 4–2. Momentum seemed to have tilted in her favor, but I had that first-set cushion to fall back on, so she was the one fighting for her tournament life. Me, I was just fighting. Here, down 4–2, I attempted a forehand passing shot that I couldn't power past Venus's long arms, and she managed to put a volley deep into the corner. I took off for it a beat or two before she played it (one of the advantages of knowing your opponent's game!), and managed to run it down and return a lob that I thought (hoped!) would clear Venus's reach, but I was just short, and she was positioned to put the point away. But here, too, I guessed correctly as Venus went into her overhead, and I fought off her smash, only to send the ball right back to her sweet spot and set her up for a put-away volley.

It was one of those points they play over and over again on ESPN, it was so incredible. The fans just went crazy, and I had to step back and catch my breath—because that last point really did take my breath away, in every respect.

Venus won the next point, which earned her another three set points—but I fought those off, too. That was the story of the match. Venus kept pushing and I kept pushing back, and at some point I pushed back hard enough so that she was the one on her heels. She missed a lot of shots, and I know she was frustrated, but it wasn't like she handed me the match with all those errors. No way. It's not even like they were errors, not really. I just kept scraping and scrapping and scratching my way through these points, running down every shot, prolonging the points just enough so that Venus was forced to be too fine with her returns. I gave her no choice. I was getting to everything deep, so she had to go a little deeper. I was getting to everything wide, so she had to go a little wider.

In the end, she just ran out of court.

When you win a match like that against your big sister, it's an enormous responsibility, because now it's on you to keep it going and win the whole thing for the both of you. Venus had been playing so well that I knew she'd have gone on to win the championship if I hadn't knocked her from contention, so now I had to win.

I didn't need any additional incentive, but here it was. There was also the carrot of returning to the number one spot in the rankings if I got past Dinara Safina in the semifinals—which I did, behind a 6–3, 6–2 effort. And past Jelena Jankovic in the final—which I also did, 6–4, 7–5.

People had been talking about that number one ranking all week long, once top-ranked Ana Ivanovic of Serbia was knocked out in the second round by Julie Coin of France. The talk was that the number one spot was up for grabs if any of the remaining top seeds managed to win, and this was very much on my mind as I stood at the net, shaking Jelena's hand right after the match. My first and foremost thought was for this particular championship, of course, because that had been my goal all along and the only result that was in my direct control, but I can't lie and suggest I was unaware of what it meant in the rankings.

I knew. Believe me, I knew.

When I held that trophy high in the night sky, I knew full well that I was doing so as the top-ranked player in women's tennis. I knew it had been five years and one month since I was in that spot—the longest gap, I later learned, between number one stints for any player in tennis history, male or female. I knew it felt good. Really, really good. And I knew I didn't want to let that feeling slip any time soon.

A footnote: it had been so long since I'd been in the top spot I'd nearly forgotten what it was like up there. Mostly, it's refreshing and rewarding. Validating, too. It's also fleeting, I'm afraid. Unfortunately, I didn't quite get the job done in my very next tournament and was dropped to the number three spot after only a couple weeks. All I could do was shrug my shoulders and think, *Oh, well* . . . because I've realized after all this time in the game that sometimes this is how you have to play it. You give it your all, and then you give it some more, and despite every ounce of sweat and effort you still might come up short, and when that happens the thing to do is set it aside and come at it even harder. Figure out what went wrong, and what you can fix, and get on it. Then, when you've done everything you can and still come up short, step back and take some small satisfaction in noting that the two girls now ahead of you in the rankings have never won a Grand Slam.

And play on.

Be positive. Have only positivity going through your body. Be the best. Being the best starts by acting like U R the best. Believing U R the best. Becoming the best. Believe. Become. Serena Williams. 8x Grand Slam winner. Only U! Stay confident. U R a winner. Watch balls. Relax. Have fun. God blesses those who work hard. God blesses U, so work hard. Work, work, work. Don't crush every ball. Don't put pressure on yourself. Don't make mistakes. U R younger sister, so pressure is on V. Toss high on serve. Don't let ball drop. Hit behind her. She likes your pace. Try high balls. Let it flow.

—MATCH BOOK ENTRY

FOURTEEN

U.S. Open, 2008— My Tournament Journal

When we were little, Daddy got us in the good habit of writing down our thoughts, our hopes, our plans. Every week, he'd find some special time with each of us, and he'd gently remind us to set down on paper what we wanted to accomplish in the days ahead.

"Meek," he'd say, when it was my turn. "Have you written down your goals today?"

We didn't have to write about tennis. We could write about school, or Kingdom Hall, or dance class, or some problem we'd heard on the news. It was wide open. All we had to do was think of something and then write about it. When my older sisters drifted away from the game, Daddy kept after them to continue setting down their goals, because he thought it was a useful enterprise. And it surely was, though it sometimes felt like a never-ending homework assignment. It still feels that way sometimes, but I keep at it. Anyway, I try. I've kept a journal, in fits and starts, for as long as I can remember. There's room in there for match analysis and insights, along with personal goals and reflections. Whatever pops into my head at the time, and makes its way onto the page. The same rules applied to Daddy's marching orders when I was a kid: think of something and then write about it.

Over the years, I've been back and forth between thinking of this keeping a journal as a burden and an opportunity, but even when I approached it like a chore I recognized the value in the exercise. Writing can be an extremely effective tool for harnessing your energies and keeping your focus, and eventually I didn't need Daddy's gentle reminders. It got to where I started reaching for the pen and paper on my own, because I found that it helped me to organize my thoughts and keep my objectives in mind. It helped me to focus. Plus, there's great power in introspection, don't you think? And what better way to turn your thoughts inward and force yourself to reflect on your day, your goals, and your blessings than to stare at a blank page and reach for some way to fill it?

Since I've been on the tour, I've almost always had a journal going of one kind or another. Those match books I've been pulling from, between chapters? That's just one outlet, one kind of writing. I also keep a more straightforward journal. I'm a little all over the place in my approach, but I'm happy just to make the approach. That's the key. If I don't step up to it, it doesn't happen. Sometimes, I don't write for weeks and weeks, and other times I might make several entries in a single day. Sometimes, my entries read more like e-mails or texts, because that's how I've been conditioned by the technology. (Or because I can only find time to write when I'm on my laptop, or fumbling with my cell phone while I'm waiting out a long match in the players' locker room.)

Usually, when things are going well on the court, I'm keeping a faithful chronicle. I don't know if that means the writing helps my tennis, or if it's the other way around, but setting down my thoughts allows me to decompress after a difficult match, and to wrap my head around what comes next, so I keep at it. Also, no two tournaments unfold along the same lines, so it's a useful thing to have all these journals piling up for my review. They're road maps I can file away for later, if I ever want to know how I got from there to here.

I thought it might be useful to share one of these journals here, because people seem to want to know what it's like to be in the middle of a Grand Slam tournament, playing for the title and the top spot in the rankings. That's how things laid out for me during my 2008 U.S. Open championship run, as you'll see . . .

Thursday, August 21, 2008

OMG. My back is killing me. I'm too cheap for my own good. It was going to cost me $2,158 to fly first from LAX to NYC, so I decided to ride coach. After all, it's a red-eye!!! I'll get an exit row and sit by a window. I'll be fine, right? *No!!!* Turns out our seats did not recline. And they were pitched at a really uncomfortable angle. The entire flight, it's like I was bending forward to tie my shoes!!! Now my back is killing me. Ugggghhhh!!! The dogs were stretched out on the floor the whole time, and I kept thinking, Oh, how I envy their spot.

Just arrived at hotel. Hoping to get in a good practice this afternoon, work out that stiffness. Then, off to a Nike event. They're opening a store downtown, and I need to make an appearance. I also need a nap, so I'll sign off for now . . .

MORE LATER . . .

Nike event went well. Saw Spike Lee. He's so cool. Would love to work with him. He keeps telling me to see Susan Babson, an acting coach in LA. It's hard, because I barely have time to practice, but as God is my witness, I am going to see Susan. Whatever it takes to do something I've always dreamed of doing.

Back to Nike, it went awesomely awesome. Went and

did my thing after hair and make-up (always a drag). Roger Federer was there. He's so cool!!! (I say that a lot, don't I?) OK, so today at practice I hit on the Louis Armstrong Stadium court. I had the worst session. I can't seem to keep a ball in play. My forehand is so off!!! I don't know what to do. My dad was there with me and that was good. He is a great help, but I'm *soooo* off. And my back is *still* killing me!!! I'm not moving well. Think I strained my groin. Went and had it taped. Hope it feels better tomorrow. After I hit, went to the gym and worked out for a while. Want to be sure my knee will be OK, too. All these moving parts . . .

God, help me and bless me. Please please please . . . Today's practice has me worried. Didn't get much of a nap, so maybe that explains it. I really want to do well here, but there's no way if I practice like I did today. Daddy says I'm trying too hard. That's often true. I over-try, because I'm a perfectionist. . . . I'm also nervous about the draw. Don't want to be on Venus's side. She's playing so well!!! It's not that I don't want her to do well. I do! But if we're on opposite sides I can root for her longer. Like at Wimbledon. Only this time *I* get to win.

I'm falling asleep as I write this, so I'll sign off . . . Good night, God. TTYT.

XXX, S

Friday, August 22, 2008

It's 5:00 a.m. Up early for a CBS "Morning Show" appearance with V. Hair and make-up on their way up to start on me. Call time is 6:30 a.m. Who makes this schedule? Don't they realize I need my beauty rest?

MORE LATER . . .

Back again. So tired when I logged that last entry. Can you believe it, up at 5:00, going into a tournament? Not complaining, though. Some people get up that early every day. Me, I've got it good, smashing tennis balls everywhere.

Speaking of smashing balls, today I did better. More consistent. More power. Forehand seems back. But back is killing me!!! OMG, that flight. Aggghhh! Starting to worry. Two hours of treatment after practice. Hoping it helps . . .

Player party tonight. Yes, another event. LOL! The bigger the tournament, the bigger the events. It's the U.S. Open, baby! The biggest!!! More events coming tomorrow, which is shaping up to be a killer day. Not looking forward to it. It's the wear and tear, so close to the tournament, the not sitting still.

Draw came out . . . I have to play Venus in the QUARTERS!!! If we make it that far. (No room for doubt, Serena . . . OF COURSE we'll make it that far!) Can you believe??? I'm so bummed, it ruined my day. Wow. Why can't I play someone else? Even the Semis would be better than the Quarters!!! Dang Dang Dang!

     XXX, S

Saturday, August 23, 2008

The week before the Open is so busy. Today was one of those wall-to-wall days. Super-long. Super-crazy. Still kinda down about the draw . . . :(

Check this out: up early for an Oreo press conference, before practice. OMG, I love Oreos. Just signed this deal with Venus and the Manning brothers, Peyton and Eli, and this was the kick-off. Really love the concept: the Williams sisters versus the Manning brothers in an Oreo-eating contest. It's *uber*-cool. The Oreo people are so happy with it. Great to do an event like this with V. Plus, all the Oreos u can eat!!! Yay!!!

Another crummy practice. Went straight from Oreo event, which might explain it. I've just been soooo busy!!! Not the best strategy. Plus, body still not right. Forehand still not right. My timing is off!!! Got to fix it, Serena. Clock is ticking.

Set it up so practice ran right into Arthur Ashe Kids Day at Flushing Meadows. Do it all in one trip. There's a concert and exhibition matches on the main court. Tons of kids come out. I have a ball, seeing them have such a good time. Saw Roger Federer again. LOL. We keep bumping into each other. Good to be out on the main court in front of a crowd again, even if it is a bunch of screaming teeny-bopper kids.

Hit the gym again for a couple hours, then raced back to hotel to get ready for Wilson launch party. Like I said, a super-long day. Wouldn't be so bad if the ride from the hotel to the tennis center wasn't an hour long. Can you believe that? One hour, each way? That kills a lot of time. There are nice-enough hotels nearby, near LaGuardia Airport, but

I need to be in Manhattan. Nothing against Queens, but mid-town Manhattan has got it *going on*!!!

Tonight I had to go to this Wilson party. They like it when they have some of their players come out. It turned out to be lots of fun. Sometimes these events can drag, but this one was cool. I saw Roger again. He's the greatest, the nic-est guy. So funny!!! We're running in the same circles. And running is the right word. Sun-up to sun-down, I'm running. Around and around. But I can't complain. It's life. Anyway, it's *my* life. I feel so blessed to be able to play and do this. Tomorrow I really want to have a good practice. That's the focus. Tournament starts on Monday, so this is it for all the hype and hoopla. After tonight, it's just tennis, tennis, tennis. My focus notes:

- Stay Positive
- Believe you can do anything, even when down
- Focus on every point
- You are the best, Serena

Believe it. Act it. Become it.
XXX, S

Sunday, August 24, 2008

Finally, an easy day. Almost got away from me, though. The CEO of the WTA asked if we could make an appear-ance at some dinner. (Me and V.) Wish I could, but I can't. Plus, it's a late ask. Need to remember why I'm here. If I plan on winning, I need to lock down. NOW!!! Tournament starts tomorrow, so the plan is to practice for a couple hours, then rest. I'll get treatment in my room. My back, my knee. Whatever ails and aches. Then I'll lay down . . . Finally, I need this. Still pissed about the draw . . . Quarterfinals? What a joke!

MORE LATER . . .

I never look at the draw other than to see where Venus is playing. After that, I don't want to know. I prefer to wait until the day of my first match to find out, but my hitting partner, Sasha, spilled the beans. He told me I'd drawn Kateryna Bondarenko. A talented young Ukrainian, ranked 46th. I've never played her, so we have no history. Best to start with a clean slate. She doesn't know my game either, so hopefully she'll think more about my game than I will about hers.

Anyway, I'm sure she'll want to go for broke. She's a younger sister, too. Her older sister, Alona, has won a bunch of tournaments. We younger sisters have to stick together, but not here. We always feel like we have something to prove. Trust me, I know. Just don't want her to go proving it on me.

Still, wish I didn't know who I was playing just yet. It's a jinx thing. Plus, now that I know, I have to do my homework. Venus knows everyone's game, so I'll have to check in with V, to see how Kateryna plays. I played her sister Alona earlier this year in Rome, on clay. Kicked her butt. 6–2, 6–0. If Kateryna asks her big sister for a report on my game, she might wish she hadn't.

Agggghhhh!!! Why am I putting so much into this? Just play your game, Serena, and you'll be OK. What really has me down is that I'll have to play Venus so early. Should have shrugged it off, but it's bugging me. So upsetting. Ruined my whole week. I'm pissed because it means one of us will be out early. The way I'm practicing, it just might be me, I'm afraid.

Really, really, really need to start having better practices. Today's session a bit better, but still feeling sluggish, slow. Highlight of my day? A turkey burger, delivered to my room. I don't eat red meat, but this burger was unbelievable!!! TDF!!! Relaxing in my hotel room, taking it easy, eating this heavenly burger, watching these old Superman cartoons to get me motivated for the tournament. I love that stuff!!! Just watched the one that shows how he was born.

Off to watch another episode. Then, sleep. Until tomor-row . . .

XXX, S

Monday, August 25, 2008

I don't play today. I'm not used to it. I'm in the top half of the draw, and we play Tuesday. All this week, I've pre-pared to play on Monday, but it's an extra day to get my body right. That's how I have to think of it, but today at practice my back was killing me again. All because of that stupid flight, I think. That's what you get, Serena, for trying to save a couple bucks. My knee is okay, though. And my shoulder was giving me some trouble, but now it seems fine.

Feeling good to go. Only practiced for an hour, then hit the gym. Another hard workout. Hope all this work pays off. Trying not to think about Bondarenko. Let her think about me. Venus says I can run her around. Don't think I'll have too much to worry about, if I'm on my game. If I'm strong. If, if, if . . .

Watched James Blake play Donald Young, both African-American players. Went to five sets. Donald Young is *so so so* young, like 20 or 21!!! Came away thinking with another year or two of experience, he'd win the same match. Oh, well . . . Great to be out there, watching. No pressure. Reminds me why I play. It's such a beautiful game. You need to be smart, graceful, fierce!!! To shut everything else out and just go for it. It's just you out there, slugging it out.

Big day tomorrow. First, a couple more Supermans, to put me in the right frame of mind. TTYS . . .

XXX, S

Tuesday, August 26, 2008

Tired. Late. Still buzzing over straight sets win over Bondarenko . . . 6–1, 6–4. In control the whole way. Strong. Great start. And yet the whole time I'm thinking about running into Venus so soon, in the quarters. Things keep going this way, that's where we are headed. Makes me SO MAD!!! And then, it bothers me that it bothers me. I want to put it out of my head, but I can't. Maybe Superman will help . . .

XXX, S

Wednesday, August 27, 2008

No match today, so I practiced early. That'll be the routine. Want to beat the traffic, the heat, the crowds . . . There's a lot to consider, playing in New York, this time of year. Logistics shouldn't be such a big part of such a big tournament, but they come into play here. Such a hassle getting around.

Back still killing me. Don't know how I'll keep going. We landed in NY, and I haven't felt right since. Just have to deal with it. Had a better practice today, which I'm really excited about. I could move, once I got warm. Trying to work on moving the ball. Those sessions can get boring, but it helps that my body is responding. Today, I'm so excited because my niece and nephews came into town. Jeffrey, Jair, and Justus. So cute. My mom's here (finally!!!) and I saw them all this afternoon at the hotel. It's like a Williams family reunion. Everyone came to my room, and we just hung out. And laughed. Always helps to laugh—it's the BEST medicine. Sent my assistant Nikki to get some clothes because I don't like to shop during a tournament. (Can u imagine? Me, not wanting to shop?) Last time I went shopping on a day off early in the tournament, I lost. Not in the next round, but during that first week. Ever since, I don't shop until I'm done. But that doesn't mean Nikki can't go for me. LOL . . .

Waiting on Nikki to get back. Ordered up some food from this really great place around the corner from my hotel. Waiting on that, too. They have really good chicken . . . Mmm mmm . . . Don't want to eat too late, but I'm hungry!!!

XXX, S

Thursday, August 28, 2008

Oh my God, I played so well today! So proud of myself. OK, so I played . . . hmmm . . . who did I play??? (I can't believe I've forgotten her name! I'll go look it up!) Elena Vesnina, from Russia. Ranked #71. I won 6–1, 6–1. Dominated the whole way. The one negative was I hadn't lost serve in that first round match against Bondarenko, and here it looked like I'd hold my serve the entire way, too. Always a nice way to jump-start a tournament, but I stumbled in the second set, up 4–0. Had a chance to go up 5–0, but I let this girl take the game from me, so I'm a little frustrated with that. Still, excited with the way I played.

Been watching some great tennis. Saw Andy Roddick beat this kid, Ernests Gulbis from Latvia, who is going to be a great player. I actually picked Ernests to win. Watched him play at the Olympics. I'm a fan! Andy played incredibly, though, and I was happy to see him win. He's been struggling but now he's back. I saw myself in his game, because that's how it is for a lot of us. You play at your peak for a stretch, and then there's a dip, and then you're back up again. Tough to stay sharp and unbeatable tournament after tournament. We're seeing that now with Roger. Everybody is so quick to write him off, because he loses a set, because he's not so invincible after all, but he's still Roger Federer!!!

I somehow managed to get in late because I played behind Ana Ivanovic and this young French qualifier. Their match went long. I can't believe it, the girl beat her! The #1 seed! Always such a shocker, when the #1 seed goes in the second round. Changes the whole field. As the tournament goes on, I'm looking to see which seed falls. I'm always thinking, Don't let it be you, Serena. The fallout here is that my match started so late. Also, it means Ana won't hold her #1 ranking. Weird!!! They're saying that if one of the top six players wins the Open, she'll be the new #1. That includes me, so how's that for incentive???

With Ana gone so early, that was all the talk. Who will be the new #1? Some reporter told me I was #3. I'd thought since I was seeded fourth in the tournament that I was #4, going in, but I guess not. Hey, #3!!! I'm excited!!! I mean, a year and a half ago, I was #143, so that's a long climb!!! WOOOO!!!

A lot to get my head around . . . Glad I played better today . . . Glad the #1 spot is within reach . . . About to put some ice on my knee and call it a night . . . Just ordered our turkey burgers, which are incredibly, unbelievably delicious. Next match is Ai Sugiyama, I think. Have to check if she won, haven't played her in forever. Last time was on clay at the French, 2003. She's tough. I never like going up against these veterans, because they can find ways to hang in there. Gotta watch some more Superman, keep my thing going . . .

XXX, S

Friday, August 29, 2008

Today I had to practice early because I have to shoot a segment for "Extra!" the Hollywood television show. Not really a typical off day, in the middle of a big tournament. Don't really like to schedule one of these when I'm in athlete mode. But I agreed, because it was at the Calvin Klein store, really close to my hotel. The paparazzi are always out, taking pictures. Always, always, always. I didn't look like I like to look, when I'm out doing my thing. Like I said, I'm in athlete mode, not walking around looking hot or anything. I like to look GOOD . . .

But what's a girl to do? There are so many great dresses. I want them all!!! So excited because after the tournament I'll be staying on in NY for Fashion Week. Then I'll get to walk around looking hot. Then I'll do it up right. I'm going to the Baby Phat show, the Calvin Klein show, and a few others. I'm good friends with Luca at Luca Luca, so I might go to that one. And then Zac Posen. I love Zac Posen! So I will go to his show, too. I'm REALLY looking forward to it!!!

MORE LATER . . .

So, I shot the piece on "Extra!" Calvin Klein gave me the most fabulous, most gorgeous gorgeous gorgeous dresses!!! (OMG!) There's a Calvin Klein party on Sunday night, so right now my plan is to make it to the finals, and to go to the party as the U.S. Open champion and the new #1. That's a good plan, right? They gave me this great black dress that I'll wear, and I'll get to keep it too!!!

Got my nails done. I'm wearing a red Nike dress, which I just love. It's really cute. I've been wearing red nails to punch it up, so I had to refresh my nails! I usually like to get a manicure every 4 to 5 days, and it's been a while, so it was great to get them done!!! It's so relaxing, to sit there and let someone else do the work. I have to make sure my nails look good on the court and good for when I play tomorrow. Sugiyama did end up winning her second round match, so that should be fun to see what happens.

Watched some more exciting tennis. It really gets me going, to watch a great men's match. I love the way these guys play!!! Their footwork is just amazing.

Thinking about another one of these turkey burgers. I should really lay off, but they're SO GOOD!!! If I keep eating them I'm going to turn into a turkey burger. Guess I should just go to bed, get ready for tomorrow. Venus is playing really well, BTW. She played this girl from Paraguay and really pushed her around. 6–0, 6–3. She's got Alona Bondarenko in the third round tomorrow, so the Williams sisters will have a chance to really take it to the Bondarenko sisters. (Sorry!) Still on track for the quarters. (Hope V's not watching Superman, too, 'cause I need all the edge I can get!) Every match is going to be tough. No free passes, rest of the way. Superman awaits! Talk to you later!!!

XXX, S

Saturday, August 30, 2008

Another seed fell! Svetlana Kuznetsova. I'm sad, because I like her. She's one of the players I get along with on the tour. So sweet, so funny. And such a strong player. She always plays me tough. Svetlana was actually seeded #3 in this tournament, but ranked #4, while I was ranked #3 and seeded #4. Weird, how that sometimes happens. I can never figure it out! She's been ahead of me for so long, but this girl from Slovenia really surprised her, so that's always a real wake-up call to the rest of the field. Can't take any of these matches lightly.

I play 3rd match on today, against Ai Sugiyama, who's been playing well. I know it'll be a battle, because this girl gets to everything. I have to keep focused, keep the pressure on, keep moving her around. Make her work for her points. Venus played first on, against Alona Bondarenko, and she finished off the other sister for us. She did her job, reaching the round of 16. Now it's on me.

I'm a little bored, waiting on Nadal. He's playing this guy whose name I can't pronounce. Still just the first set, so I've got a while. Hopefully, I'll be on soon. Would be great to get back to the hotel early, give myself an extra half-day on top of my day-off tomorrow. My back has been better, but it still hurts. The pain has gone up into the upper right side and still continues down into my lower back. I have this tape called Kinesio tape, it's what a lot of the athletes were wearing at the Olympics. The way it's supposed to work is it warms up your muscles and makes the pain subside. We'll see if it helps.

I just want to play tennis and do well. I don't want all the extras, but I'm not complaining. I'm really happy to be out here! OK, I need to get focused. G2G!!!

XXX, S

Sunday, August 31, 2008

The life of a tennis player is really boring, really repetitive. I pretty much do the same thing every day. Today I practiced at 9:00 a.m., like I do every day when I don't have a match. (Oh, I forgot to write that I beat Sugiyama. Another straight set victory. V, here I come!) After practice, I went to the gym, also like I do every day I don't have a match. Same basic exercises. Today, I actually got tired of doing the same leg exercises so I only half-way did them! I'm just so tired of doing the same things. Mix it up, Serena!!!

Anyway, I'm here at the hotel. Bored. My sister Isha is here, so we hung out. Not like we can go out and do the town, but I welcomed the company. Now I'm getting some treatment, which is always good. The treatment table is in Venus's room, so I go to Venus's room after practice. I get treatment and talk to V. We talk about our next opponents, what we liked in each other's game, things like that. Then I usually go back to my room, but I get so much treatment on my back and on my legs that by the time I get back to my room it's about 7:00 p.m.

I go to my dad's room a lot. Every night. We go over game plans, and I swing my racquet. That's a real constant, this tournament. Going into Daddy's hotel room, getting in my swings, talking strategy. Now that I've set it up as a pattern I have to keep at it. Another jinx thing, I guess, so I can't stop now. Too deep into it. Keep to the same routine, as long as it's working.

Got this French girl in my path tomorrow. Severine Bremond. Never played her before. Don't think Venus has either, so she's a real wild card. Ranked #121, but I can't take her lightly. Remember what happened to Svetlana. Ivanovic. Think like Superman. Don't let her be your Kryptonite, Serena. Remember, she's never faced you, either. Get in her head before she gets in yours.

XXX, S

Monday, September 1, 2008

Hate drawing these wild cards in the later rounds. Severine Bremond. Been around a while, beaten some good players. Have to be careful. Spent this whole tournament looking ahead to V, can't look past these players on the way.

Tuesday, September 2, 2008

Okay, so that went well. 6–2, 6–2 . . . Easy on, easy off. One good thing is there wasn't much for V to look at. It's not like there's anything new for Venus to pick apart in my game, but my serve was on. That was most of it. Another good thing is I wasn't out there too long. I'm fresh. Back feeling fine, first time all tournament. Maybe this is my year, after all. Maybe everything is lined up.

Want to be sharp, rested for tomorrow. The match of the tournament. Got my practice in this a.m. and came back to the hotel to chill. Tried to sleep. Ordered another turkey burger and tried to eat half. (Not telling if I succeeded!) Talked to V for a little, but not about tomorrow's match. Other stuff.

I've run through all my Superman episodes, but that's okay. Just as good the second time around. Positive thoughts tonight as I go to sleep.

XXX, S

Wednesday, September 3, 2008

Quarterfinals today. I play Venus. Big surprise. She beat Radwanska. I watched the match to see what Venus did so I could expose her weakness, but she beat the girl so fast! At Wimbledon, I noticed she served a lot of balls at my body. I will definitely be ready for that, but I don't want to over-think! I'm just sad we have to play each other so soon. It's only the quarters. That's my killer round. Don't know how many Grand Slam tournaments I've lost in the quarterfinals. Have to give it my all today and hope for the best. Might even need a little luck. I know I can do this! I feel like I'm the best player out there. I just have to continue to think positive and do what I do best. We have the night match, just woke up, so I'm going to get some more rest and go from there . . .

MORE LATER . . .

At the tennis center, just had a pretty good practice. Told my hitting partner, Aleksandar Bajin, to make sure he hits hard. (We call him Sasha.) Noticed when Venus and I practiced right next to each other that pace is giving her some trouble. Today I hit longer than V. She got to the court before me, though. We were going to ride together because we're staying at the same hotel, but I'm always running late so Venus left me be-hind. That's OK because I think she's taking it really seriously. I'm going to take it just as serious. I want to win this. This is it!! For me, this is the match of the tournament. If I win this match, I feel like I can win the tournament. I'm really tired of losing in the quarterfinals! Here we go! I'm going to get ready to do my thing. Unfortunately right now it's raining. We have a rain de-lay. And now a match is going over and they are trying to finish. I guess I'll be on soon, so I need to get focused!

XXX, S

Thursday, September 4, 2008

OMG!!! What a match! It was crazy. I was down the whole time! Ten set points against me and I still managed to win. Ran down everything and it was so worth it because I'm so happy to be in the semis. I haven't been in the semis here since 2002, and I won that year, so hopefully that's a good omen! The match before ours went really late and we had the night session, so we were hanging out almost 2 hours trying to get ready. Supposed to play at 7 but we didn't end up going on until around 9! Waiting upstairs in the gym. Getting my wrist taped, warming up, waiting for the match to end. Venus came in while I was warming up. We started talking and laughing. Good to know that through all of it I have my sister, who means the world to me.

We played each other so hard, and I won, and I'm so happy. I really want to win a Grand Slam tournament this year, but just where I'm at I feel blessed and honored to have this opportunity to have a sister be in this sport with me. To be so close. I had fun out there yesterday. Felt like I was watching a really good movie—with me in it!!! A little sore today, though. Didn't get home until after midnight last night, but already heading out for my 9 a.m. practice. I'm not letting anything stop me from winning this tournament. Gotta go so I can be on time! TTYL

XXX, S

Friday, September 5, 2008

Semi-finals! I'm ready. I play Dinara Safina, who's been having a great year. (Another little sister!) I'm really excited.

I feel a little pressure. I played so well the other day against Venus, and I know she would beat Dinara, so . . . now I HAVE to beat her. Don't want to let Venus down. It's like if I was going to lose, I should have let Venus win. One way to think of it. Don't know why I'm stressing about Dinara . . . maybe because I'm in the semis, and it's a big deal. I have an afternoon match, so I'm going to get up and go practice! TTYL

   XXX, S

Saturday, September 6, 2008

Been raining all morning. Sitting in my hotel room all day. Going to get some treatment on my shoulder, so I'm ready. Gotta get focused. I've got to watch my Superman episodes, since I'm superstitious. Roger plays first, and I'm rooting for him to win! We've been hanging out all week. Don't know how I'm going to play today because they have all these matches to get in. Hopefully I'll be able to play. I don't want to play the finals on Sunday, because I have that Calvin Klein party. And that dress! I get to keep it if I go to the party, so I'm desperate to play tonight. Desperate to win the U.S. Open tonight . . .

   MORE LATER . . .

Still raining!!! It's 4 p.m. and no one has played. Actually, that's not true. Roger played a little, but they couldn't finish it, and Murray was playing Nadal, in the other semi, but they had to switch courts! They put the #1 player on the grandstand court, because of all the rain. I'm still shocked to think I'll be #1 if I win this tournament. I came into the U.S. Open thinking I want to win a Grand Slam tournament, but now if I win my match I'll be #1! It's crazy: five girls with a chance, and I'm one of them. I looked up and was like, What? Me? I had no idea I was even that close. I just play, and try to win everything. But it's raining, pouring, and my agent Jill told me they might cancel, so I don't know what to do . . .

MORE LATER . . .

STILL raining . . . It's 6:30 and they canceled my match! Can you believe? Won't be able to be a champion today. Going to have to wait 'til tomorrow, and I'm going to have to miss the Calvin Klein party because the final will be tomorrow night. I'm really upset. Going to go practice. Going to hit indoors. I have to be focused. I have to stay. I have to do this! This is big! I want to do this!!

Sunday, September 7, 2008

Here we go! No rain this morning, after rain all day yesterday. It sucks because the men's final has to be played on Monday. Don't know if they've ever done that at the U.S. Open. We're playing tonight at 9 p.m. That's so late, but it's cool because it's primetime, baby!!! I'm so pumped. Worked so hard playing indoors last night. I practiced in Harlem at this great tennis facility, and I was drenched from head to toe. I was running so much. I'm so determined to do so well. That way, I have no excuses if I don't win. If I don't win, it won't be because I didn't put in the hard work! I can do this!!

XXX, S

Monday, September 8, 2008

It's over!!! (Sighs of big relief!!!) I won, I won, I won. I'm so excited. I'm the U.S. Open Champion. I'm so happy! I feel so blessed. It's so amazing. I can't even describe. Got home last night from the match at 2 a.m. Couldn't sleep because I was so excited! Couldn't do anything but crash in my bed! This is the best feeling. Now I'm a winner of 9 Grand Slam tournament titles. (WOW!!!) Growing up, I wanted to win so many tournaments. Growing up, it was so surreal to have an opportunity to do this, and I've done it! Thank God. Thank Jehovah God! Thank you, Dad. Thank you, Mom. Thank you, Venus. Thank you, Isha. Thank you, Lyndrea. Thank you, Yetunde. We did it! I'm so happy. And tired! OMG, I'm so tired. As happy as I am, I'm going to go to sleep now, because I'm so tired.

Looking forward to the Australian Open. LOL . . .

XXX, S

Hold serve, hold serve, hold serve. Focus, focus, focus. Be confident, be confident, be confident. Hold serve. Hold, hold, hold. Move up. Attack. Kill. Smile. Hold!!!

—MATCH BOOK ENTRY

CLOSING THOUGHTS

A Work in Progress

So there you have it. For now. There you have *me*, for now. A piece of my heart, at a particular moment in time. But underneath all that comes a caution: everything you've just read is subject to change. Well, maybe not everything. The facts of my life—the *who, what, when,* and *where*—are all set. But every opinion, every emotion, every insight that flows from those facts—the *how* and *why*—is still on the table.

When I set out to write this book, I never intended it to be a full-on, straight-up memoir. I'm not ready to pack it in and call it a career, and at twenty-seven I'm way too young to even think about looking over my shoulder to write a traditional autobiography. I'm not done yet! I can tell you how it's going. I can tell you how it's gone. But I can't tell you where I'm headed. I can't know how the story of my life will turn out. Heck, I don't want to know.

And so the stories I've cherry-picked from my life and career are the ones that stand now as inspiring, motivating, illustrative. These are the memories that give me shape as I pass these pages for publication. These are the touchstone moments and the formative influences that have helped to make me the person I am, the player I am, as well as the person and player I might become. Ask me in ten years to reflect on my childhood and my coming of age on the tennis court and I might reach for a different batch. Or, maybe

I'll reconsider some of these same memories but in an entirely new way, as my perspective continues to shift. Ask me in twenty, and yet another batch might rise to the surface. It's like one of those connect-the-dots drawings I used to do when I was a kid. Link these stories together and they form the picture I carry of myself in my mind at just this moment; but tomorrow I might see myself a little differently. Make no mistake, each one of these moments has given me shape. But drop one from the picture and I'd look a whole lot different. Drop a couple and you wouldn't recognize me at all.

I'm a work in progress, just like everyone else. What moves me one day might not move me the next. What helped to shape me as a child might not make a dent in my thinking now. It's all relative. And yet, when you've done the bulk of your growing up in the public eye, as I have done, people seem to want to know a little bit more about you than you might understand about yourself. That's part of the territory, I realize, and I'm happy to explore that in what ways I can.

One of the questions I'm asked all the time by reporters and fans is how I want to be remembered at the end of my tennis career, and I can never come up with a satisfying answer. Honestly, I'm not even sure I want to be remembered as a tennis player. When my body tells me it's time to stop chasing and smashing tennis balls for a living, I'll go on and do something else, you can be sure, and maybe it'll be the something else that helps me leave my true mark. Maybe tennis is just a way for me to get from where I was to where I'm going.

And yet the question keeps coming—more and more, as I continue to play and start to threaten or establish some of the all-time records in the women's game: how do I want to be remembered, after all?

I'll just have to get back to you on that one.